Housing: A Missed Opportunity
– the Tangled Story of the Kenny Report

"Property carries obligations as well as rights and the Constitution, while recognising rights of private property, provides that such rights may be delimited by law."

Neil Blaney TD, Minister for Local Government, Dáil Eireann, 22 November 1962

Tim Ryan

Grand Canal Media

www.grandcanalmedia.ie

Cover: Design Room
Grand Canal Media
Clifton House
Lower Fitzwilliam Street
Dublin 2
www.grandcanalmedia.ie

© *Tim Ryan 2023*
ISBN: 978-1-9997-139-2-8

The Author

Tim Ryan is a native of West Tipperary and graduated from UCC with an BA (Hons), H.Dip. in Ed. and M.Comm (Government & Public Policy). He was a secondary school teacher before moving into journalism, first as a freelance writer, then with the *Cork Examiner* and later the *Irish Press* where he worked in a number of positions including agricultural editor, news editor and on the political staff. Following the closure of the *Irish Press* in 1995, he set up his own public affairs consultancy where he worked for a number of clients. He also lectured in Public Affairs for the Public Relations Institute of Ireland (PRII). From 2011 to 2017 he served as a director of the Residential Tenancies Board (RTB). Now living in Dublin, he runs his own media publishing company, Grand Canal Media. He is a keen walking, cycling and gardening enthusiast.

Other books by the author

Ballinspittle: Moving Statues and Faith (Mercier, 1986)

Mara, PJ (Blackwater, 1992)

Dick Spring, A Safe Pair of Hands (Blackwater, 1993)

Albert Reynolds, the Longford Leader, (Blackwater, 1994)

Tell Roy Rogers I'm Not In – The Paddy Cole Story (Blackwater, 1995)

Quest for Quality – 100 Years of the IAWS (IAWS, 1997)

The Irish Times Nealon's Guide to the 32nd Dáil and 25th Seanad (Grand Canal Publishing, 2017)

The Irish Times Nealon's Guide to the 33rd Dáil and 26th Seanad (Grand Canal Publishing, 2020)

For Elaine

Acknowledgements

This book is based on a thesis prepared for the Department of Social Work and Social Policy in Trinity College, Dublin. I would like to thank the many people, too numerous to mention, who helped me with various aspects of the research along the way, a project that has been ongoing for the past five years. In particular, I wish to think all those who agreed to be interviewed and whose names appear throughout the following pages. Without their co-operation, the project would not have been possible.

In particular, I wish to thank Dr Lorcan Sirr of TU Dublin for his insightful introduction which sets the scene perfectly for the narrative. Thanks also to Lee Ryan for her front cover design. I wish to thank Stephen Collins for his constant help and support and for reading the manuscript.

I wish to thank Dr Erna O'Connor, Dr. Joe Whelan, Dr. Mary Murphy, Dr Pat Wallace, T.P. O'Mahony, David Davin-Power, Marie Lawlor, Gerry Crosbie, Mairead Foley, Anne McChrystal and Joe Joyce for their help and encouragement in bringing the book to fruition.

Tim Ryan

Dublin, October 2023

Contents

Foreword

Much referred to, much spoken about, accepted in principle by many, but also much feared by the powers that be, and so rarely seen and never implemented. That is the legacy of Justice John Kenny's *Report of the Committee on the Price of Building Land to the Minister for Local Government*, to give it its full title, published in 1973. The concurrent lauding of the report at the same time as it being constantly side-lined was something that frustrated Kenny until his passing in 1987, and would have no doubt continued to frustrate him given its continuing status as the rulebook that nobody plays by. Indeed, such is the trepidation that Kenny's infamous report might ever get implemented that is has been out of print for decades and currently only exists as a scan of a photocopy available online. It is highly likely that few of those who refer to it have read it.

John Kenny was called to the bar in 1940, took silk 17 years later, and was an expert in several areas of law, including chancery – a practice that includes wills, probate, trusts, property, tax, intestacy and landlord and tenant – which would undoubtedly have given him some experience in issues of land, property and its value and distribution. Kenny was also a lecturer in property and company law in University College Dublin. Unlike other solicitors and barristers who lectured at the time and regularly wrote academic tracts, Kenny wrote little. It is somewhat ironic therefore that as many of the other papers written by his fellow legal academics when Kenny was in his pre-Report years are forgotten, pages curling on the highest shelves in university libraries, Kenny's written contribution to Irish policy discourse lives on. (Politicians, in particular, have for decades juggled supporting its principles whilst simultaneously finding reasons not to implement them, usually with reference to the constitution.) For anyone involved in studies of property and land, John Wylie's quasi-biblical *Irish Land Law* will be a familiar text and Kenny was a consultant editor to the first edition published in 1975.

Kenny was therefore ideally placed to chair the Committee, convened in 1971 by then Minister for Local Government Bobby Molloy, latterly Minister of State for Housing and Urban Renewal in the 1997-2002 Progressive Democrats-Fianna Fáil coalition government. Having analysed its contents and followed its progress over the years, Tim Ryan is also ideally placed to write about it. For a report with whose contents are potentially so important, if not game-changing, as well as being so politically challenging, it is surprising how little of substance has been written about Kenny's Committee and its Report over the decades.

This book is based on assiduous research by Ryan, who has spent many hours trawling archives and documents, reviewing papers and communications which have not seen the light of day since they were first written (some of these now more than 50 years old), diligently reading and analysing hundreds of hours of political contributions to Dáil debates and committees, and travelling to warehouses of dusty old files in far-flung locations (the Irish state really needs to have a better appreciation of its records and how and where they are kept). He takes us from John B. Keane's *The Field* to the need for a land price register, something strongly resisted by successive relevant ministers.

As a housing academic, every chapter is of interest from the historical setting to constitutional issues (or not), to how things are done in other countries. I was particularly interested in the chapter on Kenny himself. Reports and their findings are often strongly influenced by their chair, and so their personality, traits and character are of more importance than is usually appreciated, especially if the chair comes from a position of respect in the first instance (for example, a judge).

Ryan records barrister Charles Lysaght's memories of Kenny as a teacher, being an "outstanding lecturer", but also one who was conscious of being a clever man and who "tended to be dismissive of the stupid", a trait not unknown amongst lecturers, for good or ill.

Kenny was apparently also courteous, and a very kindly and gentle judge on the bench. Prior to his 1973 Report, Kenny had already broken new ground in the previous decade with his introduction of the concept of 'unenumerated rights' – these are rights that do not appear in the text of the Constitution but are implied and are there to be identified by the judiciary (see *Ryan v the Attorney General [1965] IR 294*). This was, for me, important in understanding the Kenny Report as, in deciding there was such a thing as unenumerated rights, Judge Kenny had used a concept in Pope John XXIII's papal encyclical *Pacem in Terris*, which was the first papal document to highlight socio-economic rights (Kenny was a devout Catholic). Ryan writes:

> According to [former religious affairs journalist T.P. O'Mahony, what may be even more pertinent, if the Kenny Report were ever actually implemented, is the insistence in *Pacem in Terris* (and in other social encyclicals) that the right to private property is not absolute, or unqualified - it carries with it a "social function". By the same token, Judge Kenny in the Report on the Price of Building Land in 1973 would decide that some personal rights, such as the right to windfall profits from development land, are subservient to the common good as stated in Article 43.2.2°.

This is gold dust and can only be found through detailed and often painstaking and tiresome research. Such research also leads to some 'bet you didn't know that' moments, such as the fact there was a minority report in the Kenny Report, with the minority group of two consisting of two civil servants from the very government department that had commissioned the report in the first instance. They rejected the suggestion that compensation should not be based on full market value and on an existing use plus 25 percent basis as proposed by the Kenny Committee, and they felt that the idea of compulsory acquisition of land as per the Kenny recommendation would fall foul of the Constitution.

In *Central Dublin Development Association Ltd. V Attorney General [1969]*, Kenny had rejected the argument that restrictions on development were repugnant to the Constitution. According to Judge Ronan Keane:

> [Kenny] rejected the suggestion that the power given to local authorities to restrict the development by private citizens of their

property, in many instances without payment of compensation, represented an "unjust attack" on property rights.

Ryan brings us from the report's publication, through the turbulent 1970s and 1980s up to today when at least two factors concerning land are different: at the time of the Kenny Report much housing development was an expansion of greenfield land for suburban development; and we are much more conscious now of issues such as climate change on where and how we build. Both of these factors mean a better use of existing land is imperative, but also that as land is finite, its value is increasing and therefore that the principles of the Kenny, many decades later are even more relevant now than they were then: if we want housing that is affordable to most, then the cost of delivering that housing has to be made affordable, and one of the biggest costs in delivering housing is that paid for the land.

For students and practitioners involved in land, value, planning and housing, and indeed broader areas of infrastructure delivery, climate change, transport and all their associated aspects of health, gender, environment and experience, Ryan's book is the text that helps us understand what has been done, what has not been done, what is done elsewhere, and what should be done. For policymakers in particular, this book is instructive in what happens when political courage is lacking, and the consequences of doing nothing when there is much that is being done, but a lot more that could be done. Kenny, and his Report, is still very relevant.

Dr Lorcan Sirr

Dublin, October 2023

Introduction

One wet November afternoon in mid-November 2020, a new report appeared on the website of the National Economic and Social Council (NESC), the body which advises the Taoiseach on strategic policy issues relating to sustainable economic, social and environmental development in Ireland. The members of the Council are appointed by the Taoiseach, for a three-year term and it is chaired by the Secretary General of the Taoiseach's Department. The members are representatives of business and employers' organisations, trade unions, agricultural and farming organisations, community and voluntary organisations, and environmental organisations as well as heads of Government departments and independent experts.

In a written Dáil reply to Social Democrats deputy Cian O'Callaghan on 4 December 2020, the Taoiseach stated that the National Economic and Social Council is an independent statutory agency operating under the aegis of his department. "The role of the Council is to analyse and report to the Taoiseach on strategic policy issues relating to sustainable economic, social and environmental development in Ireland," he said. "The Council can consider these matters either on its own initiative or at the request of the Taoiseach. The Council's reports are submitted to the Government prior to publication. As the reports are independent, they are not Government policy but they do, of course, help inform Government policy."

The Council publishes regular reports which appear in the names of all its members. Since the establishment of the NESC in 1973 it has published a number of reports on housing policy covering all aspects of housing policy including urban development, infrastructure and the implications of Covid-19 for housing. In 2004 that the Council outlined the key role of land supply and land cost in housing and infrastructure.

The report published in November 2020 was entitled *Housing Policy: Action to Deliver Change* and set out a range of measures to solve Ireland's housing crisis. The report built on five previous reports on housing and land agreed by the Council in in recent years: *Urban Development Land, Housing and Infrastructure: Fixing Ireland's Broken System (2018); Social Housing at the Crossroads: Possibilities for Investment, Provision and Cost Rental (2014); Home Ownership or Rental: What Road is Ireland on? (2014);*

Ireland's Rental Sector: Pathways to Secure Occupancy and Affordable Supply (2015) and Housing Supply and Land: Driving Public Action for the Common Good (2015).

The opening paragraph of the Executive Summary of the 2020 report was blunt in its tone. "It is over two years since the Council set out its analysis of Ireland's system of urban development, land management and housing provision," it stated. "That research concluded that the system was dysfunctional and that a suite of actions was required to fix it. Despite the intense policy focus on housing and a range of initiatives in the interim, the broken housing system described by the Council in 2018 persists."

Among the recommendations put forward by the Report was the implementation of the principal recommendation of the Committee on the Price of Building Land (the Kenny Report) from 1973. The Kenny Report recommended that local authorities acquire designated development areas at existing use value plus a premium of 25 per cent.

"A core principle of the Kenny Report regarding the capture of the betterment remains as relevant today as it was 50 years ago," the NESC Report stated.

Indeed, there have been countless other calls too, for the implementation of the Kenny Report's recommendations. In a letter to *The Irish Times* on the 26th of September 2018, for example, a list of some 50 academics, researchers and experts in the area of housing, economics, social policy and human rights called for the implementation of the recommendations of the Kenny Report as one of a number of effective measures to tackle Ireland's housing crisis.

Despite the NESC statement and countless others, the implementation of the recommendations of the Kenny Report has been ignored by successive governments for almost 50 years. Furthermore, the endless commitments and resolutions in both the Dáil and elsewhere, resulted in no government ever seeing fit to move on this innovative and radical report. This book attempts to analyse how and why this has happened and the consequences for Ireland's housing policy.

The aim of this book is to show how carefully planned and well-researched proposals in the Committee on the Price of Building Land (the Kenny Report) to solve the escalating price of residential development land in the late 1960s and early 1970s were initially well-received and accepted by government but then placed in abeyance and never implemented at all. It will also consider the very unusual situation whereby the two civil servants from the commissioning department - the Department of Local Government - opposed the main proposal and drafted their own minority report.

The following pages, based on a thesis prepared at the School of Social Work and Social Policy at Trinity College, Dublin, place the report and events surrounding it, in the context of how housing policy was developed from the foundation of the Irish Free State in 1921 and implemented by successive Irish governments. In particular, the book contrasts the total failure to implement the proposals of the Kenny Report with other successful land policies, such as the very successful Land Commission. It also examines the Irish planning system and the process of compulsory purchase, two issues that bedevilled Judge Kenny and his committee.

The book draws on previously unreported correspondence between senior civil servants, ministers and the Taoiseach of the day to piece together an accurate analysis of how a critical piece of housing policy was drafted, debated and ultimately ignored. It assesses the fall-out from the decision not to implement the proposals and its likely impact on subsequent developments in land acquisition, culminating ultimately in the setting up of a lengthy Planning Tribunal which lasted 15 years.

Finally, it also examines the possible effects the Report's recommendations would have in alleviating Ireland's ongoing housing crisis and why the recommendations of the Kenny Report are as relevant today as they were 50 years ago.

Chapter 1

A Finite Resource

Land is a finite resource for both individuals and the community. How it is used by both can have major effects on future generations and frequently the decisions made by them are irreversible. But land, of itself, is not a productive asset. As economist David McWilliams wrote: "Unless farmed on, land generates nothing: no ideas, no new products, no creativity, no innovation, no economic value. It simply extracts value from the thing that makes the economy tick: human ingenuity. And the fundamental value of land only increases as the population increases. So, rises in the value of land have nothing to do with the input of individual landowners." [1]

The very notion of housing and urban development does not exist in nature. It has to be created through a process of physical development that is supported by infrastructure at local, regional and national level. Without these supports, land cannot satisfy the needs of humans in urban areas and cannot have economic value. However, when land is carefully managed in a way to prudently utilise useable space, it quickly acquires value.

Whereas the amount of agricultural land in any society is relatively fixed, new urban developments and higher densities are relatively flexible and can provide valuable extra supply for ever-increasing urban populations. How this is managed and administered in any society is critical to the successful development of a vibrant and stable society.

Urban areas are an amalgamation of physical assets that have been produced in response to human needs over time. They are, therefore, by their very nature, constantly changing and evolving.

Good land use and an associated transport planning is vital to the success of any urban development. Central to this is proper strategic planning and forward thinking. It must be planned, organised and controlled and must be facilitated by people, skilled with appropriate knowledge and qualifications in how the urban environment functions. As pointed out by the Joint Oireachtas

---

[1] *Irish Times* 7 November 2019

Committee on Land in 1985 (Report of the Joint Committee on Building Land), the objective of development land policy should be to ensure that land is used so as to get maximum benefit for the whole community. In some circumstances, the best use of a particular parcel may be for office development. Alternatively, it may be better to retain that parcel as open space if there would otherwise be insufficient open space available. In the latter case, the land has a higher real value to the community as open space than if used for offices.

The 2004 All-Party Oireachtas Committee on the Constitution identified a number of characteristics that are particularly distinctive to the property market. For example, the property market is cyclical and prices tend to rise and fall in cycles, often quite dramatically. But the report also pointed out that housing is a special case. It stated; "Property markets will not of themselves supply everyone with a home which they can own. Where there is an overall shortage of housing, those at the bottom end of the market will be priced out because the market rations the available accommodation among competing bidders.

On the other hand, if property prices are low, supplying those at the bottom end of the market may not be sufficiently profitable to encourage development. It follows that direct, non-market provision of accommodation will be necessary at all stages of the cycle. An approach to housing economics, therefore, which is more in tune with societal requirements than with pure market requirements is needed to deal with the challenge of providing housing for people at the lower end of the market." [2]

How best to develop land policy has bedevilled and tested modern civilisation with varying levels of success. An inherent and constant issue in this evolving process is how to balance private and common interests. Clearly many decisions in an urban environment must be made in the interests of the common good, while minimising the infringement on private rights. This necessitates the limiting of enjoyment of private rights with appropriate compensation when and where necessary.

Like many other industries, property development is very often simply engaged in the production of commodities such as housing, offices, shops, hotels and warehousing to meet the demand from end-users.

---

[2] The All-Party Oireachtas Committee on the Constitution, 2004:6

9

In any normal free society, property activity is an inherent economic component and creates its own market. In a submission to the 2004 All-Party Committee, the Irish Auctioneers and Valuers Institute commented that "as well as making a major impact on society through the provision of housing, property makes a significant contribution to economic competitiveness and the regeneration of urban areas."

At the root of this is an understanding of the various laws which dictate how property is acquired and sold. In Ireland's case, key Articles of the 1937 Constitution - and their legal interpretation in subsequent legislation - play a critical role. The law of real property or land law, is concerned with the rights and responsibilities that arise in respect of land. These rights and responsibilities are defined by the state and interpreted through the actions of individuals.

In his oral submission to the All-Party Review Committee, Tom Dunne, former Head of the School of Real Estate and Construction Economics at TU Dublin said that development land could be thought of as an amalgam of three separate property rights, "the right to occupy and use land, the right to develop, or change use and the right to connect to infrastructure."

In his book *Housing Law and Policy in Ireland*, Galway lawyer and academic Padraic Kenna stated that housing law and policy is a product of the unique history of every country. In Ireland, in particular, this involves a legacy of emotional bonds to land within a rapidly modernising globalised state. Irish housing law, he stated, has evolved from feudal concepts facilitating a few thousand large landed estates, later applied to almost half a million peasant proprietors and now addressing almost 1.5million householders in modern Ireland. The result is a complex and often contradictory situation. Indeed, it is often difficult to appreciate or sympathise with the Irish psyche that attaches an almost obsessive importance to the ownership of land.[3]

Overthrow of the landlord system

Throughout the 19th Century the aims of Fenians such as John Devoy included the overthrow of the landlord system and the redistribution of Irish lands. The legacy of insecure tenant farmers and the struggle for security of

---

[3] Padraic Kenna, *Law and Policy in Ireland*, 2006:3

tenure continues to inform much of political discourse and imagery around housing in Ireland. To this day, the desire to be free of landlordism still appears as a reason for owner-occupation.

For example, the recordings of the Irish Folklore Commission in the 1930s, 40s and 50s relating to the Great Famine mostly with people born after the event are proof of the impact of the distress on future generations.

Images such as those conjured up by Daniel MacDonald's famous painting 'The Eviction Scene' (Crawford Art Gallery, Cork) which capture the role of the bailiff and constabulary in attendance on behalf of the landlord are still engraved in the Irish mindset. Similarly, playwright John B. Keane's theatrical treatment in 'The Field' (first performed in 1965) shows the emotional association with land ownership in rural Ireland. This emotion is powerfully evoked in the words of the Bull McCabe's highly charged speech on hearing that a field that he has leased is about to be sold for non-agricultural purposes:

> I watched this field for forty years and my father before me watched it for forty more. I know every rib of grass and every thistle and every whitethorn bush that bounds it...That is a sweet little field, this is an independent little field that wants eatin'.

Right throughout the nineteenth and twentieth centuries the writings of many literary figures such as William Carleton, Charles J. Kickham, Walter Macken, John McGahern and many others explore the Irish attitude to the land in all its complexities.[4]

As recently as October 2020, three members of a family died in a murder-suicide shooting at their family home near Kanturk in north Cork as part of a dispute over a will regarding the 115-acre family holding. Tadhg O'Sullivan (59) and his two sons, Mark (26) and Diarmuid (23) died in what was described by gardai as "a terrible family tragedy" which shocked the local community of Castlemagner, near Kanturk. So bitter was the dispute that one

---

[4] William Carleton *Traits and Stories of the Irish Peasantry* (Dublin, 1833); Charles Kickham *Knocknagow or The Homes of Tipperary* (1873); Walter Macken *The Bogman* (1952); John McGathern *That They May Face The Rising Sun* (London, 2002)

of the sons was buried in a separate graveyard following a separate church service.

Therefore, largely as a result of historical factors, the growth and development of Irish nationalism in Ireland was very closely bound up with the struggle for land that continued to dominate Irish political life long after independence just as it had done for generations before.

A cursory review of the debates of Dáil Eireann reveals the amount of time given over to debates about land and land policies. For example, from 1923 to its dissolution in 1992, the Annual Vote on the Land Commission estimates attracted contributions from virtually every TD. After a long, bitter struggle that dominated the social and much of political life of Ireland from the 1880s, land ownership became a guarantee of access to social standing within the local rural community in Ireland.

The Price of Development Land

It is against this rather unique background that Irish housing and land policy has developed over the past 100 years since the foundation of the Free State in 1922. Since the introduction of the 1937 Constitution, two Articles in particular, Article 40.3.2° and Article 43 - the interpretation of which have sometimes proved extremely difficult and sometimes contradictory - have played a key role in the issue of how, and under what circumstances, land may be acquired and developed.

Key to the housing market is the provision of development land and the price paid for that land. The maximum price a developer can afford to pay for land is what is known as 'residual value'. This is determined by the estimated value of the completed project minus the cost of the land, the site preparation, construction costs, professional fees, bank interest charges and the margin of profit.

The effect of this residual land value model ensures that developers will always value the land at the top of the potential house price range. If the builder is working on the basis of a price level of €300,000 for a three-bed semi, then he can only continue to build for as long as there are people coming forward who can afford to pay €300,000. It is, of course, something of a gamble and, as a result, many developers have faced financial ruin at times of recession as, for example in the recession period of 2007 – 2012.

Speaking in the Dáil in 2016, the Labour Party leader, Brendan Howlin said the history of this State has been marked by the "insidious influence of private developers and property crashes". The biggest winner in this entire process is not usually the developer - who is normally working on a certain margin - but the landowner. The process also encourages a drip-feed system whereby houses are fed into the market over an extended period of time, thereby keeping land prices high. The result was described in rather graphic terms by economist David McWilliams in 2004 when he wrote in *Dublin Dialogue*: "Here (in Ireland) the young pass enormous amounts of wealth to the old via the housing and corrupt land market....for every five indebted first-time buyers, tearing their hair out in traffic this morning, there is an Irish sixty-year-old millionaire about to tee off in the Algarve sunshine."

Irish Examiner journalist Michael Clifford, writing in January 2019, said the reality is that as a result of Ireland's history, property-owners have enjoyed an exalted position since the foundation of the State. "Private property," he wrote "is guaranteed in the Constitution, but whenever that right comes up against the competing right of the common good, there has always been only one winner." [5]

Clifford argued strongly that central to any housing solution would have to be an acknowledgement that housing is not an issue to be left to the whims of the market. In this respect, he said one of the biggest obstacles to affordable homes is the price of land. Once land is rezoned for housing - nominally in the interests of the common good - the landowner sees the value increase exponentially. "The muck of agricultural land transforms overnight into the gold of housing land," he wrote.

Dr William Nowlan, Founder of Hibernia REIT and Urbeo Residential, said that after studying land management for over 60 years it was "still a Rubix cube" to him. "There are times I think part of the problem is greed, people wanting to make more than a fair figure. There is also a hatred of change and getting change in Irish society is difficult."

In this scenario, over many decades, property-owners reaped huge profits on the back of the alleged common good as defined in Article 43.2. The legal infrastructure set up to govern the operation of local authorities saw local councillors given major powers under what was commonly known as "Section

---

[5] *Irish Examiner*, 26 January 2019

4 motions" (Section 4 of the City and County Management (Amendment) Act, 1955) which empowered county councillors to overturn the decision of the county manager where planning permission was refused.

In many ways, these local councillors had much more powers than backbench TDs or Senators (though they often were both) in that they had the capability to turn lucky landowners, or crafty speculators, into overnight millionaires many times over.

As the demand for more and more urban housing grew, use of these Section 4 motions fuelled land speculation. Indeed, the potential for enormous financial profits inevitably created inducements for corrupt transactions between developers, local officials and public representatives.

In time public disquiet began to erupt when it emerged that huge windfall profits could be made because of this provision and the use of Section 4 motions became widespread. Furthermore, loopholes in the tax laws allowed the use of various devices which caused much of these windfall gains to go untaxed. The danger of such a regime was highlighted, for example, in an appeal ruling by Supreme Court judge, John McMenamin in *DPP v Forsey* when he stated: "The existence of a planning regime which allows for potentially huge windfall profits by land rezoning, creates a risk that financially vulnerable persons, with a role in the decision-making process, will engage in corrupt activities." [6]

Corruption and bad decisions in the Irish planning system eventually led to the Planning Tribunals. For a period of 15 years, between 1997 and 2012, the *Tribunal of Inquiry into Certain Planning Matters and Payments* heard hundreds of hours of evidence from an equally large number of witnesses. Many decisions were seen to have been simply bad, a result of pressure being put on political system by the powerful landowning lobby. Other decisions were corrupt, with some councillors being bought off for relatively paltry amounts of money.

As a result, new legislation was introduced and the powers of local councillors were curtailed, notably by the abolition of the Section 4 motions. But there has always been a reluctance among politicians and those in power

---

[6] http://www.bailii.org/ie/cases/IESC/2018/S55.html

to radically address the system and bring about a permanent solution to the issue of zoning land for development.

Today, the cost of development land still constitutes a major portion of the cost of a new house. For example, in June 2017, Irish State broadcaster RTE announced that it had sold 8.64 acres of its Montrose Headquarters in south Dublin to Cairn Homes for €107.5m. Cairn Homes subsequently announced that it planned to build 500 apartments and nine homes on the site, giving a land purchase price of in excess of €200,000 per unit.

According to builder/developer Michael O'Flynn, the only way this site could be profitable for the purchasers was if they managed to get increased density, or "a miracle" of a house price escalation. (Cairn Homes subsequently applied for, and were granted, planning permission for 611 apartments, three townhouses, two cafes and a childcare facility. In order to comply with social housing obligations, Cairn Homes proposed to sell 61 of the apartments in the plan to Dublin City Council for €30.17m. The documentation lodged with the application put a value of €521,377 on the two-bed apartments and €472,797 on the one-bed apartments, a very high price for any local authority to pay for social housing. The planning permission was subsequently quashed in March 2021 by the High Court following a challenge brought by a group of local residents.

In 2023 Ireland's housing system continues to face a crisis. While there are many aspects to the crisis, not least of which was the outbreak in March 2020 of the Covid-19 pandemic and the Ukranian war refugee crisis, the issue of how best to provide owner-occupied housing and affordable rental housing for a growing section of the population remains paramount.

The 2018 report from the National Economic and Social Council (NESC) stated that the availability of land for housing in appropriate locations, in a way that is consistent with affordability, has long been "an unresolved policy in Ireland". The supply conditions of land can vary for two main reasons: the decisions of land owners on whether they will sell, develop or hold their land; and decisions of public authorities on zoning, planning and infrastructure," the report stated. It continued: "Public decisions on zoning, planning and infrastructure often confer disproportionately large benefits on the owners of land. Planning, of the kind found in Ireland and Britain, can prevent undesired development, but lacks the ability to ensure that development takes place....The focal point for competition is land acquisition and land hoarding, rather than quality, or value for consumers. Overall, the supply of land is uncertain, patchy and costly. This tends to make the housing system risky, unstable and unaffordable."

The Kenny Report

However, over the years, there have been genuine attempts to bring about serious reform and to ensure land was rezoned in a manner that meets "the exigencies of the common good".

One such major effort was that by the Committee on the Price of Building Land which reported in 1973. Known as the "Kenny Report" it produced a number of innovative and thought-provoking measures which sought to ensure the best interests of the common good were to the forefront. At its core was a proposal that local authorities could acquire development land at the existing market value plus 25 per cent. Set up by a Fianna Fáil Government in 1971, by the time the report was submitted, the Government was about to change, as had the economic environment. As a result, the report was allowed to gather dust. Time and again when the matter was raised on the floor of the Houses of the Oireachtas, the stock response was that there were constitutional problems with implementing such a regime.

Then in 2004, just as the first findings were starting to come from the Planning Tribunal in Dublin Castle, a comprehensive study of the Kenny Report by an all-party Oireachtas Committee on the Constitution concluded, having taken detailed legal advice, that there was no apparent constitutional problem with implementing the recommendations of the Kenny Report.

Already planning legislation, notably the Part V of the Planning and Development Act, 2000, which compels developers to allocate 20 per cent of housing developments - later reduced to 10 per cent - for social housing at existing use value had, in effect, vindicated the Kenny Report. The Act was referred to the Supreme Court by President Mary McAleese and the case in its favour was argued by the then Attorney General, Michael McDowell SC. The Act was held not to be in breach of the Constitution by the court.

The Act marked a significant development in government policy and, according to homelessness campaigner and founder of the McVerry Trust, Fr Peter McVerry, was "one of the best policy decisions of the last few decades".

However, under pressure from developers and builders, the Government gradually diluted the requirements and from 2000 to 2008 only 3.5 % of residential output was allocated to social and affordable housing.

Meanwhile, Ireland's housing crisis continues right to this day, although increased building activity, slowed for a time due to the outbreak of the Covid-19 pandemic in the Spring of 2020, has increased significantly.

So, who is to blame for the recurring housing crisis over the past decades? This book will argue that successive governments and ministers must share a large portion of it for their failure over many decades to adopt and implement a clear strategy which could have seen a steady supply of housing to meet the growing demand.

Chapter 2

Housing, Land Policy and the Constitution

Policy-Making

In the Republic of Ireland today, policy is often initiated from proposals developed from reports from Joint Oireachtas Committees (joint meetings of Dáil deputies and senators) into which a range of stakeholders have made an input over a period of time. The suggestions from the stakeholders are then filtered down to 'politically' acceptable options before being refined by research, analysis, consultation and impact assessment into a single option to be drafted into legislation.

Before the Government publishes a Bill, there is usually a consultation process. The relevant Department may publish a Green Paper, setting out the Government's ideas and inviting opinions from individuals and organisations. For example, the Green Paper on Energy Policy in Ireland was launched in May 2014 and 1,200 submissions were made during the consultation process.

In Ireland, there are a number of organisations that offer their views on the process of policy-making. These include the Economic and Social Research Institute (ESRI), the National Economic and Social Council (NESC) the Institute of International and European Affairs (IIEA) and the Institute of Public Administration (IPA). In relation to housing policy, for example, in 1979 the ESRI produced a report entitled *"The Irish Housing System; A Critical Overview"* while, as outlined in the Foreword, NESC produces regular reports on a wide range of issues, including housing.

Before a Bill is finalised, a general scheme of the Bill may be published, and this is generally referred to as the Heads of the Bill. At the end of the pre-legislative scrutiny process (which does not happen to all legislation), the Committee produces a report and lays it before the Houses of the Oireachtas. The report makes recommendations on the Bill based on the Committee's scrutiny.

An example of pre-legislative scrutiny is the Committee on Justice and Equality's scrutiny of the General Scheme of the Gender Pay Gap Information Bill, 2019. The Committee invited three representative organisations to a public hearing on 21 November 2018. In February 2019 it published its report with recommendations to the Government on the final draft of the Bill.

Of course, policy problems and policy solutions frequently emerge together, rather than one after another. Decisions are rarely decided on a totally smooth basis, as the political world is full of sudden and unexpected changes and interventions. One such unexpected event was the need for swift political reaction to the global outbreak of the coronavirus, Covid-19, in the spring of 2020. C. J. Friedrich summed up this phenomenon very well by arguing that public policy is being formed as it is being executed and it is likewise executed as it is being formed (Friedrich, 1941). [7]

The making of public policy in Ireland is no different from that of many other countries, notably Britain. Key decisions are taken by the government meeting in Cabinet and then approved by the Oireachtas.

Many key decisions are made at the weekly Cabinet meeting, but are then adjusted, but rarely overturned by the Oireachtas. (However, this pattern changed radically with the 'Confidence and Supply' arrangement entered into by Fianna Fáil with Fine Gael in the aftermath of the 2016 general election when the government did not have control of the Dáil and the business of the House was arranged by the Dáil's Business Committee. This practice continued in the aftermath of the 2020 general election).

Decisions are normally preceded by a *Memorandum to Government* by a minister and his/her department proposing a particular course of action which is then agreed and which all members of the government then support, under the principle of collective responsibility.

Irish government departments tend, by their nature, to work slowly and cautiously. The Irish civil service is frequently criticised for being too bureaucratic. Its managers pay too much attention to the nitty-gritty of operations and neglect the formulation of strategy and the assessment of

---

[7] C.J Friedrich *Constitutional Government and Democracy: Theory and Practice in Europe and America.* (1941)

performance. They are focused on 'doing things right rather than doing the right things.' [8]

They also have a great deal of autonomy as they have the expertise in their area and are familiar with the interest of stakeholders. However, often dynamic ministers need to drive change and work at a faster pace than that proposed by the civil service. Examples of this include Fianna Fáil's Education Minister Donogh O'Malley's announcement of free second-level education in 1968 and Fianna Fáil's Health Minister Micheál Martin's insistence to proceed with a smoking ban in the workplace in 2004. However, such initiatives do not always have a successful outcome. When former Progressive Democrat leader Mary Harney was appointed Minister for Health in 2004, she proceeded to make major structural reform of the health services through the creation of the Health Services Executive (HSE) which is now generally seen as having failed to deliver on many promised efficiencies.

Interest Groups

A key part of policy formation is the role of interest groups, often referred to as pressure groups. They are particularly relevant in areas such as housing policy where they are well organised and focused and are a central part of the policy-making process.

As interest groups play a major role in both policy formulation and implementation, understanding how they work is crucial to knowing how modern democracies function. G. K. Wilson defined an interest group as having two distinct criteria: the organisation has some autonomy from government and that it tries to influence policy outcomes. [9]

Interest groups generally operate by attempting to influence policy through causing changes prior to, or during, the passage of legislation. This is primarily done through contact or 'lobbying' of government ministers, their advisors, key civil servants, TDs and senators, including members of the opposition.

---

[8] Litton, F. (2012) An Overview of the Irish System of Government. In *Governing Ireland: From Cabinet Government to Delegated Government* (O'Malley, E. & MacCarthaigh M. eds) IPA. pp15 – 34.
[9] Wilson, G.K. *Interest Groups* (1991)

Very often the main target is the relevant civil servants often referred to as the "permanent government" and many interest groups or lobbyists concentrate most of their efforts on this cohort of policy-makers. The existence of interest groups ultimately places constraints on governments in that the policy-making process generally involves some accommodation of the wishes of these groups.

In Ireland, a key interest group often referred to and generally seen as one of the most effective and successful is the Irish Farmers Association (IFA). It has some 85,000 members spread across the 26 counties in well organised grass-roots structure, consisting of some 945 branches. The IFA currently spends nearly half its income from farmers on its European lobbing efforts and maintains a permanent lobbying office in Brussels. (Murphy, 1992: 340). Other highly effective interest groups are the Irish Business and Employers' Confederation (IBEC) and in the property sector, the Construction Industry Federation (CIF), Property Industry Ireland, which is a division of IBEC and the more recently established Irish Institutional Property (IIP), which is largely the voice of institutionally financed investors, commonly referred to as vulture funds, with significant international backing in the Irish real estate market. (Significantly, the IIP appointed as its chief executive, Pat Farrell, a former general secretary of Fianna Fáil, senator and a banking lobbyist with a wide range of political and civil service connections).

In Ireland, the IFA is often named as the singularly most influential lobbying body on public policy. It does this through a number of carefully planned strategies. At local level, it uses voluntary officers to maintain links with local political party branches and politicians to lobby for its objectives. Nationally, when required, it can readily, at short notice, mobilize many thousands of members to protest outside a government department, or other relevant body with accompanying disruption and attendant publicity. It can do this in a successful and efficient way that most trade unions are unable to match.

Access to decision-makers is a key component of the lobbying process and often times this has been bound up with financial donations to political parties and to individual politicians. The Tribunals of Enquiry revealed that political parties and individual politicians had been in receipt of political donations for many years.

In its interim report in September 2002, the Flood Tribunal ruled that former minister Ray Burke had received corrupt payments from a succession of builders (Flood Report). (Burke was later jailed for six months for failing to make correct tax returns, thereby becoming the first ex-minister in the history of the state to be imprisoned on criminal charges.) As a result of the Tribunals, a number of pieces of legislation were introduced including the Ethics in Public Offices Act, 1995; the Standards in Public Office Act, 2001; the Electoral Act, 2012 and the Regulation of Lobbying Act, 2015.

Although politicians have always been reluctant to admit financial donations are given in the hope of receiving favours, a long-time Fianna Fail councillor and Senator Don Lydon admitted to the Flood Tribunal: "I believe that they hope to influence (them). That's my firm belief. They did it then, they did it before and they do it now."

Nowhere more was the influence of the construction industry felt than at the annual Galway Races in Ballybrit where the Fianna Fáil party hosted a tent which was basically a fund-raising initiative and served as a sort of informal annual gathering of some of the country's richest property developers and construction companies. The tent was later abandoned by Brian Cowen when he became Taoiseach in 2008.

In recent years, lobbyists have become more formalised and are now known generally as 'public affairs consultants' and since September 2015 are now obliged to register with the Standard in Public Offices Commission (SIPO) on its website www.lobbying.ie which is open to public scrutiny. In addition, three times each year they must register details of their lobbying activities with Designated Public Officials (DPOs) i.e. ministers, advisors, TDs, senators, MEPs, senior civil servants and senior local authority officials, down to the level of assistant secretary. However, as much of their work is below assistant secretary level, it does not have to be reported and continues to remain hidden from public scrutiny.

One of the earliest full-time public affairs consultants was the former government press secretary to Taoiseach Charles Haughey, PJ Mara, who lobbied government for a number of high-profile companies and individuals. Today, the list of lobbyists in Ireland includes some former TDs and senators, former government press secretaries, former officials of the main political parties and a number of former political journalists. Indeed, up to relatively recent times, many serving TDs acted as lobbyists for various companies and interest groups.

The Irish lobbying system contrasts somewhat with that which operates in the European Commission in Brussels, for example, where consulting with lobbyists and stakeholders is taken as a perquisite to the consideration of any proposed legislation (the Commission is the only body which initiates legislation within the EU).

For decades, interest groups have operated in Ireland in various formats and disguises with varying degrees of success. However, following the passage of the lobbying legislation, it would appear that Ireland is now falling very much into the mainstream of western European politics in relation to how it operates its formation of public policy and interacts with interest groups. The proliferation of cause-centred groups and private interests also seeking to influence public policy, with varying degrees of money and willing to use any means possible, adds an extra complication to the mix in attempting to assess interest group influence.

The National Mood

The national mood is always a critical factor in how governments react and make decisions. (It played a critical role in Ireland in 1973 when a number of new issues took public attention away from housing, notably the Northern Ireland Troubles and the oil crisis.) Opinion polls and surveys of all kinds are closely monitored and analysed for the latest trends and indicators as to what the electorate believes and wants.

People in and around government sense a national mood. According to political scientist John W. Kingdon they are comfortable discussing it content and believe that they know when the mood shifts. Common to all, he says, is the notion that a rather large number of people out in the country are thinking along certain common lines, that this national mood changes from one time to another in a discernible way and that these changes in mood or climate have important impacts on policy agendas and policy outcomes. [10]

---

[10] Kingdon, J.W. (2014) *Agendas, Alternatives and Public Policies.* Pearson Education Ltd. p.146

Early Urban and Rural initiatives

Housing policy specifically has a number of distinctive characteristics that makes it different from most other public policies. It has a long life and key elements of the housing situation reflect patterns of investment of 60 – 100 years earlier. Housing policy includes measures designed to modify the quality, or quantity of housing, its price and ownership, access to it and management of it. Planning restrictions/guidelines, tax incentives, the provision of services all greatly affect the viability of a project.

There is limited academic material in early State housing in Ireland. One of the people to study early State housing in Ireland was Frederick Aalen, a social geographer at Trinity College, Dublin. Aalen's work covered almost the entire span of early housing history, in particular looking at the semi-philanthropic housing companies in 19th Century Dublin as well at local authority housing in both town and country prior to the First World War.

Working class housing conditions in Dublin have been analysed by social-economic historians Joseph O'Brien and Mary Daly as part of the wider problems in Dublin prior to World War 1.

Murray Fraser was the first researcher to analyse in detail historical accounts of early State housing in Ireland and draws on a variety of source material in both Ireland and Westminster. In his book *John Bull's Other Homes: State Housing and British policy in Ireland 1883 – 1922,* his discussion on housing policy and design (Fraser is a qualified architect) are consciously interwoven and there is a genuine effort to represent the widest possible range of views of political and economic interest groups in Ireland and Britain.

Unlike mainland Britain, rural housing received as much attention in Ireland as urban and, indeed, up to the 1880s, received more attention. In fact, as Fraser points out, housing policy in Ireland was split into distinct rural and urban initiatives with the former initially fare more dominant.

In the years leading up to 1922, housing had been a significant aspect of the relationship between Ireland and the United Kingdom. The result was that Ireland, prior to 1914, was the first, and apparently, the only country to have a national policy of State housing based on centrally subsidised municipal dwellings and recommended design types. Indeed, in the context of Europe and America before 1914, it is clear that Ireland had by far the most socialised system of working-class housebuilding.

Unusually, Ireland was atypical in that it tended to be led by rural developments in contrast to most countries where urban housing got most attention. This might be expected in an agricultural economy but even before WW1, the impetus towards State subsidy in urban housing was more advanced than in most countries.

UK and other models

While Ireland has tended to be heavily influenced by UK models and legislation, other countries have taken various measures to facilitate development. In France, for example, vigorous intervention by the state from 1958 saw the creation of urbanization priority zones (ZUPs – *zones á urbaniser á priorité*) which were large tracts of land purchased at the average market price prevailing during the previous five years, normally that for agricultural land.

In Germany, an approach broadly known as 'land readjustment' is applied. There local authorities temporarily combine the ownership of land earmarked for development. The land in a designated area is pooled by the owners. The local authority then assesses the land values before existing use and after the 'readjustment'. The original owners get their land back on completion of the scheme but the local authority retains the increase in value up to 30 per cent for greenfield sites and up to 10 per cent of the value of brownfield sites.

International comparisons show that countries with similar preconditions in fact developed very different forms of housing underpinned by different legislation and different institutional and financial arrangements. Here the key factor is political action and the case for intervention. There are a number of reasons for the diverse developments, one of which is that the market cost of accommodation of a reasonable standard has tended to be too high in relation to the income of the poorer sections of society, thereby necessitating state intervention. The second is the public health aspect of housing conditions whereby the appalling conditions of the 19th and early 20th centuries, especially in urban areas, constituted a threat to health, not only of the slum dwellers themselves but to the whole population.

Also, as pointed out by Baker & O'Brien [11], passive policy, such as the basic rights accorded to owners of land, or the freedom of private enterprise banks to determine their own policies in their pattern of lending can have as much impact on the efficiency and equity of the housing system as can such active policy measures as fixing the level of local authority rents or specifying the number of houses per acre which may be built in a new housing development.

Lack of Clarity

In their report, Baker and O'Brien recommended "urgent need" for a re-definition of the basic aims of public housing policy.

> The continued existence of inappropriate laws and the present maldistribution of public housing subsidies are both the result of a failure to examine the role of the public authorities in relation to the housing system as a whole rather than to individual sectors of it.

In its review of housing policy in 1988, on behalf of the National Economic and Social Council (NESC), Blackwell stated the objective of the housing policy of the Department of the Environment was:

> to ensure that, as far as the resources of the economy permit, every family can obtain for their own occupation a house of good standard at a price, or rent that they can afford located in an acceptable environment. A secondary aim of housing policy is the encouragement of owner-occupation as the widely preferred form of tenure. [12]

The NESC report noted that the statement was very general and did not indicate the criteria by which housing policy can be evaluated nor state how the objectives could be pursued. It went on to note that "State intervention has been characterised by lack of co-ordination and continued modification

---

[11] Baker, T.J. and O'Brien, L.M. (1979) *The Irish Housing System: A Critical Review.* Economic & Social Research Institute. Dublin.

[12] Blackwell, J. (1988) *A Review of Housing Policy* (National Social and Economic Council). Government Publications Office. Dublin. p. 4

and adaption, without sufficient clarity regarding the role of the different housing tenures".

Chartered Surveyor and author Frank Ryan has stated that Irish housing policy has exhibited and continues to exhibit a strong empathic policy intent that favours ownership.

> Irish housing policy has not identified the risk that a consumer obsession for ownership matched by a policy intent to encourage ownership may prove counter-productive towards a balanced market outcome.[13]

The policy of *ad hoc* and sometimes kneejerk intervention has characterised Irish housing policy in recent decades. One example is the £1,000 (€1,270) cash grant for new houses introduced in 1977. The objective of this grant was to assist prospective owners to acquire their own home. However, the grant was not related to income and one of its effects was to increase the price of new houses.

A second example, was the introduction in 1984 of a £5,000 (€6,348) "surrender" grant for local authority tenants who purchased homes in the private sector. A study of this grant by Threshold[14] in 1987 revealed the scheme resulted in the further blight and deteriorating of municipal housing estates as tenants with higher and more secure incomes took up the offer.

The 1988 NESC report identified a number of key policy issues that needed to be addressed. These included the need for Government subsidies to be targeted more specifically. It also pointed out that the emphasis on owner-occupation in Ireland had got to the point where it could get in the way of achieving housing objectives. [15]

According to Frank Ryan, Irish housing policy is treated as a "measurement of new housing physical output". It can have an 'engineering silo', 'incremental' character as piecemeal new policies are implemented in response to current pressures in specific sectors of the Irish housing system. There is, he says, no consideration, or attention, applied to the importance of a long-term balanced housing objective for the entire housing system.

---

[13] Ryan, F.P. (2019) *Lessons in Irish Housing*. Oaktree Press. p.16
[14] Founded in 1978, Threshold is a registered charity whose aim is to secure a right to housing, particularly for households experiencing the problems of poverty and exclusion.
[15] Ibid p. 249 - 252

> In Ireland, in respect of housing development lands, where policy, the common good and the market are in conflict, the market is the winner and policy and the common good are the losers. [16]

A key issue which arises in regard to housing policy is whether it is the demand for housing that pushes up land prices, or higher land prices that push up housing costs. This has been addressed by a number of commentators including economist Peter Bacon who, in his 1998 report, stated that from an economic point of view "the balance of probability" would suggest the former channel rather than the latter.

> In other words, it is the dynamics of supply and demand for the end product -housing - that has given rise to increasing land prices, not the other way round. The contention that land costs are a rising proportion of total housing costs could reflect the relative inelastic supply of serviced development land in locations that are sought after. [17]

Today the economic value of lands for housing is calculated by reference to the house price sale less all the costs (including VAT, constructions costs, profit etc.) and hence a land economic value is arrived at. However, a major problem is that the value of the development land is based on the anticipated house sales in 24 – 36 months with estimated improving values and variable costs. In essence, it is a market gamble. In addition, market forces relating to perceptions of land scarcity, a reluctant vendor and strong competition may force the highest bidder to pay a premium to secure ownership.

In times of positive growth, high land prices are a sign of market confidence and anticipation of future growth but they create risks that high value housing must be achieved to deliver profit down the road.

> The landowner is the 'spoilt child' of new housing. He seeks to reap the housing dividend, in advance, based on projected future events, at a price level that is clearly in excess of its

---

[16] Ibid p. 44
[17] Bacon, P. (1998) An Economic Assessment of Recent House Price Developments. Government Publications Office. Chpt. iv

economic or viability measurement on current day cost/value variables. [18]

Speaking at the launch of the first Bacon report on 23 April 1998, the then Minister for the Environment and Local Government, Noel Dempsey, quoted a paragraph from page 84 of the report which stated: "there is not a simple formula available to address the issue of house price increases."

In their third and final report on the housing market in Ireland in 2000, Peter Bacon and Fergal MacCabe identified three requirements in order to have an effective supply response strategy:

- **Credibility**, in the sense that what is proposed by way of a supply response will be matched with the necessary commitment of resources to ensure that undertakings are translated on the ground into serviced sites on which necessary planning consents can be obtained.

- **Clarity,** as regards where development is to take place and that all the necessary infrastructure to facilitate the development of secure and stable community living will be put into place, including especially access to transport facilities.

- **Certainty,** as to when development can commence. At present it is difficult to predict with any certainty when making a planning application, when in fact work will be capable of commencing. Matching demand with supply in such circumstances is extremely difficult. [19]

The report also warned of the need to curb any significant speculative, or transitory component of demand, which might be present.

Department of Finance

[18] Ryan, F.P. (2019) *Lessons in Irish Housing.* Oaktree Press. p. 41

[19] Bacon, P & MacCabe, F. (2000) *The Housing Market in Ireland: An Economic Evaluation of Trends & Prospects.* Government Publications Office. Dublin.

Frank Ryan pointed out that within the housing system, the Department of Finance is the "dark horse", a hidden variable that can frustrate both leadership and policy.

> The Department of Finance has no direct interest in housing, or housing policy - as a net funding flow to government finances. Outside of the Taoiseach, it is the strongest element of government and it is not a participator in dialogue on housing with market suppliers. [20]

Ryan concluded that the intervention of the Taoiseach is normally necessary to mandate new housing policy of substance. The Irish housing system is, he says "plagued by cultural difference, separate priorities and market prejudices". Irish housing policy over the years has concentrated on a process of the physical production of houses, regular issuing of statistics and press releases. And always, there has been a reliance on the private market to deliver most of the housing needs.

> The policy has been piecemeal, incremental in character, responding to current market pressures, particularly lobby group pressure rather than a robust knowledge-based policy with continuity that anticipates rapidly-changing market trends. [21]

---

[20] Ibid p. 23
[21] Ibid p.26

Chapter 3

The Historical Setting

Colonisation

The conquest of rural Ireland by Britain dates back to the Norman feudal expansion of the 12th Century. This saw the establishment of a region around Dublin known as the "Pale" but a sustained colonisation programme was not pursued in Ireland until the 16th and 17th centuries. The surrender and re-grant policy pursued by the Tudors in the 16th century radically uprooted and abolished the land tenure system that had previously prevailed for over two millennia under Brehon law, a system that had a strong communal character.

> The English common law system was transplanted to Ireland through processes of conquest, confiscation and resettlement. It replaced the native *Brehon* system with English settlor landlords, creating 'a kind of bastardized feudalism...a feudalism not founded in a history of the evolution of mutual rights and obligations between a native peasantry and a native (or at least assimilated) ruling class'. [22]

This colonisation programme was supported by a number of plantations of both Anglicans and Presbyterians which imposed British dominancy over the large Catholic majority. Gradually Catholics were reduced to the status of tenant farmers and labourers.

An Irish Parliament governed Ireland under the authority of the English crown. After the Battle of the Boyne in 1690 and the defeat of the forces of the deposed Catholic King, James II, a series of severe restrictions known as the "Penal Laws" were introduced which remained in force for most of the 18th Century. Britain felt it necessary to maintain a tight grip over Ireland for a number of reasons, chiefly to create a cheap and reliable supply of agricultural produce and to remove the threat of attack from an often very hostile

---

[22] Walsh, R., Fox O'Mahony, L. (2018) *Land Law, property ideologies and the British-Irish relationship.* Common Law World Review. Sage Journals.

neighbour (Fraser, 1996: 2). Unrest continued and resulted in the rebellion of 1798, which was followed by the Act of Union introduced in 1800 under Prime Minster William Pitt the Younger which created the United Kingdom of Great Britain and Ireland.

However, from the start, the new system was very difficult to operate and soon the long-established motto of finding an Irish solution to an Irish problem became part of the strategy pursued by successive British governments during the second half of the 18th Century (O'Tuathaigh, 1986). Conflicts between the mainly Protestant and Unionists landlords who owned most of the land and the mainly Catholic and nationalist farmers who rented it, shaped Irish history for a long period of time. Discontent among the native Irish continued and resulted in regular outbreaks of fresh rebellion which continued right up until the Anglo-Irish Treaty of 1921..[23]

Speaking in the Dáil one hundred years later, on 3 June 1980, Labour Deputy Ruairí Quinn said:

> The land struggle of the 1880s was one of a people struggling for survival, to own land, to grow food with which to feed themselves.

He quoted the 19th Century revolutionary and writer James Fintan Lalor who, in a book on his writings published by The Talbot Press Limited in 1919 wrote: "The rights of property may be pleaded. No one has more respect for the real rights of property than I have; but I do not class among them the robber's right by which the lands of this country are now held in fee for the British crown. I acknowledge no right of property in a small class which goes to abrogate the rights of a numerous people. I acknowledge no right of property in eight thousand persons, be they noble or ignoble, which takes away all rights of property, security, independence, and existence itself, from a population of eight million and stands in bar to all the political rights of the island, and all the social rights of its inhabitants.......Against them I assert the true and indefeasible right of property - the right of our people to live in this land and possess it - to live in it in security, comfort and independence, and

---

[23] Norris, M. (2016). *Property, Family and the Irish Welfare State.* Palgrave macmillan.p.1

to live in it by their own labour, on their own land, as God and nature intended them to do." [24]

Mud Cabins

Before the Great Famine of 1845 – 1849, Irish rural housing was truly appalling and almost impossible to visualise in the 21st Century. The 1841 Census, for example, showed that 470,000 dwellings, or 40 per cent of rural housing stock, had only one room. Known generally as "mud cabins", they were poorly constructed with roofs of turf or thatch. Most had straw floors with domestic animals usually kept indoors. Chimneys and windows were rare. The next category of dwelling identified by the Census included modest cottages of between two and four rooms and these accounted for another 490,000 units, or 42 per cent of stock. By far the highest proportion of substandard dwellings were found in Connaught but Munster was wretched in many parts, too.

As early as the mid-1830s a Royal Commission examining the conditions proposed the cabins be replaced by healthy cottages. The Famine (1845 – 49) saw Ireland's population fall from 8.2 million to 5. 2 million and had a major impact on land structure in rural Ireland. In 1881, a total of 75 per cent of the population lived in rural Ireland. The predominant land structure since the Plantations had been that of Anglo-Irish Ascendancy letting out parcels of land to so-called "middle men" who would then sub-let to tenant small-holders. These parcels of land generally ranged from 1 – 15 acres, or for marginal cottiers, less than 1 acre. The farming pattern was very labour intensive with a large concentration on tillage which was necessary to feed a large population. However, this changed rapidly after the Famine when the shortage of labour caused a rapid switch to larger holdings, usually 15 – 30 acres, or more. It also saw an increase in the level of livestock farming and a gradual elimination of the middle-men. A notable exception was the West of Ireland where cottier farming continued with seasonal migration to Ulster or Britain necessary in order to earn a living. As a result of British policy, by1870 only three per cent of Irish farmers owned land and amongst the landlord ascendancy, fewer than 800 owned half the country.

---

[24] www.oireachtas.ie/en/debates/debate/dail/1980-06-03/34/)

The Land Acts

Towards the end of the 19th Century, as a result of the changing competitive balance between capitalist and family farms, a widespread reversion to smaller scale family farms took place virtually throughout the developed world as well as in many of the more backward regions of Europe. The trend was even evident in Britain where capitalist farming survived for longer than most places in Europe.

> In the face of the economic weakness of Irish landlords and the political dangers of mass discontent in rural Ireland, leading opinion in Britain lost faith in the landlord cause and began to seek means to placate the tenantry and dampen separatist agitation. The consequences crystallized in a major programme of State intervention in the rural Irish economy. [25]

In 1870, following another attempted rebellion, this time by the Fenians, the Liberal Prime Minister, William Gladstone, passed the first of a series of Land Acts which gave a measure of protection of tenure to Irish tenant farmers. The first 1870 Act had little effect and later, poor harvests, allied with an influx of cheap beef and grain from the USA, caused further rural unrest, resulting in the emergence of the Land League led by Michael Davitt. [26]

Under pressure from Charles Stewart Parnell and the Irish Parliamentary Party, Gladstone's Government introduced a more ambitious Land Act in 1881 which granted the three Fs: Fair Rent, Free Sale and Fixity of Tenure. The new Act also saw the creation of a Land Court which ruled on disputes and could set rent for up to 15 years. Most significantly, it also saw the creation of an Irish Land Commission which was tasked with organising the purchase of holdings by tenant farmers. However, only 731 farms were bought out under this Act but the fair rent was a significant change in the Liberal attitude to *laissez faire* economics. The majority of tenants who appealed their rents manged to secure a reduction of between 15 and 20 per cent which, in turn, caused a huge increase in landlord debt and 1,000 were bankrupted. [27] During the first statutory term

---

[25] Fahey, T. (2002) The Family Economy in the Development of Welfare Regimes: A Case Study. *In European Sociological Review*, Vol 18 No. 1. Oxford University Press. p. 56

[26] Further details about Michael Davitt and the Land league can be found at www.michaeldavittmuseum.ie

[27] Norris, M. (2016). *Property, Family and the Irish Welfare State*. Palgrave Macmillan. p.32

of the Land Commission after 1881 a total of 275,525 tenants with an aggregated rental of £5,883,904 (€7,414,051) availed of the new land court system to have their rents fixed. They succeeded in having their aggregated rents reduced to £4,649,918 (€5,904,177), or by 21 per cent. [28] Many labourers acquired small pieces of land, or emigrated to the USA.

The Conservative Party was back in power from 1894 until 1905 and this period saw major changes in land policy in Ireland. They radically increased subsidies to tenants and brought an end to mass agricultural landlordism in Ireland. Beginning with the 1885 Purchase of Land (Ireland) Act (also known as the Ashbourne Act), it allowed tenants to borrow the full price of land from government and repay it at lower interest rates (4pc over 49 years) than previous Acts. A total of £5 million (€6.3 m) was made available and between then and 1888 some 25,400 tenants purchased their land.

Further Land Acts followed. The Land Purchase Act of 1888 gave an additional £5 million to extend the Ashbourne Act. The Chief Secretary for Ireland, Arthur Balfour, sponsored an Act in 1887 (known as the Balfour Act) and followed up with further legislation in 1891.

This legislation provided £33m (€41m) for 100 pc loans to be repaid over 49 years. A further 47,000 tenants purchased their land as a result of these measures.

> The (Balfour) Act expressed a very different philosophical approach to the land problem. In essence, a more interventionist, state-financed system of land transfer was instituted. The Balfour Act contained a formula for buying out landlords and transferring title to tenants. [29]

This process of land purchase by tenant farmers was largely completed when George Wyndham was appointed Chief Secretary for Ireland in 1900. He supported a Land Conference held in Dublin in 1902 and this resulted in the 1903 Land Act which provided tenants with 100pc loans from government, lengthened repayment periods and further reduced interest rates. In addition, the Government also gave a 12 per cent bonus to landlords who

---

[28] Dooley, T. (2004b) *The Land for the People. The Land Question in Independent Ireland.* UCD Press. p.9

[29] Edgeworth, B. (2007) *Rural Radicalism Restrained: The Irish Land Commission and the Courts (1933 – 39),* 42 Irish Jurist (N.S.) 1

agreed to sell. Between 1903 and 1909 the Land Commission advanced a total of £23.4m (€29.7 m) to almost 73,000 tenant farmers to purchase 2.45 million acres. Thus, by 1909 a total of 270,000 tenants had bought out their farms – representing 3.9 million acres - and a further 46,000 were in the process.

The effect of this Act was widespread. For example, in his autobiography *My Fight for Irish Freedom*, former Republican volunteer Dan Breen, one of those involved in the firing of the first shots of the War of Independence at Soloheadbeg, Co. Tipperary on 21 January, 1919, recalled that "the Land Act of 1903, which enabled tenants to purchase holdings, brought great joy to the farmers. They seemed to have entered a utopia where the threat of famine no longer existed". But Breen also noted the unrest among the local farmers in West Tipperary. "I often heard my godfather, Long Jim Ryan and my uncle, Lar Breen, talking about this high rent and also the poor price paid for milk delivered to the new Cleeve's factory"

To support the purchase of land in the West of Ireland which was far poorer than the rest of the country, the Congested Districts Board (CDB), a quasi-autonomous agency was set up by the 1891 Land Act which tried to alleviate poverty and congestion. It also encouraged a host of cottage industries ranging from fish-smoking to bee-keeping. (Aalen, 1993) says it was "the earliest example of regional planning in the British Isles and perhaps in Europe".

> The particular significance of the establishment of this body was that it represented the first genuinely targeted economic aid package for Ireland, and a striking departure from the long-standing tradition of allowing the dynamics of a private law-structured economy to determine the outcome of questions of production, consumption and distribution. [30]

By 1923 the CDB had purchased around 1,000 landlords' estates which contained 60,000 holdings. Occupants of the holdings purchased and redistributed by the Board could remain CDB tenants or purchase their holdings under the terms of the relevant Land Acts. Most chose to buy.

From the mid-19th century, conflicts between Ireland's mainly Protestant and Unionist landlords, who owned most of the land, and the mainly Catholic

---

[30] Ibid

and nationalist tenant farmers who rented it, shaped much of Irish history right up to Independence in 1921. Successive British governments used land reform as a tool in order to procure nationalist political support in the House of Commons and to smother nationalist sentiment.

As mentioned earlier, in 1870 when the first Land Act was introduced, only three per cent of Irish land was owned by Irish farmers but by the time of the foundation of the State, that had dramatically increased when some two-thirds of tenants, numbering 316,000, had bought out their holdings. This change of ownership was not unique to Ireland. It was replicated in many other European countries where governments introduced measures to support the replacement of large capitalist farms with small family farms in the late 19th and early 20th centuries.

This new approach was inspired largely by the widespread depression in agriculture triggered by imports from the New World which undermined the economic viability of the farming model. But the scale in Ireland was huge and far larger than occurred elsewhere.

> "Land redistribution in many Central and Eastern European countries was rolled back by communist regimes and Swinnen's (2002) study of land redistribution in Ireland, England, Scotland, Belgium, France and the Netherlands since 1880 demonstrates that this policy was historically most ambitious in Ireland with the result that, by the late 1990s, far more Irish farmland was owner-occupied (rather than leased) than in any other of these countries." [31]

Rural housing

Running parallel to the various Land Acts were a series of measures to help rural housing which were dealt with under separate legislation known as the Irish Labourers' Acts. The period is divided broadly into two phases 1883 – 1906 and 1906 – 1914. Under the terms of the 1883 Labourers Act, twelve or more ratepayers could apply to the local Board of Guardians who were responsible for sanitation to ask them to carry out a housing scheme. If this was approved by Irish Local Government Board (ILGB), the Guardians could

---

[31] Norris, M. (2016). *Property, Family and the Irish Welfare State.* Palgrave macmillan.

apply for a loan to the Board of Works to be repaid over 60 years. This early measure relied heavily on the British model. In addition, each cottage was given a half-acre of land, later extended to one acre. Thus, measures initially designed to clear slums of London were used to house Irish rural labourers.

The second Labourers Act in 1885 eased and broadened conditions whereby existing cottages could be repaired as well as new units built.

As rural labourers helped the Irish Parliamentary Party to sweep to victory in the 1885 General Election, further easing of conditions were offered. Another Act in 1886 extended terms of the schemes to part-time agricultural labourers.

As a result, a total of 2,188 cottages were built between 1888 and 1889. The schemes continued so that by the time World War 1 started in 1914, Irish local authorities had built 44,055 social rented cottages at a cost of £1.6m (€2m). Much of the success of the schemes depended on the relative strength of the local economies as much of the funding depended on the rates for support.

When the Tories returned to power in 1894, they showed less concern for housing but were very progressive in other areas. They introduced a policy known as "constructive Unionism" in which they tried to show that Ireland's best future was with Britain. Under successive Chief Secretaries in Dublin Castle, including Arthur Balfour, Gerald Balfour and George Wyndham, they reformed Irish local government along British lines. The Department of Agriculture and Technical Instruction had been set up in 1891 and proved to be very successful as did the Congested Districts Board in stimulating growth in the West. It provided limited housing, about 3,000 cottages, and consolidated land holdings in Connaught and parts of Munster.

As a further measure to stimulate rural housing, Arthur Balfour in 1890 introduced an Act to launch a pilot scheme for local authorities to house rural labourers. Initially, a sum of £40,000 (€51,000) was divided between all the counties in Ireland and this figure was later increased.

The rate of cottage building increased with 1750 completed between 1904 and 1905, for example. "If the Irish nation is to be healthy, energetic, hopeful and independent, then up to a third of the population would have to be rehoused," said Chief Secretary George Wyndham.[32] Wyndham's constructive unionism eventually ended when he tried - and failed - to introduce a limited degree of self-determination for Ireland. His successor as Chief Secretary, Sir Walter Long, returned to a policy of imposing law and order.

At this time, the typical rent for a rural cottage plus half an acre was 11 – 12d (1s 5d to include rates) and wages were about 10s (63c) per week. However, the rent was insufficient for most local authorities where the cost of building an average cottage was £1,000 (€1,270). In some counites there was a "housing rate" of 8d in the £ which proved a major disincentive to expansion.

The second phase of building rural cottages began when the Liberals returned to power in 1905. They knew the Irish Home Rule Bill would be vetoed by the House of Lords, so instead concentrated on social reform.

The 1901 Census showed that there remained just 9,000 one-roomed cabins in Ireland which represented just 1 per cent of rural housing stock.

The 1906 Labourers Act gave further loans which, this time, was administered by the Irish Land Commissioners and not the Board of Works. This time the State met 36pc of loan repayments. A maximum spend of £170 (€215) per cottage was stipulated, broken down into £130 (€165) for the house and £40 (€50) for the land. As rural wages were increasing, local authorities could now build more houses. In 1911 the re-elected Liberal Party, with the IPP and Labour Party holding the balance of power, reduced the House of Lords' veto to delay only. This was a critical move as it now cleared the way for the Third Home Rule Bill in 1912. The Tories agreed to pass it, provided it was suspended for the duration of World War 1 and a clause to exclude Ulster agreed.

Urban housing

While considerable progress was made in rural housing, a different scenario existed in the urban areas, notably Dublin which had barely grown since the Act of Union in 1800. In fact, only since the mid-1960s has more than half the population of the Republic of Ireland lived in towns. [33] Dublin had only a few

[32] Fraser, M. (1996). *John Bull's Other Homes. State Housing and British policy in Ireland, 1803 – 1922*. Liverpool University Press.
[33] The All-Party Committee on the Constitution, 2004. p. 67.

successful industries such as the Guinness Brewery and Jacobs Biscuits. As a result, half the workforce were unskilled labourers, living for the most part in appalling tenement conditions.

"The whole city outside a few leading streets is in the process of decay", the *Irish Builder* magazine report in 1913 (25 October) while *The Times* commented: "The slums of Dublin are the worst in the kingdom. Such conditions would not be tolerated even in a modern Oriental city without desperate attempts to remedy such a deplorable state of things...yet people die like flies in its squalid slums" (4 September 1913).

The mid-1850s saw the first housing schemes built by employers for their workforce. These were mainly by the transport companies such as the Great Southern and Western Railway Company and the Guinness Company. However, their impact was very limited (Fraser, 1996: 69). In 1865 came the first legislation with the Labouring Classes (Lodging Houses and Dwellings) Act whereby the Board of Works could make public loans at 4pc interest over 40 years to private companies and even municipalities for up to half the cost of a housing scheme.

In 1884 Dublin Corporation built its first housing scheme at Benburb Street (then Barrack St) when it constructed 144 small flats between one and three rooms at a rent of 1.s 6d to 5s. Other local authorities followed suit and availed of the benefits of further legislation. Another significant piece of legislation was when the 1890 Housing Act was extended to Ireland and urban local authorities began to develop greenfield sites for the first time. By the time the next major piece of legislation came in the form of 1908 Housing Act, the Irish urban authorities had built approximately 5,000 dwellings.

In the meantime, 1890 saw the establishment of the Iveagh Trust with a donation of £50,000 (€63,500) from Sir Arthur Guinness. Initially, it provided 586 dwellings between one and three rooms each in the Bull Alley area of Dublin, next to St Patrick's Hospital. It also included public baths and a recreation building, making it an enclave of Unionist reform in a decaying nationalist city.

The Irish Housing Act 1908, known as the Clancy Act (after JJ Clancy, a North Dublin MP) extended loan periods for housing to 80 years. It created the first direct subsidy through an Irish Housing Fund. Despite some restrictions, house completions boomed from 80 per year prior to the Clancy

Act to 710 in 1910/11. In Dublin almost 5pc of housing stock was built between 1908 and 1914 as a result of the Clancy Act.

The 1916 Easter Rising proved yet another turning point in housing. From this moment on, first the Castle Administration and then Westminster gradually took control of Irish state housing and began to use the issue as a political tool. The 1920 Government of Ireland Act showed Westminster had still not given up on its intention to finance Irish housing but the formation of the first Dáil led to conflict and a degree of paralysis.

Chapter 4

The Land Commission[34] 1: A Public Policy which Compulsorily Acquired Land Successfully

A story of success

One of the major success stories of the land policy in Ireland was the success of the Land Commission which acquired thousands of acres from large estates and redistributed them to small tenant farmers. Significantly, when compared to the fallout from the Kenny Report from 1973 onwards, never were its powers, derived from a series of Land Acts, successfully challenged as being adverse to the new Constitution of Ireland, *Bunreacht Na hÉireann*, which came into force in December 1937. (Between 1921 and 1937 there were a small number of court challenges to the work of the Commission but these were cleared in a new Act in 1939 which enabled the Land Commission "to proceed with normal expedition and regularity").

Pre-independence its powers had been challenged when the Marquess of Clanicarde, the holder of a number of estates in Co Galway, challenged the Land Act, 1909 (the "Birrell Act") which conferred on the Land Commission powers to compulsorily acquire land in designated counties for the relief of congestion. He applied to the High Court for an injunction which was granted but was later overturned by a unanimous Court of Appeal. The Marquess then appealed to the House of Lords but was unsuccessful although he was granted

---

[34] Almost 30 years after its closure in 1992, there were no immediate plans to make the eight million or so records of the former Irish Land Commission generally available to the public for research or other purposes, as they are still classified as working documents and have not been handed over to the National Archives. Thus, it is impossible to know who, and on what grounds was allocated land. Land Commission documents are the largest single collection of Irish records covering the late 19th and early 20th centuries outside of the National Archives.

a £10,000 (€12,700) increase in the purchase price, up from £228,075 (€289,595) to £238,211 (€302,465). [35]

The powers of the Land Commission are referred to in the Kenny Report on some occasions. In Chapter 8 dealing with the Constitution, the Report refers to a significant Supreme Court decision in *Fisher v The Irish Land Commission* [1948] I.R. 3. In this case, Mr Fisher, who owned lands the Land Commission wished to acquire, brought an action in which he claimed that Section 39 of the Land Act, 1939 was repugnant to the Constitution because it authorised the exercise of judicial powers by a tribunal whose members were not judges. The Supreme Court ruled that the Oireachtas had given the Land Commission general power to take land for the purposes of the Land Acts provided certain specified steps had been taken.

> The decision of the Lay Commissioners did not therefore involve a ruling on whether a legal right existed but was to be based on considerations of public policy only; the Lay Commissioners had not to decide a conflict of legal rights and so their power to decide whether the Land Commission should be allowed to resume (acquire) the holding was not an administration of justice. [36]

In Chapter 10, outlining details of the proposed Designated Area Scheme, the Kenny Report specifically refers to the powers of the Land Commission under the Land Acts of 1927 and 1953 which allowed the Land Commission to take possession of land even if those in occupation refused to leave them.

> The State was involved in basically appropriating lands, at what they euphemistically called "fair value", which is basically whatever they felt like paying for it. In most cases, taking it from what are euphemistically called Anglo-Irish landlords and giving it to small farmers. None of this was ever deemed unconstitutional and that went on right until the late 1980s, but on a large scale to the end of the 1960s. So, under the

---

[35] Edgeworth, B. (2007) 2007) *Rural Radicalism Restrained: The Irish Land Commission and the Courts (1933 – 39),* 42 Irish Jurist (N.S.) 1
[36] Kenny Report, Par. 95

current Constitution, the arguments about (Kenny) being unconstitutional are just not convincing. [37]

The following is a brief overview of how successive governments used the Land Commission to acquire and redistribute private land.

The role of the Land Commission was to implement one of the most successful policies of the new fledgling government which oversaw the break-up of hundreds of large estates and the transfer of in excess of two million acres of land to tenants. The policy helped set in place the basis for today's Irish agricultural industry.

> ...the Land Commission became the most important state institution of the 20th Century – its impact on rural society matched only by the Catholic Church – and the most important vehicle of social engineering in modern Ireland. [38]

Speaking in the Dáil during the winding up of the Commission in 1992, Minister of State Liam Hyland TD described it as "the body responsible for the dismantling of the landlord system and the conversion of tenants into proprietors". [39]

From rent-fixing body to purchasing agency

Established under British rule in 1881, it was originally a rent-fixing body with the objective of alleviating the lot of Ireland's tenant-farmers *vis-a vis* the dominant landlord class. Having completed this task, it soon developed into a purchasing agency which proceeded to eliminate landlords and transform the tenants into proprietors of their holdings.

> It thus led to the elimination of the of the 19th Century landlord system and made independent small family farmers into the largest class in the Irish social structure....It was widely regarded as offering a more natural and wholesome form of social protection than state welfare in the usual sense. This

---

[37] Interview with Prof. Michelle Norris
[38] Dooley, T. (2004b) *The Land for the People. The Land Question in Independent Ireland.* UCD Press. p. 230
[39] https://www.oireachtas.ie/en/debates/debate/seanad/1992-10-21/10/)

view became an important strand in Irish thinking on social issues and provided an armoury to those opposed to the extension of British welfare measures to Ireland. [40]

In May 1923, introducing the new Land Law (Commission) Bill, the new Minister for Agriculture, Patrick Hogan TD told the Dáil that as "a result of the operations of the Transfer of Functions Order, which transferred the administration of the Land Acts, the Office of the Commissioner of the Irish Land Commission ceased to exist, and we were under the necessity of reconstituting the Land Commission.....There is one body now - the lay Land Commissioners and they administer the Land Acts and the Land Purchase Acts." [41]

From 1923 onwards, under the terms of the significant 1923 Land Act, the Land Commission, under the direction of Minister Hogan, emerged as a purchaser and distributor of untenanted land, taking on the huge challenge of alleviating rural congestion. This Act enabled the Land Commission to compulsorily purchase the holdings of the tenants who had not purchased their holdings under the terms of the pre-independence Land Acts. This rectified the situation of approximately 114,000 tenants.

But the 1923 Act went further and conferred on the Land Commission the power to compulsorily acquire non-tenanted land from large holdings and redistribute it to smallholders where deemed necessary. It also abolished the Congested Districts Board and transferred its redistribution responsibilities to the Land Commission. Further legislation in 1933 (Land Act, 1933) and 1936 (Land Act, 1936) removed the last remaining loopholes which had enabled landlords to avoid compulsory acquisition.

UCD Professor Michelle Harris argues that operating this land policy required government intervention in the property rights of landowners "which was just as radical as the taxation applied to the incomes and assets of middle and higher earners to establish welfare states". Without doubt, the 1923 Act was one of the most important pieces of legislation passed by an independent Irish government and probably the most important piece of social legislation.

---

[40] Fahey, T. (2002) The Family Economy in the Development of Welfare Regimes: A Case Study. *In European Sociological Review*, Vol 18 No. 1. Oxford University Press. p. 57 - 58
[41] https://www.oireachtas.ie/en/debates/debate/dail/1923-05-30/9/#spk_15

Under the terms of the 1923 Act, landlords were not paid market value but rather "fair value" and neither were they paid in cash but rather in "Land Bonds". These Land Bonds yielded a fixed rate of return, payable twice yearly with the rate being determined by the year of issue (e.g. in 1923 it was set at 4.5 per cent). To generate the capital to fund these Land Bonds, the fledgling government negotiated a £30 m (€38m) loan facility. Due to the lack of creditworthiness by the new State, the loan had to be backed by a British government guarantee.[42]

Over time, governments bought back a proportion of the bonds for their original value and any remaining bonds were redeemed after 30 years by the Minister for Finance. Bondholders who did not wish to wait for the government to buy them back could sell them on the stock market but there was no guarantee they would get the original value of them. Under Section 24 of the 1939 Land Act, the Land Commission also had the power to partition commonages as much of the land in the West of Ireland was in commonage.

New Impetus

Between 1923 and the coming into office of the Fianna Fail-led government in March 1932, the Land Commission acquired and divided 330,825 acres among 16,587 allottees, or an average of 36,758 acres per annum. In contrast, under Fianna Fáil, during its first five years in government, the Land Commission divided almost 353,0000 acres among 25,802 allottees, or an average of 70,600 acres per annum. At its peak, it employed 1,350 people. During the 1930s the Department of Lands budget accounted for approximately 5.4 per cent of the total annual government budget, which was a significant sum.

> When the Fianna Fáil government was re-elected in 1933, it
> embarked on what was not unreasonably described at the time
> as a revolutionary approach to rural and agricultural policy.[43]

A new Land Act was introduced which gave the Land Commission more widespread powers. Whereas the Land Act, 1923 had provided that land could

---

[42] Norris, M. (2016). *Property, Family and the Irish Welfare State*. Palgrave macmillan. p.81

[43] Edgeworth, B. (2007) 2007) *Rural Radicalism Restrained: The Irish Land Commission and the Courts (1933 – 39)*, 42 Irish Jurist (N.S.) 1

not be acquired for the relief of congestion without the consent of the owner if other suitable land in the district was available, Section 29 of the 1933 Act removed this restriction. *The Irish Times* reported that "the Land Commission is to be given a freer hand to purchase untenanted land for the relief of congestion or for division among the classes of approved allottees specified in Section 31 of the Land Act, 1923." [44]

One reason for the success and extent of the land redistribution schemes was the numerical power of small farmers which drew on a strong political tradition which stretched back to the Land War. Small farmers were, in fact, far more skilled and effective advocates of their concerns and demands than their urban counterparts. Irish farmers continued to be a very successful lobbying body and eventually evolved into the National Farmers' Association (NFA) and finally the Irish Farmers' Association (IFA).

In 1933, the new Fianna Fáil majority government gave a commitment to increase land division to 100,000 acres per year. Fianna Fáil had already built up an impressive electoral machine and part of this strategy required attracting the support of small farmers. Indeed, it could be argued that Fianna Fáil's majority victory in the second general election in 1932 was helped by small farmers and the promise of radical land reform proposals. The Fianna Fáil leader, Eamon de Valera viewed land distribution as a key social policy and this was clearly evident in the party's objectives as revealed at its inaugural meeting in 1926 which committed to "establish as many families as practicable on the land."

With a new Fianna Fáil Minister for Lands and Fisheries, P.J. Rutledge, in charge, an Appeal Tribunal was set up under the 1933 Land Act and two new Commissioners were added to the existing four (subsequently reduced again to four by the 1950 Land Act) to cope with the increased workload. The change of government also saw an innovative idea whereby Gaeltacht migrants who heretofore were installed on reclaimed blanket bog in the West of Ireland were installed on lush holdings in Co. Meath.

The 1933 Act was interesting in that it clarified the distinct powers of the Minister and the Commissioners. The "excepted matters" where the Commissioners had complete control were set out:

---

[44] The Irish Times, 4 July 1933

1. The persons from whom the land was to be acquired and the area to be acquired
2. The price to be paid for acquired land
3. The selection of allottees and the resale price of parcels of land

The Minister had no power over the new Appeal Tribunal. Another major feature of the 1933 Act was the funding of arrears of land annuities. Arrears in excess of three years were waived altogether with the shortfall being funded by the Exchequer. (The land annuities were not specifically mentioned in the 1921 Anglo-Irish Treaty and the question was whether they were/were not included under the heading of "Public Debt").

On being allocated land, the new owner had to sign a purchase agreement which bound him "to work the parcel of land in accordance with the proper methods of husbandry and not to sell, assign, or sub-let it without the consent, in writing, of the Land Commission."

The outbreak of World War II in September 1939 had a profound effect on the work of the Land Commission and its programme of land division was severely curtailed. Many of the staff were transferred to the Department of Agriculture to work on the compulsory tillage programme which was introduced to ensure basic food supplies for the population. For example, in 1940 a total of 41,472 acres were allocated but by 1948 this had reduced to 12,615, a long way from the 100,000 per annum Fianna Fáil aspiration. [45]

Following the ending of World War II hostilities in September 1948, staff on secondment returned to the Land Commission and normal work resumed, although the rate of increase in and allocation was modest.

The 1948 General Election saw the first inter-party government take power and the appointment of Joseph Blowick, a Clann Na Talmhán Dáil deputy, as Minister for Lands. The new government embarked on a policy of tree-planting with a target of 25,000 acres per annum and this new project attracted some of the Land Commission staff. A new Land Act in 1950 introduced some significant changes including requiring the Land Commission to pay "market value" for compulsorily acquired land rather than "fair value" as heretofore.

---

[45] Sammon, P. J. (1997). *In the Land Commission: A Memoir 1933 – 1978.* Blackhall Publishing Ltd. P. 17

Fianna Fáil returned to power after the 1957 general election and a new Minister, Erskine Childers (later to serve as President of Ireland from June 1973 – November 1974) arrived at the Department of Lands. According to Patrick Sammon, who worked in the Commission, the new Minister immediately began to issue queries on all aspects of the work.

> We were dealing with a new Minister who, from the beginning, gave the firm impression that he was going to do a root and branch examination into the Land Commission and all his queries merited, and got, priority treatment.[46]

The Minister, clearly with new ideas in mind, also called for a full review of land policy, with an emphasis on assisting medium-sized farmers. However, a subsequent conference resulted in no change.

Having come to office with high hopes for reform and innovation, Childers, according to Patrick Sammon in his autobiography, must fall into the category of ministers who "allowed themselves to be won round to the *status quo* by hide-bound top civil servants."

This problem of tension between the minister of the day and the civil servants was to recur again and again in the Irish government system - not least in the reaction to the Kenny Report in 1973 and following years. Childers was replaced by Mayo deputy Micheál Ó Moráin who was far more traditional in his approach and who remained in the Department of Lands from 1959 to 1968. His term saw major increase in the amount of land redistributed. In a radical 1965 Land Act, elderly farmers were offered an annuity which would allow them a pension for allowing their land to be redistributed.

Wind-down and Closure

Ireland's membership of the EEC from 1973 saw a change in the operation of the Land Commission and in land policy generally. In 1976 the Fine Gael-Labour Government merged the Land Commission with the Department of Agriculture. This changed the way the Commission operated as in future it was viewed through the eyes of civil servants accustomed to protecting the lot of farmers, big and small, through price maintenance and the new challenges of the European Economic Community (EEC).

---

[46] Ibid. P.48

For small developing farmers, or trained young farmers seeking to obtain some land, the writing was on the wall. Due to the small scale of parcels of land distributed earlier, some of these people were now finding it difficult to survive in the modern high-cost environment and were gradually squeezed out while hard-working and successful farmers had bought more land and were well equipped to benefit from the EEC's agricultural policy. Top quality land increased in price fourfold and this put it outside the realm of the Land Commission.

The 1983-87 Fine Gael/Labour coalition instructed the Land Commission to cease its land distribution activities and considered closing it altogether but the loss of the 1987 general election left it to a Fianna Fáil government, who had so championed its activities over the decades, to finally bring the curtain down.

In 1989 all outstanding Land Bonds were redeemed at par value by the Minister for Finance at a cost to the Exchequer of £76m (€96.5m). As a result of this action, interest payments out of the Land Bond Fund were no longer payable to former owners of land acquired by the Land Commission. Under provisions of the Land Bond Act, 1992, the Land Bond Fund was dissolved and land annuities now went directly to the Exchequer. [47]

The Land Commission had finally run its course. Since its inception in 1881 to its handover to the Free State Government in 1921 and to its final abolition in 1992, it proved to be a very successful instrument of government land policy, whereby millions of acres of land were distributed to Irish tenant farmers and the basis of a modern viable farming system set in place.

> Since 1923 over 108,000 tenants were assisted in purchasing almost three million acres and over two million acres were distributed among uneconomic small-holders, migrants and others. In addition, the Land Commission carried out extensive improvement works. It built houses and out-offices, it carried out drainage, reclamation and fencing and it provided roads and water supplies. (Minister of State for Agriculture & Food, Liam Hyland TD).[48]

---

[47]Sammon, P. J. (1997). *In the Land Commission: A Memoir 1933 – 1978*. Blackhall Publishing Ltd. p.111

[48] https://www.oireachtas.ie/en/debates/debate/seanad/1992-10-21/10/

Its success over a period of more than 100 years and the lack of any successful Constitutional legal challenge to it stands in marked contrast to the attitude adopted to the recommendations of the Kenny Report which were published in 1973 while the policy of land acquisition by the Land Commission was still in full sway.

Chapter 5

Judge John Kenny

Building background

The central figure in the entire Kenny Report is the chairman, John Kenny, then a High Court judge and later appointed to the Supreme Court. According to the *Dictionary of Irish Biography*, Judge Kenny's reputation lies chiefly in his work as a High Court judge. In the entry on Kenny, written by Gerard Hogan SC, it states "Kenny must rank as one of the greatest High Court judges in the history of the State." His finest contributions were in the realm of constitutional law.

John Joseph Kenny was born in 1917 and grew up in Dublin's Rathgar area where his father, John Kenny, was a well-known building contractor. Mark FitzGerald, son of former Taoiseach Garret FitzGerald and chairman of the Sherry FitzGerald Group, recalls John Kenny's father who built a large part of the Mount Merrion area of Dublin county.

> I think it was a difficult time in the 1930s and his father was obviously a great craftsman when you look at the houses in Mount Merrion. He used a famous architect, Felix Jones. So, between Jones and Kenny, they helped to shape Mount Merrion which set a new standard in modern Irish houses at the time. But he went broke two or three times, I think. So, we often thought that Judge Kenny would have been impacted by that because he was about 20 at the time and would have seen his father make all this huge effort only for things to unravel and then have to put it back together again. I'm not sure what exact impact it had on him in terms of his approach to the Kenny Report. [49]

---

[49] Interview with Mark FitzGerald, 2020.

According to barrister and author.[50] Charles Lysaght, Kenny was not especially nationalist but his family history would have made him unsympathetic to Fine Gael. "His builder father had had acrimonious litigation with the Cosgrave government."

UCD

John Kenny was educated at Catholic University School and UCD where he graduated with a BA in legal and political science, an LLB and an MA. He was called to the Bar in 1940 and became a senior counsel in 1958. As well as practising at the Bar, John Kenny also lectured on Company Law and Property Law at UCD and acted as consultant editor of Professor J.C.W. Wylie's seminal work *Irish Land Law*.

Charles Lysaght first met John Kenny when attending his lectures in UCD in 1959-60 where he was a part-time lecturer on the Law of Property.

> He was the outstanding lecturer in a faculty that included Paddy McGilligan.[51] and Seamus Henchy.[52] and put a lot of himself into his lectures. It was clear that he had a love of the law for its own sake not that common in practitioners. He was quite dogmatic and could be vitriolic in his denunciation of wrong-headed judgments or statutes. Conscious that he himself was a clever man, he tended to be dismissive of the stupid.[53]

It was while as a legal academic at UCD that he first came to prominence when, in 1959, he clashed with the university leadership over some of the academic appointments made by the UCD governing body. He proposed that the Government have someone appointed to investigate the matter and while this was accepted, it deeply angered the then UCD President Michael Tierney.[54] Tensions worsened between the two men in 1960 when Kenny

---

[50] Interview with Charles Lysaght 2021
[51] Patrick Joseph McGilligan was a Fine Gael TD and lawyer who served as the 14th Attorney General of Ireland from 1954 to 1957, Minister for Finance from 1948 to 1951, Minister for External Affairs from 1927 to 1932 and Minister for Industry and Commerce from 1924 to 1932.
[52] Seamus Henchy was a barrister and judge. He served as a member of the Supreme Court from 1972 – 1988.
[53] Interview with Charles Lysaght 2021
[54] MacCormaic, R. (2017) *The Supreme Court*. Penguin Ireland.

gave advice to the College's Literary & Historical Society (the L & H) in a bitter confrontation over college regulations regarding membership of student societies.

Under Tierney, UCD was seen at the time as something of a Fine Gael bastion. Having been Professor of Greek for a number of years, he served as President of UCD from 1947 to 1964 and was the prime mover of UCD from Earlsfort Terrace to its current location in Belfield. He had also served as a Cumann na nGaedheal TD for Mayo North in the 1920s and had come up with the name "Fine Gael" when Cumann na nGaedheal merged with the National Centre Party and the National Guard (commonly known as the Blueshirts). Tierney was known for his independent temperament and found it difficult to co-operate even with the sister colleges of the National University. .55

Kenny's stand-off with Michael Tierney appeared to do him no harm and may even have helped his career. He was subsequently praised in the Dáil for his courage in standing up against the UCD system of appointments and this may have endeared him to the Fianna Fáil government who appointed him to the High Court in 1961 (Oscar Traynor was Minister for Justice and Charles Haughey, who succeeded Traynor later that year, was Parliamentary Secretary in the Department).

Kenny belonged to a group of young judges, which included Brian Walsh and Seamus Henchy who were appointed to the High Court in their early to mid-forties and were to lead a creative appraisal of the Constitution and the courts' place in society.

High Court Judge

Senior Counsel and former Attorney General Dermot Gleeson remembers Judge Kenny as a very kindly and gentle judge on the bench and whom he holds in very high esteem. "His judgement in the Ryan case (see below) would certainly be in the top 10 judgements of the Irish courts." According to Lysaght, Judge Kenny was acclaimed as a High Court judge not only for his ability but also his courtesy which contrasted with a number of his colleagues at the time.

> He worked hard reading the papers in advance of hearings. He examined issues other judges might have ducked. So it was that

---

55 Gaughan, J.A. (1992) *Alfred O'Rahilly. Part III Controversialist*. Kingdom Books.

he went into the scientific arguments on fluoridation (see below) and offered an opinion instead of just finding that it was a reasonable decision with which the court would not interfere. [56]

As a barrister John Kenny specialised in Land Law and in Company Law. "This area of the law was then still dominated by Protestants for whom he had great respect and with whom he had good relations. His wife was a Methodist and he was one of the few UCD graduates in the Dublin University Club," says Lysaght.

Unenumerated Rights

Two years later, in 1963 Judge Kenny established himself as one of the most innovative voices in the higher courts when he introduced the ground-breaking concept of 'unenumerated rights', i.e. rights that do not appear in the text of the Constitution but are implied and are there to be identified by the judiciary.

The decision arose when a housewife from Drumcondra, Gladys Ryan, became a household name when she took a unique High Court case. Gladys McConaghie grew up on Dublin's Leeson Street and studied to become a singer before later marrying Corkman John Ryan. The couple became deeply involved in the emerging ecology movement. In 1960 Fianna Fáil introduced the Health (Fluoridation of Water Supplies) Act, 1960 which allowed local authorities to add fluoride to the country's water supply largely in an effort to prevent tooth decay in children. However, a movement claiming the practice was actually damaging to health emerged and Gladys Ryan, through her solicitor, Fine Gael TD Richie Ryan (later Minister for Finance), brought a High Court case, *Ryan v the Attorney General [1965] IR 294* seeking to declare the new law was unconstitutional. The judge appointed to hear the case was John Kenny. The three formidable senior counsel arguing the case were Seán MacBride, Tommy Connolly and Seamus Egan who claimed the new law was a breach of Ryan's personal rights and those of her children. They claimed preventing tooth decay in their children was purely the responsibility of Ms Ryan and her husband.

The key section of the Constitution at issue was Article 40.3 (later to feature prominently in the Kenny Report itself) which states:

---

[56] Interview with Charles Lysaght 2021

1° The State guarantees in its laws to respect, and, as far as possible, by its laws to defend and vindicate the personal rights of the citizen.

2° The State shall, in particular, by its laws protect as best it may from unjust attack, and, in the case of injustice done, vindicate the life, person, good name and property rights of every citizen.

The phrase "in particular" was critical to Kenny who later suggested it implied that there were other rights that did not appear in the text itself.

> In Article 41, the State recognises the family as 'a moral institution possessing inalienable and imprescriptible rights, antecedent and superior to all positive (i.e statute) law.' But what were these rights that were superior to the legislation passed by the Oireachtas? On that, the Constitution was silent.[57]

The Ryan case lasted 65 days in the High Court with a plethora of medical and scientific evidence analysed. But the case finally centred on Seán MacBride's claim of implicit rights, which he referred to as personal integrity.

In a two-hour judgement, delivered on 31 July, 1963, Judge Kenny rejected almost all of Gladys Ryan's arguments. He was not convinced she had shown that fluoridated water could damage your health and that there were ways of removing it, if she so wished. However, most significantly, Judge Kenny decided there was a right to 'bodily integrity', a phrase he took from a recently published papal encyclical *'Pacem in Terris'* or 'Peace on Earth' from Pope John XXIII. The concept of unenumerated, or implied rights, in the Constitution was born.

According to Hogan[58], this was Judge Kenny's most striking and distinctive judgement when he held that the personal rights referred to in Article 40.3 of the Constitution were not confined to the constitutional rights expressly enumerated elsewhere in that document but extended to such implied rights "which result from the Christian and democratic nature of the State". The subsequent development of the unenumerated rights doctrine, says Hogan, to extend to rights such as the right to privacy and basic fairness

---

[57] MacCormaic, R. (2017) *The Supreme Court.* Penguin Ireland.
[58] Hogan, G. (2009) 'Kenny, John Joseph' in Dictionary of Irish Biography (McGuire and Quinn eds). Royal Irish Academy and Cambridge University Press

of procedure, "bears ample testimony to the singular importance of this remarkable decision". Gladys Ryan appealed to the Supreme Court which, to the surprise of many, in a judgement delivered by Cearbhall Ó Dalaigh (who later served as President of Ireland) upheld that there were, indeed, implied rights in the Constitution.

> It was a watershed moment. The Constitution contained rights that didn't actually appear in the text. And that meant the only people with the authority to identify them – the judges of the Supreme Court – had just made themselves immeasurably more powerful. [59]

According to former religious affairs journalist T.P. O'Mahony, of all the great social encyclicals, beginning with Pope Leo XIII's *Rerum Novarum* in 1891 which addressed the unjust conditions created by the Industrial Revolution, the greatest is *Pacem in Terris* from Pope John XXIII in 1963, not least because it highlighted what have come to be known as socio-economic rights.

The key passage reads: "Beginning our discussion of the rights of man, we see that every man has the right to life, to bodily integrity, and to the means which are necessary and suitable for the proper development of life; these are primarily food, clothing, shelter, rest, medical care, and finally the necessary social services". [60]

O'Mahony pointed out that we still have a situation in Ireland where these rights await constitutional protection, the exception, of course, being the right to "bodily integrity" because of the now famous case of *Ryan v the Attorney General* (1963). "In this case, Kenny J. in the High Court delivered a seminal judgement, availing of *Pacem in Terris* which had been issued a month into the hearings that lasted sixty-five days. He ruled that the general guarantee of personal rights in Article 40 of *Bunreacht na hEireann* extended to rights that were not actually specified in the Constitution. Among these was the right to "bodily integrity", a phrase the judge took directly from the encyclical. This opened the way for the doctrine of unenumerated (or unspecified) rights," he said. "Because of the judgement in *Ryan v AG*, according to David Gwynn Morgan, emeritus professor of constitutional law at UCC, Article 40 came to

[59] MacCormaic, R. (2017) *The Supreme Court.* Penguin Ireland.
[60] http://www.vatican.va/content/john-xxiii/en/encyclicals/documents/hf_j-xxiii_enc_11041963_pacem.html

be regarded as a "reservoir of unspecified rights". However, whether the right to bodily integrity (properly understood) can be adequately vindicated in a society that prizes cupidity over social justice remains a moot point."

According to O'Mahony, what may be even more pertinent, if the Kenny Report were ever actually implemented, is the insistence in *Pacem in Terris* (and in other social encyclicals) that the right to private property is not absolute, or unqualified - it carries with it a "social function". By the same token, Judge Kenny in the Report on the Price of Building Land in 1973 would decide that some personal rights, such as the right to windfall profits from development land, are subservient to the common good as stated in Article 43.2.2°.

Judge Kenny also made a landmark judgement in the *Central Dublin Development Association Ltd. V Attorney General [1969] 109 IL TR 69* when he rejected the argument that the restrictions on development were repugnant to the Constitution. However, as pointed out by Judge Ronan Keane, it was significant that in the judgement, Judge Kenny placed a greater emphasis on the provisions of Article 40.3 with its guarantee against unjust attacks on property rights than his predecessors.

> He, nevertheless, rejected the suggestion that the power given to local authorities to restrict the development by private citizens of their property, in many instances without payment of compensation, represented an "unjust attack" on property rights.[61]

Later Life

Judge Kenny also commented occasionally on social issues of the time. In 1975, for example, he told a UCD law society meeting that the Republic's position on divorce had become a symbol to the North that the Republic was a Catholic-dominated State. He suggested there was no reason why divorce should not be available in the case of registry office marriages, or in civil law for religions which did not allow divorce.

Three years later, in 1978 he told a TCD meeting that a referendum on divorce would produce an enormous victory for those opposed to it.

---

[61] Keane, R. (1983) *Land Use, Compensation and the Community*, 18 Irish Jurist (N.S.) 23

Interviewed after the meeting he said: "You would have every woman over 40 voting against it, as well as all the socialites, confraternities, Roman Catholic old boys and every source of influence possessed by the Catholic Church would be marshalled for the occasion." [62]

In October 1975, two years after the publication of the Kenny Report, Judge John Kenny was appointed to the Supreme Court by the National Coalition Government (Patrick Cooney was now Minister for Justice) but his finest judgements are generally regarded as from his time as a member of the High Court. He retired due to ill-health in 1982 and died in March 1987, aged 69.

Upon his retirement, the then Chief Justice, T.F. O'Higgins said Mr Justice Kenny had brought to the interpretation of the Constitution a refreshing clarity of thought which had contributed significantly towards those provisions which dealt particularly with personal rights. The President of the High Court, Mr Justice Finlay said Mr Justice Kenny's 14 years on the High Court bench had produced a massive contribution to the jurisprudence of the Chancery Court, the law of bankruptcy and the problem of custody of children and family law.

In his private life, John Kenny was a shy and retiring individual with an interest in literature and horse-racing. Mark FitzGerald, remembers John Kenny from his holidays in Rosslare when both families stayed in Kelly's Hotel for the month of August. "I knew him because we used to go on holiday in Rosslare when I was a child in the summers of 1964, 1965 and 1966. I was only eight and nine but he struck me as a very careful man. He dressed impeccably and he would wear a three-piece suit on holidays and was a very shy man."

Charles Lysaght said that while he was oecumenical in his views, he was a pious Catholic often to be seen praying long after Mass ended at his local church. "He was never a man for pubs and would have been counted as something of a loner. His life-style was austere, apart from a Rover car."

Kenny lived with his wife Marjorie on Dublin 4's Nutley Lane. They had two sons, Roger John, a noted barrister in his own right and Stewart, who became a famous bookmaker and co-founded the Paddy Power betting chain.

---

[62] The Irish Times, 26 March 1987

Chapter 6

The Committee on the Price of Building Land

A key cause of the commissioning of a report into the price of building land by the Minister for Local Government, Robert Molloy TD in January 1971 was the increase in the price of serviced land suitable for building and the failure by his department to come up with any practical solution.

Between 1966 and 1971 successive ministers in the Department of Local Government asked that studies be undertaken on the issue of land prices. Much attention was focused on finding a mechanism by which the cost of building land required for housing and other purposes for local authorities could be reduced from its open market value.

A Memorandum for Government in March 1968 from the Department of Local Government stated that the Minister (Kevin Boland) "expressed concern at the indications of speculation in potential building and at the prospect of the substantial cornering of such lands by interests seeking to make handsome and unearned profits from the value added to such lands by public works and the promotion of planning policies." [63]

Already there were plans to exclude the value of "betterment" from lands acquired by the local authorities. The proposals recommended by Minister Kevin Boland [64] to deal with the situation were:

-   That local authorities should be encouraged to undertake substantial advance acquisition of land due to become ripe for development;
-   That maximum compensation for compulsory acquisition by local authorities should be on the basis of 150% of the existing use value, or the agricultural value, of the land, whichever was higher: and

---

[63] Dept. of Housing File No. PL 4/2/10/1
[64] Kevin Boland served as Minister for Local Government from 1966 – 1970.

- That the programme of acquisition be financed through the co-operation of the banks or by the issue of local authority bonds.

Significantly, the Memo added: "As an alternative to compensation on the basis of (b), no account would be taken of any increase in value in the land due to works carried out by the local authority within the previous seven years, or to proposals for such works."

Minister Boland requested the Attorney General at the time, Colm Condon SC, to state whether he considered that the proposals submitted to the Government were compatible with the Constitution, and "if not, in what respects they were considered to be repugnant".

According to the Memo of March 1968 "the Attorney General had not indicated the final outcome of his consideration of this matter, when, at a meeting of the Government held on 12 Eanair (January), 1968, the item was withdrawn from the agenda."

The Memo noted that the price of serviced building land around Dublin was in the region of £3,500 (€4,444) per acre. Prices at the rate of £1,700 (€2,158) and upwards were freely being paid for un-serviced land which normally for agricultural purposes would fetch in the region of £400 (€507) to £500 (€634) per acre.

The issue of the scarcity of housing was often raised in the media where, in 1969, there were 20,000 people on the approved housing list which required a family to have two children before becoming eligible for inclusion.

In a series on poverty in Ireland, the November 1969 issue of *Nusight* magazine reported that Ireland had the lowest number of houses built per 1,000 of population in all of Europe in 1967.

> In the last five years or so Ireland has developed a housing crisis of unparalleled seriousness and intensity. This crisis is a comparatively recent phenomenon. In previous decades the chronic failure of the Irish economy partially obscured the inadequacy of the State's effort to provide adequate housing for the people. Emigration ensured that the natural need of the working class in the city for decent housing was minimised.

Describing the situation as "critical", it said the government estimated rather conservatively that there was an accumulated need for 59,000 new houses and that each year another twelve thousand houses were needed due to loss of dwellings from demolitions and obsolescence, marriage and migration. It also noted that the Government in its White Paper on *"Housing in the Seventies"* admitted that there was a problem in the cost of serviced land, which often comprised more than 20% of the price of a house. It stated that "while the obvious solution to this problem might appear to be to bring all building land into public ownership, this would entail the most serious constitutional, legal, financial and administrative problems." Among the solutions proposed in the article was the implementation of strict rent control and the nationalisation of building land.

The issue of land prices was frequently the subject of Dáil questions. For example, on 15 December 1970, Labour Deputy Dr David Thornley asked Minister Robert Molloy if he would consider the introduction of legislation to control the price of building land. The Minister replied that "consideration is being given to the possibility of introducing legislation". But he added that there were "considerable administrative, financial and legal problems involved" and these were being studied by "the Departments concerned". [65]

Speaking during a Private Member's motion on the same issue on 20 April 1971, Fine Gael Deputy Tom Enright complained about speculators buying up land on all sides of Dublin city and in the larger centres throughout the country. "They sell the land at enormous prices to local authorities and to individuals throughout the country," he said. "It is a very common occurrence to see sites offered for sale at figures ranging from £1,000 (€1,230) to £2,000 (€2,540). It is often around £1,500 (€1,900) that couples must pay for sites on which to build their own houses. Anybody will realise how difficult it is for young married couples to obtain such an amount of money to purchase a site. Unless they can do that, they must coop themselves up in small flats at exorbitant rents in Dublin and some towns throughout the country. Their life is one of misery and dreariness in which love and the proper relationship that should exist between young couples are stifled. [66]

Speaking during the same debate, Minister Molloy noted that the cost of land was not the only factor contributing towards the increase in house prices but if it could be controlled, it "would make a substantial contribution".

---

[65] https://www.oireachtas.ie/en/debates/debate/dail/1970-12-15/34/#spk_311
[66] https://www.oireachtas.ie/en/debates/debate/dail/1971-04-20/61/#spk_443

He told the Dáil he put the full resources of his department to work on the problem and after many months of study they had been unable to come up with a solution. It was at that point "in a last-ditch effort to find some practical solution" he established the Committee on the Price of Building Land. He chose Judge John Kenny, he said, because he had already "expressed a keen interest in the problem".

The Minister revealed that he had also considered in depth the provisions of the Constitution and the legal position with regard to the compulsory acquisition of land and the assessment of compensation for land compulsorily acquired for public purposes. Having considered all these various aspects and having obtained the best legal advice available to him he said he came to the conclusion that a solution was legally, administratively and financially impracticable.

Having read Article 43 into the Dáil record, he said he understood that the rights of landowners could be restricted, or delimited, with a view to reconciling their exercise with the exigencies of the common good. Then, perhaps pre-empting the eventual fall-out to the Kenny Report, he added:

> The whole crux of the problem is the question of compensation. Under existing law, the basic rule for the assessment of compensation for land compulsorily acquired is that the value of the land is taken as the amount the land might be expected to realise if sold on the open market by a willing seller. The owner is entitled to expect to get from the acquiring authority the sort of price he would receive if he sold his land freely on the open market.....If it were possible to empower local authorities to acquire such land at less than the prevailing market value, there would then be a two-tier price system in operation and the man selling in the open market would get one price, the market price, while the man whose land was being acquired compulsorily would get considerably less. It should be obvious, even to the Labour Party.....

Between 1963 and 1971 the Kenny Committee noted price of serviced land increased by 530% while the Consumer Price Index during the same period increased by 64%. In County Dublin, for example, it increased from £1,100 (€1,397) per acre to £7,000 (€8,888). (KR: Par 6). Factors cited include the increase in population, increase in the proportion of people living in cities, increase in household forming age group, increase in income and inflation. Also cited were improvements in food production methods, high-rise, improved transport, planning uncertainty, lack of serviced lands and advance acquisition of greenfield sites.

The Report noted that the amount of capital available to local authorities for housing was limited and if the price of land went up, the number of houses which could be provided must be less.

To try and get around the problem, the then Minister for Finance, Charles Haughey TD, made £3 million (€3.8m) available to Dublin Corporation to purchase land in advance. A total of 1,902 acres were purchased at an average price of £1,604 (€2,036) per acre. However, the Kenny Committee found this caused a further scarcity of development land as services were not being provided quickly enough.

Robert (Bobby) Molloy

The Minister responsible for commissioning the report, Robert (Bobby) Molloy (1936 – 2016), was a TD (member of the Irish Parliament or Dáil) for the constituency of Galway West from 1965 until 2002. He was an important political figure and was involved in many of the biggest political events during this period, not least of which was his decision to leave Fianna Fáil and join the fledgling Progressive Democrats party. First elected in 1965, he was part of a wave of younger TDs who were to play a significant role in Fianna Fáil and in Irish political life in the decades that followed. He was appointed a Parliamentary Secretary (Junior Minister) after the 1969 General Election and was promoted to Minister for Local Government after the 1970 Arms Crisis which saw two senior ministers, Charles Haughey (later Taoiseach) and Neil Blaney sacked and Kevin Boland resigning from his post as Minister for Local Government in protest.

Fianna Fáil lost power in 1973 immediately after the Kenny Report was published and when it regained power in 1977, Molloy was appointed to the Cabinet as Minister for Defence. A lifelong opponent of Fianna Fáil leader Charles Haughey, he joined the fledging Progressive Democrats party in January 1986 and served as Minister for Energy and later as Minister of State (Junior Minister) at the Department of the Environment where he spearheaded a campaign to tackle homelessness. He retired from politics at the 2002 general election. When he died in October 2016, President Michael D. Higgins, a former constituency colleague in Galway West, said that on every platform Bobby Molloy served, "he delivered his contribution, which was always well informed with great distinction." [67]

Molloy took over the Local Government portfolio from Kevin Boland in 1970 shortly before commissioning the Kenny Report. Boland had served as Minister for Local Government from 1966 when Jack Lynch succeeded Seán Lemass as Taoiseach. He, in turn, succeeded Neil Blaney who had been a remarkable reformer in the Department and had spearheaded the first detailed planning legislation in 1963.

The Committee

The appointment of a High Court judge and a number of civil servants from relevant departments was totally in accordance with government practice.

The full membership of the Committee on the Price of Building Land was as follows:

The Hon. Mr Justice J. Kenny, High Court – Chairman

Mr. M.J. Murphy, Department of Local Government

Dr. M. O'Donoghue, Department of the Taoiseach

Mr. J. T. O'Meara, Department of Local Government

Mr. L. Reason, Office of the Revenue Commissioners

Mr. D. F. Ryan, Valuation Office

Michael Murphy was the legal officer in the Department of the Environment. He was noted for his strong and forthright views and was mainly responsible for drafting the Minority Report of the Committee.

According to barrister and former legal advisor to the Department of Foreign Affairs, Charles Lysaght, Murphy "would not have been highly rated in the profession or in the public service". He mainly disagreed with the Majority Report because he did not consider that there was "any justification

[67] The Irish Times, 3 October 2016

for a radical departure from the basis compensation principle on which the present code is founded." [68]

Dr Martin O'Donoghue was elected a Fellow of Trinity College Dublin in 1969 and promoted to Associate Professor of Economics there in 1970. Between 1970 and 1973 O'Donoghue was economic adviser to the Taoiseach Jack Lynch during which time he was a member of the Committee on the Price of Building Land. At the 1977 General Election, O'Donoghue was elected to Dáil Éireann as a Fianna Fáil TD for the Dún Laoghaire constituency. He was chief author of the election manifesto which saw Fianna Fáil achieve an unprecedented 20-seat majority. O'Donoghue was appointed Minister for Economic Planning and Development on his first day in the Dáil. In 1979, Charles Haughey became Taoiseach and O'Donoghue's ministerial position was abolished. In 1982 O'Donoghue was returned to Cabinet as Minister for Education. He resigned from the government in October 1982, when he refused to support Haughey in a leadership challenge, and in November 1982 lost his Dáil seat at the general election. He remained in the Seanad until 1987. Later he left Fianna Fáil, becoming a supporter of the Progressive Democrats.

Ted O'Meara, Liam Reason and Denis Ryan were middle-ranking civil servants in the Department of Local Government, the Revenue Commissioners and the Valuation Office respectively. The secretary to the Committee was a civil servant from the Department of Local Government, Ms Beth Ann O'Byrne who, despite the volume of material sent to it, was not assigned full-time.

Once established, the Committee, on the 13th of February 1971, sought written submissions from interested parties by way of advertisements in the daily press. It also wrote to the organisations the members thought had a special interest in the terms of reference. In total 42 written submissions were received. Three submissions were from government departments, namely Agriculture & Fisheries, Lands and Transport & Power; 16 were from local authorities and the remainder from other organisations and private individuals, including one Fine Gael TD, Mark Clinton, who later served as Minister for Agriculture in the 1973 – 77 Fine Gael/Labour coalition government. Officials from Dublin Corporation and a delegation representing the Construction Industry Federation supplemented their written

---

[68] Kenny Minority Report, Par. 2.2

submissions by oral evidence. The Committee met 59 times and heard oral evidence at two meetings.

In carrying out their work, the Committee reviewed a great deal of documentation from Europe, the United States, Canada, Australia and New Zealand where similar problems had arisen with regard to land prices.

> The suggestion sometimes made that these increases are a feature peculiar to Ireland and that they are the result of some defect in our institutions, or in our system of government and laws, is inaccurate. [69]

The Report noted a report in the *Estates Gazette* of 15 April 1972 where land suitable for building and sold with planning permission within a 40-mile radius of London rose from £11,800 (Sterling) an acre in 1965/66 to £43,030 in 1971.

In trying to prove allegations of speculation made to it, the Committee was hamstrung in a number of ways in sourcing information. Firstly, they could not ask the Revenue Commissioners as the annual returns from the public are confidential. The Registry of Deeds also proved fruitless as it does not show the purchase price. Nor could they access the Land Registry as it only allowed inspections in particular circumstances. Instead, the Committee relied for its evidence on land price increases in cases heard in the courts and from details obtained from the Valuation Office and from Dublin and Galway Corporations.

Among the examples of increases in land prices suitable for development pointed out by the Committee in its Report was the sale of 60 acres in Castleknock, Co. Dublin in March 1965 for £160,000 (€203,158). These lands had been bought in October 1964 for £67,000 (€85,072), representing a profit margin of 140% in a few months. A second example showed how in Ballyfermot in 1963, lands were sold by A to B for £195 (€248) per acre. In 1964, B sold them to C & Co. Ltd for £258 (€327) per acre. However, in September 1970, C & Co. Ltd sold them to M. Ltd for £6,480 (€8,228) per acre. Often these sales were carried out through complicated inter-company transactions which ensured the profit was not liable to tax.

---

[69] Kenny Report, Par. 8

The Committee concluded that these huge increases would not have occurred if the services (water, sewerage and drainage) had not been, or were not intended to be, provided by the local authority.

It added:

> Therefore, the provision of the services by the local authority is largely responsible for the difference in price between agricultural land and serviced and potential building land and so, it is said, the community which provided the services has a legitimate claim to all the profit. [70]

Causes for price increases

In its examination of the causes of the huge increase in development land prices, the Committee had access to Volume 1 of the 1971 Census which showed a sharp increase in the population over the previous decade (from 2,818,000 to 2,978,000). For housing purposes, the most relevant demographic was the number of married couples which had shown a dramatic increase of 900% in the decade leading up to the report compared to the previous decade, which, according to the Report "produced a totally new situation in relation to housing needs".

A second key factor was the rapid increase in income which the Committee found to be £645 (€819) in 1971, an increase 38% per head compared to 1961.

The Report identified increasing population and rising incomes as the two key factors in the upward trend in the price of development land. Other factors identified such as inflation and credit could accelerate, or slow it down, but not arrest it completely. It also identified the advance purchase of tracts of land by local authorities - in 1967 a special allocation of £3m (€3.8m) was made to Dublin City Council to enable it to purchase land - as a contributory factor. [71]

The Report also noted that a number of large firms in the building industry had purchased 4,000 acres of un-serviced land near Dublin and this process of "advance acquisition" helped to increase land prices in the short term. The

---

[70] Kenny Report, Par. 10
[71] Kenny Report, Par. 16

Report noted that in 1971 the total number of houses in the State was about 730,000 of which 355,000 had been built since 1922. Of these, 194,000 were built by private builders and 161,000 had been provided by local authorities.[72]

Planning Act

The Report identified the 1963 Planning Act as a further cause of land price inflation as, in its initial phases, it slowed down the availability of building land while planning guidelines were satisfied, thereby driving up the price of the number of sites that were available. "From the information available to us, it appears that there is substance in that view." [73]

Compensation

The Report also argued that the rules for assessment of compensation by local authorities under the Acts of 1919 and 1963 tended to inflate land prices as official arbitrators tended to make their decisions based on an award for the potential development value of the land even though this was purely speculative. ".... each owner claims that his land should be valued on the most favourable basis." [74]

Betterment

In any formal planning system, the Report noted development rights are granted to some land owners and denied to others. If the amount of zoned land is scarce, then the value of the zoned land increases and the cash bonanza given to the owner distorts the market. This increase in value is often referred to as "betterment". It also sends a signal to developers and would-be entrepreneurs to acquire as much zoned development land as possible and hoard it until the time is right to gain maximum profit. As a result, developers often compete with each other to acquire scarce development land in good locations leading to a distortion of the market and spiralling house prices.

---

[72] Kenny Report, Par. 19
[73] Kenny Report, Par. 18
[74] Kenny Report, Par. 22

While zoning huge areas of land for development might seem an obvious solution, local authorities are reluctant to choose this route as it can result in servicing vast quantities of land that may not be required for a generation or more.

Speculating on prime zoned land and hoarding some, or all, of it was a trend that emerged in urban areas in Ireland post the 1963 Planning Act and was something that the Kenny Report sought to tackle. It also tried to define "betterment".

> When a local authority carries out a scheme for sanitary services or builds a road or does other improvements, the land which benefits from these will get a higher price when sold. This increase in price is called "betterment", an ambiguous term because it is sometimes used to describe the increase in price brought about by all economic and social forces including planning schemes and sometimes to describe the part of the increase which ought to be recoverable from the owner.[75]

Tracing the origin of the term "betterment" to the 1885 Royal Commission on the Housing of the Working Classes, the Kenny Report noted that in 1894, a Select Committee of the House of Lords on Town Improvement (Betterment) defined the principle as "that persons, whose property has clearly been increased in market value by an improvement effected by local authorities, should specially contribute to the cost of the improvement".

Subsequently, the Scott Committee in a report in 1918 recommended that "as a general principle where the State, or a local authority, by a particular improvement has increased the value of neighbouring land, the State, or local authority, should be entitled to participate in such increased value." This widening of the concept of betterment was reflected in Section 58(3) of the Housing and Town Planning Act, 1909 - which did not apply to Ireland - and which provided for the recovery of betterment in cases where any property was increased in value by the making of a town planning scheme. However, nothing was ever recovered under this section.[76]

---

[75] Kenny Report, Par. 27
[76] Kenny Report, Pars. 28 & 29

70

The Kenny Report noted that in Ireland, Section 72 of the Town and Regional Planning Act, 1934 provided for "whatever the value of any property was increased by the coming into operation of enforcement of any provision in a planning scheme, or by the execution of any work by a planning authority under the scheme, every person having any estate or interest in the property became liable to the local authority for a payment for betterment of three-fourths of the amount by which the value of the estate, or interest of the person in the property, was increased." Sections 73, 74 and 75 contained elaborate provisions for the recovery of this. However, similarly to Britain, no collection in respect of betterment was ever made and when the 1934 Act was repealed by the 1963 Planning Act, no similar provisions were included.[77]

British Legislation

In drafting the legislation, the Kenny Committee reviewed legislation elsewhere, notably in Britain. The Report also thanked the Hon. Mr Justice Robert Megarry of the High Court in England for his help in providing information. However, it noted that many of the changes, while attractive, were so complicated in detail, that they were unworkable.[78]

The first attempt in the UK was in the 1910 Finance Act when a land tax was introduced at a rate of £1 for every £5 of incremental value. It proved too complicated and was repealed in 1920. In January 1941, a committee was set up to consider compensation, betterment and development. This was under the chairmanship of Mr Justice Uthwatt and its report, the "Expert Committee on Compensation and Betterment" was very influential on the deliberations of the Kenny Report Committee. The final report "includes a masterly examination of the subject of betterment."[79]

As mentioned elsewhere, the Uthwatt Committee recommended that local authorities be given powers to compulsorily acquire land which would be used by them at a price determined by reference to its use value before the works were carried out.

The Committee recommended that all land outside built-up areas should become vested in the State after the payment of fair compensation. The price

---

[77] Kenny Report, Pars. 30 & 31
[78] Kenny Report, Par. 34
[79] Kenny Report, Par. 37

was to be fixed on the basis that the development potential was to be ignored. The recommendation that all development rights in undeveloped land should vest in the State was accepted by the British Government and extended to all land by the 1947 Town and Country Planning Act. The development rights in all land in Britain were valued at £300 million which was to be distributed among owners of the rights and a development charge of 100% on the increase in the value of the land caused by the grant of planning permission became payable when the land was developed. Compensation for compulsory acquisition was to be assessed on the 'existing use' principle and the development potential was to be ignored..[80]

However, the system did not work well as land owners were very reluctant to sell at 'existing use' value and developers ended up paying far more. The system was ended by the Town and Country Planning Act, 1954. Since then, a number of other pieces of legislation have been introduced in Britain including the large and detailed 1971 Town and Country Planning Act which was again amended by the Town and Country Planning (Amendment) Act, 1972.

Alternative Options

The Kenny Committee considered and rejected 11 possible schemes for dealing with the increases in the price of building land before finally recommending one.

These were:

- A system by which all building land would be controlled - rejected on the grounds that it would mean an elaborate structure of tribunals that would be costly, cumbersome and slow.
- Nationalisation of all building land and payment of compensation – rejected on the grounds that the amount of compensation which would be payable if all building land was nationalised would be enormous and which neither the State nor the local authorities could bear.
- Nationalisation of the development rights in all building land and payment of compensation for these. The land when required for

---

[80] Kenny Report, Par. 41

development would then be purchased by a Central Agency or a local authority at its existing use value – rejected on the grounds that it was found to be totally unworkable when tried by the British Government in The Town and Planning Act, 1947 and had to be abandoned.

- A special gains tax on profits arising from the disposal of land suitable for building - rejected firstly, because it would give rise to major problems of defining the land where liability would arise and secondly, that methods of arranging transactions so that tax would not be paid, would be discovered.

- A betterment levy on the difference between the price realised on the disposal of land after planning permission had been granted and the market price of it based on its existing value – rejected because the Committee felt the immediate effect of the levy would be to increase the price of serviced and potential building land.

- The right of pre-emption whereby the owners of land suitable for development who wished to sell it would be obliged to offer it first to the local authority – rejected on the grounds that it would not secure any of the increase in price for the local community.

- An amendment to the Planning Act, 1963 so that planning permission would be granted on the condition that the developer would pay the local authority the total cost of the works which have, or will have, to be carried out in connection with the proposed development – rejected on the grounds that the costs of any such works would ultimately be passed on to the house purchaser.

- A high rate of Stamp Duty payable by the vendor on the transfer or lease of land suitable for building – rejected on the grounds that an increase in Stamp Duty would ultimately be passed on to the house purchaser.

- The imposition of a new tax levied annually at a progressive rate on the site value of lands suitable for building for which planning permission (including outline permission) has been granted. The site value would not be present rateable valuation but a modern assessment of the letting value – rejected on the grounds that the tax yield would be very small and that the cost of its assessment might well exceed the ultimate proceeds.

- A system under which land would be zoned by the planning authority for different uses and the compensation paid to owners on compulsory acquisition would be related to the specified use – rejected on a number of grounds but principally because the local authority acquiring the land would be determining the scale of compensation payable which the Committee deemed highly undesirable.

The Pre-emption and Levy Scheme

This was the Minority Report scheme put forward by the two representatives from the Department of the Environment, Mr Murphy and Mr O'Meara. It was rejected by the majority of the Committee on a number of grounds but principally because the history of levies and taxes in Britain since 1947 showed they invariable increased the price of land. Also, the majority concluded that "tax lawyers and accountants are very ingenious and they would quickly discover ways of carrying out the transaction so that the heavy levies would not be payable.".[81]

The Designated Area Scheme

The scheme favoured by the Majority of the Committee was a scheme whereby the High Court would acquire new powers to designate areas which, in the opinion of the Court, would probably be used for development (houses, factories or other development works) and which would be increased in value because of the works carried out by the local authority which were commenced not earlier than 1 August 1962 (the date on which the 1963 Planning Act was published as a Bill).

The High Court judge would sit with two other assessors, at least one of whom would have valuation experience and the other would have town planning qualifications. The two assessors would simply advise and the final decision would be the judge's alone. The report favoured the decision being made by a High Court judge rather than by a judicial tribunal on the grounds that judicial procedure has the disadvantage that everything has to be proved and this can cause delays in decision-making..[82] The notion of sitting with two assessors was a long-standing practice and a number of precedents are cited in Paragraphs 126 and 127, including the hearing of appeals from the

---

[81] Kenny Report, Par. 66
[82] Kenny Report, Par. 124

Registrar of Political Parties in connect with the registration of political parties.

Once the land was designated, the local authority would have the power to acquire all, or any part, of the land within a 10-year period after it had been designated at its-existing use value at the date when the application to assess the compensation was made plus some percentage of that value together with compensation for reasonable costs of removal but without regard to its development potential. If agreement was not reached when the local authority applied to have the price fixed, it would then be assessed by the High Court judge sitting with the two assessors. Until the local authority made this application to the court, the land owners could continue to use the land, lease, or sell it but any development would require planning permission.

The Report also proposed an amendment to Section 26 of the 1963 Planning Act to allow a planning authority, or the Minister on appeal, to refuse to grant planning permission for any development of lands in a designated area on the grounds that the authority intended to acquire the land within a 10-year period. If planning permission was refused, then the land owner would be entitled to appeal to the High Court to compel the local authority to acquire the land at existing land use value plus 25 per cent. An appeal to the Supreme Court was envisaged but on a point of law only and not on fact. The Committee recommended that where planning permission was refused, the Planning Act, 1963 should be amended so that there could be no right to compensation under Part VI of the Act in a designated area.

Exempted lands from the Designated Areas Scheme would be those owned by any religious denomination, or educational institution in accordance with Article 44.2.6° of the Constitution, existing dwellings, shops and offices etc and property used for community, recreational and sporting purposes.

When the lands were so acquired by the local authority, it was proposed that they would either be leased for private development, or used by the authority for its own purposes. In order to allow for the local authority to retain ownership and review it at the end of each seven or 10-year period, it was further proposed to amend the Landlord and Tenant (Ground Rents) Act, 1967 to prevent the developer purchasing the interest of the local authority.

The arguments for 25%

The Kenny Report Committee believed the community was entitled to the whole of the increase in price in undeveloped land which was attributable to the works carried out by the local authorities. However, as the land, in part at least, would be increase in value by general economic influences outside of the concept of betterment, the Committee agreed that the owners had a right to something more than existing use value.

They recommended a figure of 25% as "a reasonable compromise between the rights of the community and those of the landowners."

> We agree with the view of the Utwhatt Committee that purchase for recoupment is the most effective of the methods available by which public authorities may secure for the community the increases in price of property which their works have created.[83]

The Report listed the benefits of such a scheme:

- It would give the community most of the betterment element in the price of development land.
- It would end speculation on the sale of land suitable for development as nobody would pay more than existing use value plus 25%.
- Land for social purposes such as housing or schools could be made available at a price which covered costs only.
- Local authorities could impose conditions as to the type of building erected and its ultimate price.
- It would allow for an orderly land acquisition programme.
- It would increase the revenue for local authorities because of the profits made from commercial and business lettings.
- It would end the disproportionate rise in the price of undeveloped land suitable for development.
- Arguments against the scheme were also listed:
- It was repugnant to the Constitution (dealt with in a separate chapter)

---

[83] Kenny Report, Par. 68

- There would be two codes of law dealing with compulsory acquisition of land by local authorities, one outside and one within the Designated Areas.
- The scheme would not apply to built-up areas where large profits are made in connection with redevelopment.
- Delays in land acquisition by local authorities would result in fewer houses being built.

The Kenny Report devoted an entire chapter to the Constitutional question and in particular, the relevant Articles, 40.3° and Article 43. The Report argued strongly that 43.1.2° is a guarantee that the State will not pass any law which will attempt to abolish the right to private ownership or the right to transfer or to bequeath and inherit property. The Report's recommendations did not query any of these rights. Section 2 of Article 40, argued the Committee, recognises that the rights given by Section 1 ought to be regulated by the principles of social justice and that the State may delimit (Irish version: *teorainn a chur*) the exercise of these rights so that their exercise will be regulated by the principles of social justice.

It seems to us that it is contrary to the principles of social justice that the owners of land should make large profits from works carried out by local authorities when these are paid for by all the citizens and partly by ratepayers. The Constitution does not give to each citizen the right to get full market price for any of his property which he decides to sell.[84]

Court Precedents

The Kenny Report in its deliberations on the Constitution cited a number of relevant Supreme Court decisions including Buckley *v the Attorney General (The Sinn Féin Funds Case)* [1950] I.R 67], *Foley v The Irish Land Commission* [1952] IR 118 and *The Attorney General v Southern Trust Limited* [1960] 94 IL TR 161.

Having reviewed the various powers conferred on the Land Commission and on local authorities to compulsorily acquire land, the Report concluded that the courts would hold the decision as to whether lands should be included in a Designated Area was an administration of justice and, therefore,

---

[84] Kenny Report, Par. 88

must be decided by a judge and recommended that jurisdiction be conferred on the High Court.

> ..the power to include lands in a designated area would not be "limited" within the meaning of the word as used in Article 37; its exercise could affect in a far reaching way the fortunes and property of the owner.[85]

Two-Tier System

The Report also dealt with suggestions that the recommendations could be repugnant to the Constitution on the grounds that they discriminated against the owners of land in a designated area who would be paid far less for their land than those outside it. (Article 40.1 states that "All citizens shall, as human persons, be held equal before the law"). However, the Report concluded that Article 40.1 relates only to the "essential attributes as persons, to those features which made them human beings" and has nothing to do with property rights.

Religious and Educational Institutions

The Kenny Report also had to deal with Article 44.2 which reads:

> The property of any religious denomination or any educational institution shall not be diverted save for necessary works of public utility and on payment of compensation.

After due consideration the Committee concluded that the new powers proposed in the Report would not apply to the property of any religious denomination, or any educational institution.

Refer to the Supreme Court

Finally, the Report recommended that as a speedy judgement on the validity of the legislation was desirable, that the President, when asked to sign the Bill,

---

[85] Kenny Report, Par. 100

78

should refer it to the Supreme Court under Article 26 of the Constitution for a decision on whether or not it was repugnant to the Constitution.

If this is not done, the constitutional validity of the legislation will almost certainly be challenged by the ordinary process of an action in the High Court and an appeal to the Supreme Court and this will result in uncertainty for a considerable period.[86]

Legislation in Italy and Northern Ireland

While admitting that the Designated Area Scheme might seem radical, the Report pointed to similar legislation in both Italy and Northern Ireland. Legislation had been passed by the Italian Parliament in October 1971.

The Italians are attached to their land and property as are the Irish and if the principle that the development potential is to be ignored when assessing compensation for compulsory acquisition has been accepted by the Italian Parliament, we cannot see any reason why a system based on this concept should not be accepted by the Oireachtas.[87]

The Report also pointed to the New Towns Act (Northern Ireland) 1965 which, when dealing with compensation, stated: "...no account shall be taken of any increase or diminution in the value of the land that is attributable to the existence of the new town."[88]

Additional recommendations

A number of difficulties were set to arise immediately if the scheme was implemented. Chief among these was the status of land granted planning permission before any orders were made for designated areas. The solution proposed by the Report was that such permission should continue to be effective and to authorise the development of such land even in a designated area. However, any subsequent application to the courts by a local authority to assess compensation should have the effect of revoking the planning permission except where work had started at the date of the application.

---

[86] Kenny report, Par. 110
[87] Kenny Report, Par. 112
[88] Kenny Report, Par. 113

Given the expected reluctance of some local authority members to apply for an order designating an area, the Report proposed that this power should be an executive function of the city or county manager. The manager should not require sanction from the council, nor should the members have the power to control his decision under the then Section 4 of the City and County Management (Amendment) Act.[89]

The Report recommended that the new legislation should as far as possible be "a complete statement of the new jurisdiction" and should only refer to the 1963 Planning Act. All rules in relation to determination in the Land Clauses Consolidation Act, 1845, the 1919 Act and in the 1963 Planning Act itself should be excluded.

The Report recommended new rules for the assessment of compensation which should be included in the new legislation (See Appendix 4).

The Report also recommended:

- Details of dealings in land in a designated area should be transferred to local authorities and available to the public
- Public access to all documents in the Land Registry
- The Central Bank should examine the question of banks making loans for purely land speculation purposes
- The specifying of a time limit for completion of works in all grants of planning permission
- The granting of power to the local authorities to obtain injunctions for breaches of planning permission
- Restrictions to the granting of compensation for refusals to grant planning permission
- The amending of the 1919 Act so that the Official Arbitrator should be obliged to show the division of compensation under the heads: the value of the lands; compensation for disturbance; compensation for severance; injurious affection; loss of goodwill and interest
- The consolidating of all law relating to compulsory acquisitions by local authorities into one Act

---

[89] Kenny Report, Par. 117

The Minority Report

In their Minority Report the two representatives from the Department of Local Government, Michael Murphy and Ted O'Meara stated that they agreed generally with the findings of the Report, other than the principal recommendation that local authorities be empowered to acquire land in areas designated by the High Court and that compensation should be based on existing use value. In particular, the writers subscribed to the idea that much of the problem was caused by inadequate investment in sanitary services.

However, they regarded any legislation which would give effect to the main recommendation in the Majority Report as unjust.

> We do not consider that is any justification for a radical departure from the basic compensation principle on which the present code is founded.[90]

In making this decision, they claimed they were influenced by the results of studies in the Department commissioned by Ministers Kevin Boland and Bobby Molloy from 1966 onwards. One of the first ideas considered by the Department they stated was the notion of compulsory acquisition of land at existing value but it had to be abandoned "because of what appeared to be insuperable Constitutional difficulties".

> ....The critical point in the advice given to the Minister and the Government was that the relevant provisions of the Constitution must be interpreted as meaning that while the exigencies of the common good can readily require compulsory acquisition from an unwilling property owner, it is virtually impossible to show how the common good requires that he should not be paid market value for it.[91]

According to Judge Ronan Keane, in the view of the Minority Report writers, any such legislation would almost certainly be held by the courts to be invidiously discriminatory, and repugnant having regard to both to Article 40.3.2° (forbidding unjust attacks on property rights) and Article 40.1 which provides that all citizens shall be held equal before the law.[92]

---

[90] Kenny Minority Report, Par. 2.2
[91] Kenny Minority Report, Par. 2.4
[92] Keane, R. (1983) *Land Use, Compensation and the Community*, 18 Irish Jurist (N.S.) 23

The writers were also concerned that a dual price system would emerge - for land that was compulsorily acquired and land that was not - and that the Government was advised that such discriminatory legislation would be held by the courts to be repugnant to the Constitution.

They pointed to the 1963 Planning Act which they said was "based on acceptance of the fact that the potential development value of land is an inherent part of its value." [93]

> We do not believe for one moment, however, that extreme
> measures of this kind would be justified or that they would be
> likely to command public acceptance. [94]

The Pre-emption and Levy Scheme

The Minority Report proposed a 'Pre-emption and Levy Scheme' whereby planning authorities would be given the power to designate land required for urban expansion. The owner would not be able to dispose of the land unless it was first offered to the local authority and it declined to purchase it. Development land in designated areas would attract levy payments in certain cases.

The Minority Report proposed that the order for designation should be made by the city, or county manager and it should not be subject to Section 4 of the City and County Management (Amendment) Act 1955. A number of exceptions were proposed including, for example, the disposal of land to a state authority, or to a member of the owner's family. [95]

Subject to certain exemptions, a levy would be payable on the disposable of any land required for urban expansion proper. A figure of 30% was suggested but the Minister for Finance should have the power to vary the amount of the levy and a number of exemptions would be allowed such as the disposal of land of less than one acre, or the disposal of land to a member of the owner's family. [96] Alternatives to the levy were also suggested including a charge at the granting of planning permission, or a levy based on the capital cost of the development. [97]

---

[93] Keane Minority Report, Par. 2.6
[94] Kenny Minority Report, Par. 2.8
[95] Kenny Minority Report. Par. 4.18
[96] Kenny Minority Report, Pars 4.25 & 4.30
[97] Kenny Minority Report. Par. 4.44

Chapter 7

The Irish Constitution

Constitution of the Free State

Much of the difficulties for the Kenny Committee and for various ministers seeking to implement the main recommendation later, arise from two Articles in the 1937 Irish Constitution, namely Article 40 and Article 43. As many commentators have pointed out, the difficulties arose because both seem, at least, partly contradictory and a number of reviews have suggested the need for revision to bring clarity.

Although the importance of property rights has been repeatedly reiterated by the courts, there has been considerable discussion surrounding the nature of property rights, in particular the extent to which Article 43 of the Constitution regulates those rights. Article 43 acknowledges the right of individuals to private ownership of property and provides that the Oireachtas is prohibited from enacting legislation that would abolish that right.[98]

The Constitution of the Irish Free State of 1922 contained no general provisions whatever in relation to property rights other than Article 8 which dealt purely with religious denominations and educational institutions. In addition, Article 11 set out the State's rights over natural resources within the national territory.

Article 8

'Freedom of conscience and the free profession and practice of religion are, subject to public order and morality, guaranteed to every citizen, and no law may be made either directly or indirectly to endow any religion, or prohibit, or restrict the free exercise thereof or give any preference, or impose any disability on account

---

[98] Law Reform Commission (2017) *Compulsory Acquisition of Land.* (LRC IP13 – 2017) Law Reform Commission.

of religious belief or religious status, or affect prejudicially the right of any child to attend a school receiving public money without attending the religious instruction at the school, or make any discrimination as respects State aid between schools under the management of different religious denominations, or divert from any religious denomination or any educational institution any of its property except for the purpose of roads, railways, lighting, water or drainage works, or other works of public utility, and on payment of compensation.'

The 1937 Constitution

The right to fair procedures, or to constitutional justice for all citizens derives from Article 40.3.2° of the 1937 Constitution. Initially, principles of social policy formed part of the core property rights guarantee but were moved to Article 45 on the basis of government fears concerning their potential cost implications. [99]

The Constitution protects the right to private property in both Article 40.3.2° and Article 43. Article 43.2 echoes closely the sentiment proclaimed in the Democratic Declaration of the First Dáil (21 January 1919) which stated that "all right to private property must be subordinated to the public right and welfare." [100]

Article 40

3.2° The State shall, in particular, by its laws protect as best it may from unjust attack and, in the case of injustice done, vindicate the life, person, good name, and property rights of every citizen.

---

[99] Hogan, G.W., Whyte, G.F., Kenny, D., Walsh, R. (2018) *Kelly: The Irish Constitution.* Bloomsbury
[100] See Appendix 5

Article 43

1.1° The State acknowledges that man, in virtue of his rational being, has the natural right, antecedent to positive law, to the private ownership of external goods.

1.2° The State accordingly guarantees to pass no law attempting to abolish the right of private ownership or the general right to transfer, bequeath and inherit property.

2.1° The State recognises, however, that the exercise of the rights mentioned in the foregoing provisions of this Article ought, in a civil society, to be regulated by the principles of social justice.

2.2° The State, accordingly, may as occasion requires delimit by law the exercise of the said rights with a view to reconciling their exercise with the exigencies of the common good.

Delivering a Thomas Davis lecture in 1988, Judge Ronan Keane commented that Article 43 probably owed its appearance in the Constitution to the influence of Catholic and social teaching.

In its rejection of communist or utopian visions of a property-less society on the one hand and unbridled *laissez-faire* on the other, it reflected, then as now, the broad political consensus in Irish society. The framers of the Constitution, I suspect, would have been surprised to find that Article 43 had in fact been so frequently invoked in litigation and, had they foreseen that development, might have been happier to see it tucked away among the social policy directives, which are not within the ambit of the courts, rather than be the subject of painstaking judicial exegesis. Had they contented themselves with the forthright protection of the citizen against unjust attacks on property rights contained in Article 40, there might have been a less tangled history to unfold. At least the damaging impression could not have taken so firm a hold that the Constitution imposes unnecessary barriers against progress to social justice.[101]

In *Blake v Attorney General [1982]1 IR 117* the High Court held that Articles 40.3.2 and 43 should be read in conjunction with each other, with reference to the preamble so as to have full regard to the "principles of social justice, exigencies of the common good, the principles of justice generally and the attainment of true social order".

The case involved controlled rents and the restriction on landlord's possession of their property due to statutory restrictions imposed during World War I. The plaintiffs claimed successfully that such legislation represented an unjust attack on their property rights.

The Supreme Court held that on the one hand, Article 43 "is an article which prohibits the abolition of private property as an institution but at the same time permits, in particular circumstances, the regulation of the exercise of that right and of the general right to transfer, bequeath and inherit property". On the other hand, it held that Article 40 deals with a citizen's right to a particular item of property. The Court actively rejected the decision of the Supreme Court in *Attorney General v Southern Industrial Trust* which held that there was no differentiation between Articles 40 and 43. In the case before it, the Court found Article 40 to be applicable; therefore, the test was that of "unjust attack".[102]

In its report in 1996 the Report of the Constitution Review Group[103], noted that the fact there are two separate constitutional provisions dealing with property rights has itself given rise to much confusion.

---

[101] Keane, R. (1988) Property in the Constitution and the Courts. In *De Valera's Constitution*

[102] Law Reform Commission (2017) *Compulsory Acquisition of Land.* (LRC IP13 – 2017) Law Reform Commission.

[103] The Constitution Review Group was a group established by the Irish government in 1995 to review the Constitution of Ireland and to recommend alterations. The group was chaired by T. K. Whitaker and had fifteen members selected from different backgrounds. Their report was published in July 1996, comprising within its 700 pages the most thorough analysis of the Constitution from the legal, political science, administrative, social and economic perspectives ever made. The members were: Dr T.K. Whitaker (Chairman), David Byrne SC, Dr Alpha Connelly, Mary Finlay SC, Dermot Gleeson SC., James Hamilton BL, Mahon Hayes, Gerard Hogan FTCD, BL, Professor Áine Hyland, Dr Finola Kennedy, Professor Michael Laver FTCD, Dr Kathleen Lynch, Diarmaid McGuinness BL, Dr Dermot Nally and Dr Blathna Ruane BL.

It also noted that the language of Article 43 in particular is "unhappy". Several commentators had drawn attention to the contrast between Article 43.1 and Article 43.2. It quotes a famous *dictum*: 'Where are contrasted the stress placed on the right of private property in Article 43.1 – calculated to lift up the heart of the most old-fashioned capitalist – with that placed on the principles of social justice and the exigencies of common good in Article 43.2 – 'the Constitution of [former] Yugoslavia hardly goes further than this'.

In addition, the Review Group noted comments by Mr Justice Keane who had spoken of the 'unattractive language' and 'tortured syntax' of Article 43.

The Review Group also noted that both Article 40.3° and Article 43 are particularly open to subjective judicial appraisal, with phrases such as 'unjust attack', 'principles of social justice' and 'reconciling' the exercise of property rights 'with the exigencies of the common good'.[104]

The Review Group commented:

> ..whatever formulation might be devised to replace Article 40.3.2° and Article 43, it could probably not avoid entrusting a degree (even a high degree) of subjective appraisal to the judiciary. However, the Review Group considers that, for reasons examined below, it would be preferable to recast these provisions in a manner which provided for a more structured and objective method of judicial analysis.[105]

The Constitution Review Group recommended that the Constitution be amended so that the provisions dealing with property rights are contained in a single Article. It also recommended:

> The Constitution should expressly provide that such property rights can be qualified, restricted etc by legislation where there are clear social justice, or other public policy reasons for doing so.[106]

---

[104] *Report of the Constitution Review Group (1996).* Government Publications Office.
[105] Ibid p. 38
[106] Ibid P. 361

To date, none of the above recommendations have been implemented.

In their report, the 2004 All-Party Oireachtas Committee on the Constitution noted that although constitutional change may not be strictly necessary, the Committee thought that change "along the lines recommended by the Constitution Review Group may be desirable".[107]

The All-Party Committee report noted that Article 40.3.2 is directed at the personal and individual rights of citizens and expressly protects the right to property while Article 43, on the other hand, is exclusively concerned with the right to property. It continues:

> The existence of these two separate constitutional provisions has caused the courts considerable difficulties over the decades. In the end, however, the courts have concluded that the two provisions inform each other so that both have to be taken into account when considering constitutional protection of property rights.[108]

The Committee also noted that a significant number of constitutional challenges in the area of property rights fail and cited as examples the restrictions on the use of gaming machines *Cafolla v O'Malley, [1985]1 IR 486,* challenges to the taxi licensing regime affecting the capital value of a taxi plate *Hempenstall v. Minister for the Environment [1994] 2 IR 20* and the operation of the red zones adjacent to airports which may have the effect of impairing the rights of landowners to obtain planning permission *Liddy v Minister for Public Enterprise [2004] I ILRM 9.*

As pointed out by the All-Party Committee Review, early case law in this area created considerable difficulties with the Supreme Court placing a difference in emphasis from time to time. Two of the cases - both of which are referred to in the Kenny Report - are *Buckley v the Attorney General* in [1950] IR 67 and the *Attorney General v Southern Industrial Trust Ltd* [1960] 94 ILTR 161. In the first case, (usually simply called the Sinn Féin funds case) the principal plaintiff, who was the then President of Sinn Féin, Margaret Buckley, claimed ownership of certain funds deposited by the former trustees of Sinn Féin after the Civil War split. The Oireachtas enacted

---

[107] The All-Party Oireachtas Committee on the Constitution. Ninth Progress Report: Private Property (2004). Government Publications Office. P.62
[108]Ibid P. 21

the Sinn Fein Funds Act, 1947 which directed the High Court to dismiss the action and transfer the funds to a charitable board which would distribute the monies to veterans of the War of Independence. The Supreme Court found the legislation to be unconstitutional in that it breached constitutional property rights.

In the *Attorney General v. Southern Industrial Trust Ireland* case, an Irish citizen, a Mr Simons, had bought a motor car with the aid of a hire purchase loan from the plaintiffs so that they became the owners of the vehicle. Mr Simons later exported the car to Northern Ireland without a licence, which he had been required to obtain. When the car was subsequently brought back into the State, it was confiscated by Customs authorities who claimed the right to forfeit it under Section 5 of the 1945 Customs Act. The Attorney General then brought an action seeking a Declaration that the car was forfeited. Southern Trust Ireland opposed the action claiming the section of the Act was repugnant to the Constitution on the basis compensation must be paid. The company claimed it had not itself been involved in any illegal export of the vehicle and it was being deprived of its property rights. This argument was rejected by both the High Court and Supreme Court. The Supreme Court ruled that the delimitation of rights was in line with the exigencies of the common good as set out in Article 43.2.2.

The All-Party Committee Report noted that this case was very much at odds with the *Buckley* case. [109] As noted in *Kelly; The Irish Constitution*, the "whole tone and effect of the *Southern Industrial Trust* case did not seem easily reconciled with the Supreme Court's strong words in the *Sinn Féin Funds* case and for the following 12 years it was not possible to state clearly what exactly the property guarantees of the Constitution amounted to."

The All-Party Committee also noted that the system of restricting compensation was upheld by Mr Justice Kenny in *Central Dublin Development Association Ltd v the Attorney General* [1975] 109 ILTR 69. There he concluded:

> Town and regional planning is an attempt to reconcile the exercise of property rights with the demands of the common good and (Part IV of the 1963 Act) defends and vindicates, as

---

[109] Ibid p. 23

far as practicable, the rights of the citizen and is not an unjust attack on their property rights.

The Kenny Report states that the Sinn Féin Funds case is sometimes stated to be "authority for the proposition that when the State, or a public authority, acquires property compulsorily, the Constitution requires that they must pay the full market price for it". The report notes Mr Justice O'Byrne, who gave the judgement, pointed out "that the power of the Oireachtas to delimit the exercise of the rights of property so as to reconcile that exercise with the exigencies of the common good arose only when there was a conflict between the exercise by the citizens of their property rights and the exigencies of the common good and as there was no conflict in relation to the Sinn Féin Funds, legislation was repugnant to the Constitution."

But the Kenny Report adds:

> There is however, clearly a conflict between the exercise of rights of property and the exigencies of the common good in the case of services and potential building land. The free-market principle means that the owners of such land get unearned profits to which they have not contributed in any way and which result in substantial additions to the cost of the buildings subsequently erected. The community, however, has got a legitimate claim to such profits because citizens, in their capacity as taxpayers, bear the costs of servicing such lands and hence has a right to be recouped.
>
> The alleged right of landowners to get the full market price for something in limited supply (a right which we believe does not exist) is not consistent with the common good.[110]

2.16 Equality and Proportionality

In addition, to the above, Article 40.1 of the Constitution states:

1° All citizens shall, as human persons, be held equal before the law.

---

[110] Kenny Report, Par. 89

2° This shall not be held to mean that the State shall not in its enactments have due regard to differences of capacity, physical and moral, and of social function.

The relationship between the equality guarantee and the principle of proportionality in the context of property rights was analysed by the Supreme Court in *Re Article 26 and Part V of the Planning and Development Bill, 1999*. Under Part V of the Act a local authority can reserve up to 20 per cent, later reduced to 10 per cent, of land zoned for residential development to meet the identified needs for social and affordable housing and this percentage of land can be made available to the local authority at existing use value. The wording echoed the recommendations of the Kenny Report of 27 years previously.

The Act was referred to the Supreme Court by President Mary McAleese under Article 26 of the Constitution to test its constitutionality. The case for the State, argued by the then Attorney General, Michael McDowell SC and accepted by the Court, was that the Bill: '...was doing no more than requiring the landowner, if he wished to develop the land, to surrender some part of the enhanced value of his property which had resulted from the operation of a planning regime intended for the benefit of the community as a whole.'[111]

The operation of Part V was found to be in compliance with the Constitution and the outcome has a major bearing as to whether the recommendations of the Kenny Report were repugnant to the Constitution.

In *re the Planning and Development Bill 1999*, the Supreme Court held that "it can scarcely be disputed that it was within the competence of the Oireachtas to decide that the achievement of these objectives would be socially just and required by the common good". The "novel" approach of the Oireachtas in the matter of planning was found to be entirely within its competence. The Court concluded "that the presumption that every Act of the Oireachtas is constitutional until the contrary is clearly established applies with particular force to the legislation dealing with controversial social and economic matters". This approach is certainly reflective of a higher level of deference to the Oireachtas. However, the Court did not actively state that the

---

[111] Re Article 26 and Part V of the Planning and Development Bill 1999 [2000] 2 IR 321, 343

determination of the common good is beyond the scope of the Court's jurisdiction.[112]

Indeed, one of the cases referred to by the Supreme Court in the Part V reference in support of the right to private property not being absolute was *Dreher v Irish Land Commission* in which the plaintiff had insisted on being compensated in cash rather than in Land Bonds for land compulsorily acquired. The Supreme Court held that the statutory requirement of compensation in Land Bonds was not unconstitutional.

The Supreme Court decision in the 1999 Planning & Development Bill case was extremely significant having dealt with the central question as to whether the price paid amounted to an interference in property rights given that the amount was below market value.

> The Supreme Court commenced its analysis by stating that, where land is compulsory acquired by the State for social objectives, the owner is usually entitled to compensation at market value. However, it held that, in the particular circumstances of the case, this was not necessary for two reasons. The first was that value of the land had indeed been enhanced by zoning and the grant of planning permission and the second was that the law was needed to meet serious social problems.[113]

This view was supported by Feichín McDonagh SC in a legal opinion provided to the Labour Party in February 2021.

> The court held that all persons acquiring or inheriting land did so subject to the general restrictions on use imposed by planning law, which could increase or decrease the value of land, depending on the particular form of development permitted. The court concluded that the Bill required an owner "...to cede some part of the enhanced value of the land deriving both from its zoning for residential purposes and the grant of

---

[112] Law Reform Commission (2017) *Compulsory Acquisition of Land.* (LRC IP13 – 2017) Law Reform Commission.

[113] Gwynn Morgan, D. (2012) Government and the Courts. In *Governing Ireland: From Cabinet Government to Delegated Government* (O'Malley, E. & MacCarthaigh M. eds) IPA. pp. 232 -233

permission in order to meet what is considered by the
Oireachtas to be a desirable social objective". This, it regarded
as constitutional.

The use of the Part V legislation in providing for a social and affordable
component in all developments gives effect to the fact that the legislation is a
living thing or a living process, according to Planning Regulator Niall Cussen.

It is not so much absolute in time but a response to different
socio-economic contexts and indeed I think that was a key part
of the referral of the 2000 Act Part V provisions to the Supreme
Court for determination in relation to its constitutionality
because maybe in a previous generation, or previous era, there
would have been a sense probably that Part V went too far over
the edge, or the margin between common good and an
unreasonable intrusion into constitutionally protected
personal freedoms and liberties like property rights. The State
was going through another housing pressure in the early
noughties, arguably, some might say, it's never quite come out
of it. It was either a feast or a famine. So, the legislation, to
some extent, ebbs and flows around this, depending on the
issues and the pressures of the day._[114]

Principal conclusion

The Kenny Report was delivered against a relative paucity of case law and an
uncertain background but in Chapter VIII on the Constitution, it considered
relevant cases including those mentioned above.

The principal conclusion of the Kenny Report is contained in Paragraph
93 of the report:

Our proposal is not that a local authority should have the power
to acquire land anywhere at a price below its market value. It
is that a court should be authorised to operate a form of price
control in designated areas. In that sense the proposal involves
a delimitation of property rights but one which is no more

---

[114] Interview with Niall Cussen 2020

restrictive than other forms of price control. We believe that the limitation is not unjust because the landowners in question have done nothing to give the land its enhanced value and the community which has brought about this increased value (through the provision of these additional services) should get the benefit of it.

In an earlier paragraph (84) the Kenny Report also recommended that a local authority should have the power to acquire lands contained within a designated area and compensation would be assessed by the High Court and would be the existing value at the date of the application plus 25 per cent.

In justifying its conclusions, the Kenny Report noted:

.....The Constitution does not give to each citizen the right to get full market price for any of his property which he decides to sell. If it did, then all price controls would be repugnant to the Constitution and we are convinced that this is not the law. Moreover, if each citizen has the right to get the full market price for any part of his property which he decides to sell, each owner of house property must have the right to get the full market rent for it when he lets it. But if this is the law, the Rent Restrictions Acts and the Landlord and Tenants Acts, both of which regulate the amount of rent which a landlord may lawfully get for some types of property and which, in effect, prevent him from realising the full market price of sale of the property by giving privileges to tenants are repugnant to the Constitution. Nobody has ever suggested this in the thousands of cases under those Acts which have come before the courts."[115]

However, some eight years later in *Blake v the Attorney General* [1982] 1 IR 117 the Supreme Court held the Rent Restrictions Acts (1946 – 1967) to be unconstitutional.

In this case, the Supreme Court found that rents had been fixed at absurdly low levels, no allowance had been made for inflation and there was no regard to the income of the landlord or the tenants.

---

[115] Kenny Report, Par. 88

Commenting on this in their 2004 report, the All-Party Oireachtas Committee stated that, contrary to what many had argued, this decision did not decide that all forms of price control were unconstitutional and all it decided was that "the form of the rent control sanctioned by the Rent Restrictions Acts 1946 – 67 was unconstitutional.....The proposals in the Kenny Report appear to the Committee to be very much at the opposite end of the spectrum, in particular, given that the landowner will receive the existing land use value plus 25 per cent.[116]

A number of similar cases followed including *Brennan v the Attorney General* [1984] ILRM 355 where the system of determining rates for farmers was found to be arbitrary and unconstitutional and *Electricity Supply Board v Gormley [1985] IR 129* where the absence of a system of enforceable compensation to landowners for works carried out on property by the ESB was found to be unconstitutional. Whether these decisions were a significant factor in why subsequent governments never acted on the Kenny Report is a matter of some speculation.

In its 2004 Report, the All-Party Oireachtas Committee asked if the conclusions of the Kenny Report were still valid. It quoted from the Labour Party submission to its deliberations which argued that:

the only way of finding out whether such proposals will survive constitutional challenge is to incorporate them into legislation and await the outcome of the constitutional challenge.[117]

Most significantly, the Report stated:

Judged by contemporary case-law, it is nevertheless very difficult to see why the recommendations contained in the Kenny Report would not survive constitutional scrutiny. In the *Planning and Development Bill* the Supreme Court held that the Oireachtas was entitled to conclude that 'the provision of affordable housing and housing for persons in special categories and of integrated housing' was rationally connected 'to an objective of sufficient

---

[116] The All-Party Oireachtas Committee on the Constitution. Ninth Progress Report: Private Property (2004). Government Publications Office. p. 40
[117] Ibid p. 39

importance to warrant interference with a constitutionally protected right, and given the serious social problems which they are designed to meet, they undoubtedly relate to concerns which, in a free and democratic society, should be regarded as pressing and substantial.' By extension, therefore, the imposition of price controls on building land would be regarded as an objective of social importance which would warrant interfering with a constitutional right.[118]

In its conclusions, the All-Party Oireachtas Committee stated that it seemed clear from the Supreme Court decisions in the 1991 European Court of Human Rights decision in Pine *Valley Developments Ltd and Others v Ireland* [1991] 14 EHRR 319 and the Planning and Development Bill that a landowner's property rights only extend to existing and permitted land uses.

Accordingly, in many instances, there is no constitutional right to receive compensation where planning permission has been denied and this is certainly so where the application for permission would involve a material contravention of a development plan.[119]

The Report made two further significant conclusions:

The Committee is of the view that, having regard to modern case-law, it is very likely that the major elements of the Kenny Report recommendations - namely that land required for development by local authorities should be compulsory acquired at existing use values plus 25 per cent - **would not be found to be unconstitutional.** Indeed, it may be that in certain respects, the Kenny Report was too conservative, since there seems no necessity that either the act of designating the lands in question, which are to be subjected to a form of price control, or the payment of compensation to the landowners thereby affected, would require to be performed by a High Court judge.

---

[118] Ibid. p.39
[119] Ibid p. 43

Existing land use plus 25 per cent

On the question of the 25 per cent extra to existing use value, the All-Party Oireachtas Committee admitted that while the figure was an arbitrary one, a line had to be dawn somewhere and the Kenny Report was anxious to ensure the land owner received fair compensation beyond existing use value. The Report added:

> While this Committee is not necessarily wedded to the 25 per cent figure, we are nonetheless of the view that the landowner should receive a figure in excess of the existing land use, if only to assist in the repelling of any constitutional challenge. [120]

In this regard, the Committee concluded

> The Committee is not, therefore, persuaded that the existing constitutional provisions place any unjustified impediment to infrastructural development. It does not, therefore, consider that constitutional change is necessary before any reform of the existing system of compulsory purchase and acquisition is attempted. The Committee suggests instead that there should be a thorough-going revision and reform of the complex and byzantine legislation in this area, not least matters such as the necessity for property referencing in every area (no matter how trivial the interference) and the rule whereby every landowner is deemed to own from the centre of the earth to the sky. [121]

Urban Regeneration and Housing Act 2015

Since the publication of the All-Party Oireachtas Committee Report on Private Property, a number of amendments were made to the Part V obligations, notably by the by the Urban Regeneration and Housing Act, 2015 with the aim of making more social housing available and to provide for transparency in the Part V process. Since the 2000 Act, developers were required to reserve up to 20% of land zoned for residential use or residential and other uses, for social and affordable housing, or fulfil that obligation by

---

[120] Ibid P. 40
[121] Ibid P. 43

one of the permitted alternative means, including cash payments, or making land available elsewhere as had been the widespread practice.

The 2015 Act removed the affordable housing element but retaining a requirement for 10% social housing. While the Act provided that the overall percentage was reduced to a maximum of 10%, the provision for social and affordable housing was kept on the statute books.

In addition, future Part V agreements must be put in place prior to lodgement of a commencement notice in respect of the development to which the planning application related. The 2015 Act also provides that the relevant date for calculating the *"existing use value"* is the date of the grant of the planning permission. Prior to the 2015 Act, the relevant date was the date of the transfer of the lands to the local authority. According to Dr. Padraic Kenna of the School of Law, NUIG, in effect, the principles of the Kenny Report were now partially written into law 42 years after its publication. "We now have a version of the Kenny Report in force since the 2015 Act which requires all developers to provide 10 per cent of each development for social housing."

The European Convention on Human Rights

Article 1 of Protocol No. 1of the European Convention on Human Rights states:

> 1. Every natural or legal person is entitled to the peaceful enjoyment of his possessions. No one shall be deprived of his possessions except in the public interest and subject to the conditions provided for by law and by the general principles of international law.

> 2. The preceding provisions shall not, however, in any way impair the right of a State to enforce such laws as it deems necessary to control the use of property in accordance with the general interest, or to secure the payment of taxes or other contributions or penalties.

Article 1 of the First Protocol of the European Convention of Human Rights guarantees the right to private property in terms which are not, in substance, dissimilar to Article 40.3 and Article 43. In its report, the 2004 All-Party Oireachtas Committee stated that the case law of the European Court of

Human Rights on the topic of property is in many ways, along the lines of modern Irish case law. "Certainly, the methodology applied by the Irish courts on the one hand and the European Court on the other is very similar".[122]

A report in 2017 by the Law Reform Commission concurred.

> The provision is similar in nature to Article 43. It also provides that this right does not impair the right of a State to enforce such laws as it deems necessary in order to control the use of property "in accordance with the general interest". Article 43 and A1P1 (Article 1 of Protocol 1) thus appear broadly consistent with one another. It is also the case that both have been held to apply to corporate bodies as well as individuals.[123]

Since the enactment into Irish law of the European Convention of Human Rights Act 2003 (ECHR Act 2003), the Irish courts are now empowered to grant a declaration of incompatibility with the Convention.

This, in effect, means that any domestic legislation restricting, or interfering in property rights, can be tested by reference to the guarantees outlined in Article 1 of the First Protocol. Dr Padraic Kenna commented that in the Supreme Court ruling on the 2000 Planning & Development Act, Judge Keane ensured that it was not in breach of the Convention.

"In effect, Judge Keane in his judgement cut off any possible route to the European Court by dealing comprehensively with Article 1 and there never was a further challenge."

- NB: Further details on areas which were considered by the Committee on Building Land including Planning, Compulsory Purchase, Zoning and Betterment are dealt with in Appendices 1 and 2.

---

[122] Ibid P. 36
[123] Law Reform Commission (2017) *Compulsory Acquisition of Land.* (LRC IP13 – 2017) Law Reform Commission.

Chapter 8

International Comparisons

British Influence

For historical reasons and as explained in previous chapters, the Irish planning system for housing is based on the that of the UK. As mentioned previously, the Kenny Report was heavily influenced by the Uthwatt Committee in 1942 which recommended that the uplift in land value, commonly referred to as "betterment", arising from planning permission be treated as belonging to the community and so could be taxed. However, the Conservative government elected in 1951 saw the development charge as an impediment to housebuilding and abolished it. Since then, successive British governments introduced various measures to capture windfall profits from land speculation.

However, in the 1980s there was a sea change from the post-war period when most infrastructure was paid for by the state to a position where local authorities increasingly applied planning obligations on private developers to pay for it. The legal basis for these obligations were codified by the 1990 Town and Country Planning Act and are commonly referred to as 'Section 106 Agreements'.

The use of planning agreements brings together funding of infrastructure and services at a local level and the capture of development value. They include the requirement to provide or fund 'affordable' and market housing on the same site (Jones and Stephens, 2020). According to Jones and Stephens, a parallel initiative was introduced in the United States during the housing boom of the noughties in the form of 'inclusion zones'. In these zones developers provide a percentage of affordable housing, usually on a mandatory basis but sometimes they receive an incentive in return.

However, there are other systems that operate throughout Europe and the wider world. For the purposes of this book, it is worth taking a brief look at how some operate and how successfully.

Broadly speaking, three types of planning systems exist across the developed world. They are firstly, discretion-based; secondly, autocratic and thirdly, rules-based. The first type is commonly found in Commonwealth, or former Commonwealth countries, including the Republic of Ireland. Under this system local residents have considerable power to stop development plans and frequently exercise this power. According to Paul Cheshire, Emeritus Professor of Economic Geography at the London School of Economics, it may be no con-incidence that those countries have in recent decades seen the fastest growth in house prices. [124]

Autocratic planning systems boost housing supply quickly. Russia, for example, raised its annual rate of housebuilding from 400,000 per annum in the early noughties to over one million in 2018. In Moscow, there were 58,544 apartments built in 2018, up almost 10 per cent from a year earlier.

The third system, a rules-based planning system, is often found in European countries such as France and Germany. If the developers tick all the boxes, then construction is permitted despite local objections.

This system appears to work better than that which operates in the British and Irish system. Since the 1950s, for example, Germany has built twice the number of houses as Britain, despite having only a slightly higher population.

The Netherlands

The Netherlands is widely regarded as having an effective system of land-use planning. For example, Peter Hall in a comparative study, placed the Netherlands in first place. [125] Most people there appear to have good houses in good residential areas with facilities such as schools, shops and health centres, all within easy reach. Central to the Dutch system is an active system that goes beyond the passive planning system used in many other countries whereby planning permission is required for changes in land use.

> The Dutch see active spatial policy as the only way of creating the towns, cities and countryside that they want. Put negatively, they do not think that they should accept a physical environment that

---

[124] *The Economist*, January 18 – 24, 2020
[125] Hall, P. (2014) Good Cities, Better Lives: How Europe Discovered the Lost Art of Urbanism Routledge. New York

is shaped predominantly by market forces. In their opinion, the physical environment, even nature can and should be constructed.[126]

Up until around 30 years ago, housing in the Netherlands was heavily subsidised including rental housing as well as houses for sale. Much of the housing was built by housing associations and social housing now represents around one-third of the housing stock. The exact locations for houses were determined by the national government in consultation with local government who, in turn, collaborated with the housing associations. In addition, the Dutch generally opted for generous allocations of open space.

Critical was the fact that the price at which land was sold to housing associations was determined by government regulation. As a result, the municipalities were able to recover the costs involved in the necessary public investment – in effect the 'betterment' - by selling serviced land plots. Developers earned their profit from the building of homes rather than from speculative land development. Generally, each residential estate would comprise of a mix of owner-occupied houses, more expensive rental home and cheaper rented homes.[127]

By the mid-1990s things began to change in the Netherlands. Lower interest rates in the EU, combined with easier access to credit, saw an increasing cohort of people wishing to own their own homes and less demand for social housing. All these factors combined to increase land prices and municipalities found it more difficult to acquire land.

Gradually the Netherlands adopted three broad approaches to enable municipalities to pursue active land policies: the building claims model, joint ventures and concessions. The building claims model involves the developer selling un-serviced land voluntarily to the municipality at a price the same, or sometimes lower, than he paid for it. In return, the municipality then commits to selling the developer an amount of serviced land later. The developer buys a piece of land, not necessarily because he wants to build there on that land, but because he wishes to build in that plan area.

---

[126] Needham, B. (2012) Institutions for Housing Supply in Smith, S.J. (Ed.) *International Encyclopaedia of Housing and Home*. Elsevier, Amsterdam. p.19
[127] Cahill, N. (2018) International Approaches to Land Use, Housing and Urban Development. NESC Dublin. p.4

The joint ventures model is not unlike the private/public partnership model in Ireland whereby a company is established with the shares divided between the developer and the municipality. The company then acquires the land, services it and sells it on for development to an agreed purchaser.

The concession model involves the land being acquired, service and developed by one or more developers. The onsite infrastructure costs are born by the developer while the offsite costs are a matter for negotiation. According to Cahill, all three development models have resulted in a lack of competition in the building market. While a number of proposals were put forward, including a law to allow compulsory purchase of land at existing use value, municipalities are still able to acquire land at less than commercial value.

New legislation introduced in 2008 gave municipalities enhanced powers to recover costs when they did not own the land as well as the power to require developers to include affordable housing in their plans.

Compulsory Purchase

Compulsory purchase of land for residential development is permitted in the Netherlands where a land-use plan has been adopted by the municipality. It can be used, for example, where a landowner is unwilling to develop the land in accordance with the land-use plan or to sell it to the municipality. In the process of compulsorily acquiring land, two points are worthy of note, firstly, the price paid for an individual plot of land is the average price with the whole plan area and secondly, the land value is reduced to take account of the cost of providing services.

In a method similar to that of the Minority Kenny Report, since 1985 Dutch municipalities have been able to designate areas in which they intend to use pre-emption rights, that is, the owner has to offer the land for sale to the municipality before it can be offered to another buyer. The price paid is the same as under the compulsory purchase offer but the process is much quicker. In recent years, these powers have been increased. To prevent a rush of sales prior to pre-emption being applied, it is usually put in place before a land-use plan has been put in place.

In some Dutch cities such as Amsterdam, active land management is complimented by a system of public leasing whereby ground leases are provided by the municipality rather than outright sales. As a result, the city of

Amsterdam now owns 80 per cent of the land. The leases are regulated by law and can be sold on to new parties but the same conditions apply. The system allows housing associations and others to provide social housing with the avoidance of having to pay for the land.

The Dutch experience illustrates that leasing of public land at scale in a European country is a feasible proposition and one that yields benefits. At a time when Ireland is planning to allocate a substantial volume of publicly-owned land to housing, the option of leasing the land is well worth considering.

Dr William Nowlan has long argued that the Dutch approach to land management, strategic planning and infrastructure provision is a potential exemplar for Ireland.

> If such a system were implemented here, it could facilitate a very rapid doubling of our housing output. The Dutch model is based on a partnership between the planning authorities and landowners with linkage to the construction sector.... Such an approach is quite workable in Ireland without the requirement for new legislation as the Irish Planning Acts already provide for such arrangements. They have been used several times in the past with an example being the partnership development of the ILAC Centre by Irish Life and Dublin City Council in the 1970s.[128]

Germany

Following German re-unification in 1990 house building, notably apartment-building doubled, aided by subsidies to both private landlords and not-for-profit housing associations. According to Cahill, this was achieved mainly through the provision of low interest loans and tax relief on rents. The generous development policies in Germany after the unification contributed to a gross housing surplus, with around 500,000 more homes than house-holds by 2002. This was most notable in East Germany as more and more people moved to the West, chasing new economic opportunities.

---

[128] Interview with Dr Bill Nowlan 2021

In recent years, housing output slowed down and is currently below the level needed. In addition, much of the subsidised housing has reached the end of its rent-restriction period. Germany was expected to have a requirement of 270,000 new homes by 2020 which was close to output. However, new figures to take account of the influx of refugees increased that figure.

In Germany, it is normally the responsibility of the municipality to service the land and to provide the local infrastructure for development. In return, the municipalities are entitled to recover up to 90 per cent of the cost of this work from the landowners with the local authority paying 10 per cent (section 129 of the Federal Building Code).

There are special local laws used by local authorities to vary the level of charges for landowners or developers. Landowners and developers cannot legally require an authority to provide local infrastructure, but they can offer to do it by making a legal agreement with the authority which authorises the developer to provide the local infrastructure.[129]

Where housing development is required but has not taken place by other means, municipalities may designate an 'urban development zone' which allows for the swift acquisition of land, both brown and greenfield sites, for development. Here, the municipality has the right to acquire the land at existing use value. It then provides the infrastructure before selling it on in plots to builders. While this measure is not widely used, its very presence acts as an incentive to develop land.

House-building in Germany is also stimulated by a complex range of subsidies. These subsidies can be availed of by anyone including individuals, not-for-profit organisations and private builders. Profit is not the main motive in the provision of housing which is not dominated by large developers or building companies.

In recent years the federal government has taken a stricter approach to contain urban development and not unlike recent Irish planning policy, has adopted the principle of 'brownfield first' in an effort to re-develop existing sites in urban areas.

Germany has, of course, a very large private rental sector where renting is an attractive long-term option. This is caused by providing a very strong

[129] Davies, B., Turner, E. & Snelling C. (2016) *German Model Homes? A Comparison of UK and German Housing Markets.* Institute of Public Policy Research. London. p.20

degree of security to tenants where tenancies are typically indefinite with lengthy break clauses on the part of the tenant and there are also strict limits on how, and when, a landlord can evict a tenant. Secondly, rents are regulated with both limits on how much a landlord can raise the rent on a sitting tenant and limits on how much a landlord can charge to a new tenant.

In 2015 a new law was introduced to slow down rising rents via controls on new contracts. This so-called 'rent-brake' or *Mietpreisbremse* means that new rents cannot be set at more than 10 per cent above the level of the local reference rent, or the rent previously charged for the property, whichever is the higher.

In January 2020, Berlin's parliament passed a law to freeze rent prices for five years, becoming the first federal state in Germany to introduce a rent cap. The new law put a cap on residential rental prices in the German capital, where the cost of rent had doubled in the previous 10 years. The cap was pegged to freeze rent prices until 2025, following which, the law limited increases to 1.3% per year in line with inflation.

Austria

Housing output was sustained in Austria during the 2006 - 2011 economic recession and the country continued to provide a continuous supply of affordable houses. According to a NESC 2018 report, State subsidies are modest but are concentrated on the supply side by engineering cost-effectiveness.

Limited-profit housing associations use modest subsidies in the form of low-cost finance to provide rental accommodation at affordable rents based on costs; they provide a leading example of an effective cost rental housing sector.

In Austria, land policy plays an integral role in supporting the development of affordable housing. In Vienna, for example, a special Housing Fund (*Wohnfonds Wien*) was set up in 1984 to provide land for subsidised housing and to supervise the restoration and upgrading of old buildings.

However, this Fund does not have any legal rights in buying land but does enjoy a monopoly position in some areas where it is not in competition with private developers. (Lawson). In addition, the Housing Fund also organises competitions to purchase larger sites which are open to limited-profit associations and developers. The winning proposition buys the land at a moderate cost and receives a low-interest loan that covers 35% to 40% of the project costs.[130]

Dr William Nowlan argued the best cost-rental model currently operating in Europe, is the Vienna Cost-Rental Model whereby cost based rents of about €800 per month are charged and for those on very low incomes who cannot afford €800 rental a month, a State-funded housing allowance is available to bridge the deficit.

He added: "The providers of such 'affordable rental housing' rely on direct and indirect State support to bring down their rents in the form of loan guarantees and grants. Such support structures enable charitable and other housing organisations to secure long-term funding at low interest rates. Some such providers are philanthropic, others are limited profit or semi-charities and yet others use low-cost Impact Capital."

---

[130] Holeywell, R. (2013) Vienna Offers Affordable and Luxurious Accommodation http://www.governing.com/topics/health-human-services/gov-affordable-luxurious-housing-in-vienna.html

Chapter 9

The Turbulent 70s

Political Change

During the period 1971 to 1973 while the Committee on the Price of Building Land was sitting and deliberating, there was a lot of turbulence in the Irish political world. Without doubt, this pushed the issue of escalating land prices down the agenda. The country and Fianna Fail were still reeling in the aftermath of the 1970 Arms Crisis when two senior government ministers, Neil Blaney (responsible for the Local Government (Planning & Development) Act, 1963) and a future Taoiseach, Charles Haughey, were sacked by the Taoiseach, Jack Lynch and two other ministers resigned.

The impact of the Troubles was reflected, for example, in a letter dated 20th April 1972 which Judge Kenny wrote to Minister Bobby Molloy as he was finalising his report. He wrote: "It is not easy to do hard work with the daily chronicle of sorrows in Northern Ireland" (See Appendix 6).

The fallout from the Arms Crisis and the Troubles in Northern Ireland were to totally dominate the agenda of Irish politics for the next 10 years. Former Labour Party General Secretary, Senator, TD and MEP, Brendan Halligan, recalls that lots of things did not happen because of the North.

> From 1968 onwards it began to take over the national psyche
> and it became the number one issue. I spent as much time away
> in Belfast and London as I did here in Dublin. People forget
> how short the time was. [131]

On 17 May, 1974 three bombs exploded in Dublin (Parnell Street, Talbot Street and South Leinster Street) during the evening rush hour and a fourth exploded in Monaghan almost 90 minutes later. The bombs killed 33 civilians and injured almost 300. The bombings caused outrage and the follow-up dominated the Government's attention for many months as it was feared

---

[131] Interview with the late Brendan Halligan 2020

other bombings could follow. Many years later in 1993 the Ulster Volunteer Force (UVF), a loyalist paramilitary group, claimed responsibility but no-one was ever charged.

Also, in 1973 the Provisional IRA began a bombing campaign in mainland Britain beginning with the Old Bailey courthouse in March 1973 and continued with the Guilford pub bombings in October 1974 and the Birmingham pub bombings in November 1974. The bombings strained British-Irish relations and a huge amount of government time on both sides of the Irish Sea was spent in trying to bring an end to these acts and to find solutions. In Dublin the new National Coalition Government concentrated on domestic security and the threat posed by the IRA to the Republic itself.

In the Autumn of 1973, the Ministers were told that they and their families now faced the threat of kidnap by extreme Republicans. The Taoiseach Liam Cosgrave initiated a cabinet discussion of the issue and it was agreed that if any member of their family was kidnapped, they would opt out of the discussion on the matter and that regardless of the threats, no concessions would be made to the kidnappers.[132]

Then, on 12 March 1974, the IRA murdered a sitting politician, Fine Gael Senator Billy Fox, a former Dáil deputy and a Presbyterian from Monaghan, making him the first member of the Oireachtas to be killed since the Minister for Justice, Kevin O'Higgins was killed by Anti-Treaty republicans in 1927.

On 1 January 1973, Ireland also joined the European Economic Community (EEC) and this also caused major changes in how the government ran its business, with decisions in a number of areas now being made in Brussels. Furthermore, in October 1973, the world got hit by an oil crisis when the Organisation of Arab Petroleum countries proclaimed an oil embargo. The Arab-Israeli war of October 1973 caused the first oil crisis. This led to massive inflation and unemployment right across the western world and it threw the Cosgrave Government's economic calculations out the window. By the time the embargo ended in March 1974, the price of oil had risen by 400%, another major headache for the fledgling National Coalition.

Farmers, too, had their particular problems. Con Lucey, who was the IFA chief economist in the 1970s, recalls that the optimism arising from EEC

---

[132] Collins, S. (1996) *The Cosgrave Legacy* Blackwater Press. Dublin. p.180

accession was quickly shattered by the cattle crisis of 1974, which was felt particularly hard in the West of Ireland and linked to a fodder supply crisis.

> The new Fine Gael - Labour government, in its first Budget in March 1974, started the process of extending Income Tax to farmers, while also retaining the system of rates on agricultural land. They also dramatically reformed capital taxation, by ending Death Duties (which IFA had campaigned for) but also introducing three new taxes, Capital Acquisitions Tax (CAT), Capital Gains Tax (CGT) and a Wealth Tax. The above two issues dominated IFA policy from 1974 onwards, and while cattle prices recovered in 1975, taxation was permanently on IFA's agenda for the following decade. [133]

The notion of a Wealth Tax had been a pet project of Garret FitzGerald. He had failed to have it included in Declan Costello's 'Just Society' programme in 1965 but finally managed to get it into to Fine Gael-Labour election manifesto. Its introduction proved a major source of conflict at Cabinet, particularly between FitzGerald, now Minister for Foreign Affairs and Richie Ryan, the Minister for Finance.

> At a political and financial level, the Wealth Tax was a disaster for the Government...The net effect was to further narrow the tax based and place a bigger burden on ordinary citizens. When Fianna Fail returned to power, the Wealth Tax was abolished. [134]

Former political journalist Joseph O'Malley says it was very difficult to understand the reasoning for introducing a Wealth Tax in a recession when there were very few wealthy people to tax. But it also worked to the detriment of the Kenny Report as that would have been seen as the introduction of a further unpopular measure.

By the time the General Election was called on 28 February, 1973 Fianna Fáil had been in power for almost 16 years. The Labour Party leader Brendan

---

[133] Interview with Con Lucey. 2020
[134] Collins, S. (1996) *The Cosgrave Legacy* Blackwater Press. Dublin P. 162

Corish in a speech in Tullamore in 1968 had ruled out coalition as an option.[135]

However, the left wing of the Fine Gael party (which included Garret FitzGerald, Tom O'Higgins and John A. Costello) believed coalition with Labour was the only way to get into government and believed Fine Gael on its own would not be progressive enough and needed the Labour Party to counter the more conservative elements in their own party (Collins, 1996:92). Not long after the general election was called, both parties agreed to a pre-election pact to fight the election together on the issues that united them. One of the commitments was to build more houses.

> The Government fought the election on the basis of the 14-Point Plan and had made the assumption that it was going into government... The reason it was going into government was to get rid of Jack Lynch as Taoiseach and to get rid of Fianna Fáil.[136]

While Fianna Fáil actually increased its percentage of the vote, it lost seats. Fine Gael won 54 seats and Labour 19 giving them a total of 73 seats, a bare majority in the then 144-seat Dáil. According to history Professor Joe Lee, Fianna Fáil would almost certainly have won the election, despite the happenings of the previous four years but for the electoral pact.[137]

National Coalition

The National Coalition, as it was known, offered the electorate the first credible alternative government in many years.

> Largely untroubled by the type of inter-party wrangling that characterised previous coalitions, the 'National Coalition' under Liam Cosgrave as Taoiseach, with Brendan Corish as Tánaiste, proved a more formidable combination than its predecessors. It needed to. Not only did the dark shadow of Ulster continue to

---

[135] Corish's strong opposition to coalition was based on his experience of the 1954 – 57 coalition and in his experience of the right-wing Fine Gael Minister for Finance, Gerard Sweetman while he was Minister for Social Welfare. (Collins, 1996: 93).
[136] Interview with the late Brendan Halligan, 2020
[137] Lee, J. (1989) *Ireland 1912 – 1985.* Cambridge University Press P.468

loom over Southern affairs, but the industrial world was about to suffer a serious shock with a quadrupling of oil prices from the end of 1973.[138]

The Labour Party was allocated five Cabinet seats in the new government, among them James (Jimmy) Tully who was given Local Government. (He was later to serve as Minister for Defence in the short-lived 1981 – 82 Fine Gael-Labour coalition government.)

A native of Carlanstown, near Kells, Co, Meath, Jimmy Tully was first elected to the Dáil in 1954, lost his seat in 1957 but regained it in 1961. A former general secretary of the Federation of Rural Workers (later the FWUI), he is best remembered for an attempt to gerrymander the constituencies to ensure the re-election of the National Coalition at the 1977 General Election, a project that spectacularly backfired.

> Tully was a man of the people. He came from the country in County Meath, from among agricultural workers. He was honest, he was very much committed to the public good. He could be best summed up that he was in the army. There were no airs, or graces, or pretensions about him at all.[139]

Former Labour TD, Senator and MEP John Horgan recalls Tully as "one of the most powerful rural political barons and an able, if conservative, Minister for the Environment". Frank Cluskey, a former party leader, regarded Tully as "a sort of litmus test" for whatever course of action he happened to be proposing. "If Tully was onside, or at least neutral, the other conservatives posed less of a problem." [140]

Tully also had a mischievous sense of humour. The Labour Party faced considerable ongoing criticism from its grassroots members during this period in government for failing to deliver in many areas. John Horgan recalls that frequently at meetings of the parliamentary party at that time, a missive would be read out from local branch, or constituency, calling on the parliamentary to immediately implement a socialist state, or face the threat of mass defections, or worse.

---

[138] Ibid. p. 469
[139] Interview with the late Brendan Halligan 2020
[140] Horgan, J. (1986) *Labour: The Price of Power*. Gill and Macmillan. Dublin p.55

> Into the pool of silence generally created by the reading out of such sentiments, Jimmy Tully's voice would drop with the accuracy of a well-lobbied stone. "Tell, me", he would ask the general secretary, with an air of concerned and earnest enquiry which was betrayed only by the wolfish grin which accompanied it, "Who is the TD for that constituency?"[141]

Tully was one of the Labour ministers who was close to the Fine Gael Taoiseach Liam Cosgrave. Here, according to Brendan Halligan, the link was a psychological link. "It was the army. Now Tully had only been an NCO, but Tully had the NCO's respect for an officer." According to Stephen Collins, Labour Ministers Conor Cruise O'Brien and Jimmy Tully were closest to Cosgrave but again nobody got too close.

> Tully took his new job at his department very seriously and was determined to deliver on the commitment for housing. In all some 100,000 houses were built during the coalition's four years in office, an increase of 50% in both the public and private sectors. This was an extremely impressive performance by any minister for Local Government given the political and economic circumstances of the time.[142]

Inter-Departmental Committee

On 24 May, 1973, in the immediate aftermath of the publication of the Kenny Report (the Report was submitted to the Minister on 7 March, one week before the change of government), the newly elected Fine Gael/Labour Coalition Government decided to set up an inter-departmental committee representing the departments of Local Government, Finance, Agriculture and Fisheries, Industry and Commerce with a mandate to report by Friday, 8 June, 1973.

Their brief was to enumerate the problems which would arise in implementing the Kenny Majority Report and to suggest how they might be

---

[141] Ibid p.107
[142] Collins, S. & Meehan, C. (2020) *Saving the State: Fine Gael from Collins to Varadkar.* Gill Books p.145

overcome. The Department of Local Government recommended that both the Department of Lands and Justice be added.[143]

The Committee consisted of Mr. E.T. Sheehy, Department of Local Government (Chairman); Mr P. Gill and Mr D. Kennedy, Department of Finance; Mr R. Hayes and Mr K. O'Grady, Department of Justice; Mr C.A. Blair, (later replaced by Mr. K. Cregan), Department of Industry& Commerce; Mr J. Gaul, Land Commission; Mr. J.C. Doherty, Department of Agriculture and Fisheries along with Mr. B. J. Kiernan and Mr B. Drury, Department of Local Government. Mr Niall Calnan was appointed Secretary.

The Committee held its first meeting on 30 May 1973, the day the government decision was received. As a result, few had time to have it read properly. A second meeting was convened on 6 June, 1973 where a widespread discussion took place on the basis of written submissions from members and they agreed that a draft report be submitted to the next meeting.

On 8 June, the new Minister for Local Government, James Tully TD, advised the chairman that a government meeting had decided the Committee should consider the following questions:

- The immediate consequences of adopting the report
- Would the implementation of the majority report hold up development?
- Would it result in a sudden increase in price?
- How long would it take to have the necessary legislation prepared?
- What would be the effect on areas being acquired which are contiguous to areas already being developed?

The Committee was asked to have a report ready for Government by 15 June, just seven days later. The Committee completed a draft report on time but noted it was minimal time and that "shortcomings are likely to be found in any report on such complex matters which is prepared at short notice".

One of the problems identified by the Committee was the absence in the Kenny Report itself of information which was essential to gauge the impact of the Majority proposals if put into effect. With the consent of the Minister, "discreet requests" were made to the Dublin City and County Manager and to the Secretary of the Valuation Office "for information which would partly fill

---

[143] Dept. of Housing file DOH PL 4/2/10/1

the gaps". The report summarised the main proposals from the Majority Report.

In regard to its constitutionality, or otherwise, the Committee noted the Majority report suggested the President refer it to the Supreme Court.

> It is for the AG to advise on the constitutionality, or otherwise of any proposals for legislation which comes before them and on the merits, or otherwise, of an early reference of the Bill to the Supreme Court. We are concerned with the time-element if there is to be adjudication on the constitutional issue. From the time point of view, the most favourable assumption is reference of the Bill to the Supreme Court direct by the President.[144]

On the issue of a timeframe, the Committee commented that with the best of progress and assuming the Bill got priority, it was unlikely that a satisfactory Bill could be circulated in less than 12 months and passed by both Houses of the Oireachtas in less than 18 months. "Any attempt to rush the process is likely to produce a faulty Bill, all the more vulnerable to court action," it added.

Taking a decision would be issued by the Supreme Court in one or two months, the Committee concluded that it would take two years in total before knowing whether the new Bill would, or would not, be constitutional. In the event of it being found to be unconstitutional, the Committee suggested the Government could either seek some other solution to the issue of building land, or hold a referendum to amend the Constitution. If the people did approve, then "the process of an implementing Bill would start all over again". In a worst-case scenario, the Committee concluded the whole process could take "about four years".

The Committee suggested there was no point in undertaking the administrative measures "and in particular the expensive build-up of staff" until the constitutional issue was decided. In relation to the special protection for religious and educational property as outlined in Paragraph 105 of the Majority Report, the Committee suggested there was little justification for such an exception "nowadays" but did not think it would raise any immediate difficulties as the amount of land involved was not significant.

---

[144] Dept of Housing file DOH PL 4/2/10/1

The Committee were concerned at the use of the courts to designate an area rather than the local authority, or the minister. They asked that the AG carefully consider this as the local authority would concurrently be exercising functions under the Planning Act "which do not appear to differ in principle, or effect, from that of designating an area". They also suggested that there was a risk to jamming the courts with individual compensation appeals and suggested the Attorney General might consider an arbitral tribunal which could, if necessary, have a judge as chairman.

The Committee also noted that agricultural prices were rising in areas and in five years' time the "existing value plus 25%" could be worth much more. The Committee concluded that "the implementation of the Designated Areas Scheme may have little effect on building land prices in the short term" and particularly so to local authorities.

On its effect on house prices, the Committee concluded that while the effective operation of the Majority Report would reduce the price of building land, it would not necessarily reduce the price of houses as other factors such as wages, cost of material and inflation would impact on these. They concluded that house price control was a separate subject and not part of their function.

The Committee favoured early publication so that the public could see the arguments in favour of the Majority Report. They did not think there would be a rush of planning permission applications as the Majority Report provided that they could be revoked later. They suggested that while the price of building land near towns and cities would not rise suddenly, land in the country which might secure planning for scattered housing might rise as it would not be affected by the Designated Area Scheme.

The Committee also suggested possible issues with land transfers to family members as well as highlighting various administrative problems that could arise in the implementation of the Majority Report.

Acceptance in Principle

On 15 January, 1974 the Attorney General, Declan Costello SC, (who was also the serving Fine Gael TD for Dublin South-West) sent a letter to Minister Tully with a draft press statement. In the letter, he said the major problems appeared to him to be as follows:

- Whether the High Court should be used to designate areas.
- Whether the basis of compensation (existing use value plus 25 per cent) is correct. It occurs to me a way out of this difficulty would be to provide that more than existing use value could be given by way of compensation provided a reasonable case can be made for it and a ceiling of existing use value plus 25 per cent fixed.
- Whether in the case of land purchased before the Report is published "purchase price plus interest" should be the basis of compensation instead of existing use value plus 25 per cent. This point was raised by you and it is referred to in the inter-Departmental Committee report at paragraph 5.12.
- It may be possible to avoid taking final decisions on these and other important matters until all the different representations have been considered and what I suggest is that the statement could be non-committal on such matters but indicates that the general concept of the Designated Areas Scheme is accepted and that existing use value be the basis for compensation.[145]

The subsequent Government statement of 26 January 1974 announced acceptance in principle of the Majority report but left many major issues unresolved. The Government indicated that the problem of the high cost of building land was a complex one and it involved remedies "which are far-reaching and comprehensive". They made no commitment as to the amount of compensation payable in a designated area and left open the questions as who should be the Designation Authority.

The Government also considered that an increase in the value of lands could result not only in works undertaken by local authorities, but also from other public authority works, or because of decisions of planning authorities and indicated that the scheme to be introduced would ensure that these factors would be taken into account by the designated authorities.

The Government advised that the principles did not infringe the Constitution but concurred with the view in the Majority Report that the opinion of the Supreme Court on the legislation should be obtained pursuant to Article 26 of the Constitution. They indicated that before taking final decisions on many of the more important matters of detail they would take

---

[145] Dept. of Housing file DOH PL 4/2/10/1

into account the views of interested parties and expressions of views were sought. Many views were expressed as to the merits or demerits of the recommendations in the Majority Report.[146]

Vested Interests

A number of bodies and organisations which submitted views questioned the whole basis of the proposals e.g. they expressed doubts as to their constitutionality. They opposed them also on grounds of equity and the use of existing use value as a basis of compensation. The Incorporated Law Society pointed out that the Majority Report itself recognised that its proposals would be unconstitutional having regard to Article 37 of the Constitution unless they were exercised by the High Court.

The Society expressed its doubts that this new jurisdiction of the High Court "would be held to be constitutional because in its efforts to be so, it may itself erode the fundamental rights of the individual under the Constitution."

The Law Society added:

> The Majority Report considered that the advantages of a Statutory Tribunal would be obtained if the Judge exercising the new jurisdiction was obliged by the Act to sit with two Assessors, one with Town Planning experience and the other with qualifications in valuation matters. We do not share the views of the Majority Committee and believe that if the High Court is made use of in the way suggested that the independence and dignity of the Court will be seriously damaged. [147]

While the main objection from the Incorporated Law Society was on the basis that the Kenny Report proposed to make "the High Court a tool of the Executive and thereby bring it into disrepute", it also raised the constitutional question.

> ... in this report it is recognised by the Author of the Majority Report that as they envisage, there will be such a radical departure from the present law that it will be contested as unconstitutional

---

[146] National Archives file NA 2012/90/418
[147] National Archives file NA 2014/23/27

and therefore, before signing, it should be referred by the President to the Supreme Court for a decision as to whether, or not, it will be unconstitutional. It is an unhealthy start to the life of a law when its promoters admit the certainty of the legislation being challenged by the ordinary process of an action in the High Court on grounds that it is unconstitutional.

In keeping with its traditionally conservative approach to change, the Incorporated Law Society objected to the Majority Report on the basis that the public would freely be able to obtain information on the price at which property changed hands.

> There is far too much invasion of privacy at the present day without extending it and we think that the suggestion of the Majority Report that the public should be able to find out what prices have been paid for land is unwarranted and unnecessary. A purchaser should be entitled if he so wishes, to keep private from the world at large the cost of a land acquisition. Such a desire for privacy is deeply embedded in human nature and we see no reason why it should be disturbed.

The building, auctioneering and some of the professional bodies saw the scheme as creating uncertainty and disruption in the building industry. Concern was expressed about the hardship to landowners if the scheme was to be implemented; the use of the High Court as a designation authority was opposed; opposition was raised to giving local authorities a monopoly of the supply of building land and doubts were expressed as to the capacity of local authorities to administer the scheme having regard to their staffing and financial position.

A preliminary scheme outlining the legislative provisions that would be required to give effect was prepared by the Dept of Local Government. The preliminary scheme highlighted major legal, financial and administrative implications which would require detailed study. It did not deal with the level of compensation and the designation authority.

Further questions which arose requiring Government decision included the phasing of the introduction of the proposals in the Majority Report, the constitutionality of certain aspects, whether to modify or restrict application of Capital Gains Tax (CGT) and Wealth Tax to land transactions affected by the scheme and whether resources (financial and staff) on the scale required to successfully implement the scheme would be made available.

The notes attached to the Heads of Bill drafted by the Department in 1974 repeat many of the concerns and reservations raised by the inter-departmental committee in their report. For example, in a note attached to Head 1, attention was drawn to the Inter-Departmental Committee's concern about the use of the courts. It warns of the danger "that a bottleneck might develop and that the scheme might be bogged down by further delays arising out of the provision for appeal to the Supreme Court on a point of law (DOH, PL 4/2/10/1). The note also suggests asking the attorney general whether compulsory arbitration falls within Article 37 of the Constitution.

Another difficulty was found as to why houses and factories were mentioned in the Majority Report but not other forms of development such as offices, shops or commercial developments generally. Yet another difficulty was found under Head 2 in relation to whether the Court would hear objections. It notes Paragraph 96 of the Majority Report seems to infer it would. If so, a procedure would then need to be put in place for public notice of application and hearings. "In view of all these, the preliminary scheme was not processed to a definitive stage," states a draft Memo to government. [148]

At the outset there had been public enthusiasm for the proposals. *Business and Finance* magazine, for example, went so far as to congratulate the "admirable detailed and lucidly presented review of an extraordinarily complex problem which has defeated the ingenuity of successive governments". [149]

However, builders, developers and speculators all began to rail against the Kenny Report and invariably used their political connections to lobby against it. As mentioned earlier, the timing was unfortunate as Ireland entered a period of recession in the mid-70s and house-building declined. The *Irish Press* newspaper noted that house building in the first three months of 1974 had dropped by 43 per cent compared to the previous year. The Government set up a sub-committee to look at the steps to be taken to increase output and employment. By Autumn 1975 *Business and Finance* magazine predicted the emerging mood "...Kenny, like old soldiers, may now slowly fade away". [150]

---

[148] National Archives file NA 2012/90/418 PD 76/33
[149] *Business and Finance*, 14 February, 1974
[150] Ibid 16 October 1975

Opposition to Kenny appeared to be cross-party. The Labour Party generally championed the Report but one Dublin Labour Party councillor, Dermot O'Rourke, who was chair of Dublin Corporation's Housing Committee, told *The Irish Times* the Kenny Report "would inflict unique hardship on the owners of land in the periphery of the cities and towns of Ireland".[151]

As regards the Kenny Report's recommendation that the legislation be referred by the President to the Supreme Court to test its constitutionality before being implemented, the Secretary to the then President of Ireland, Erskine Childers, M. O'Flathartaigh wrote to the Department of the Taoiseach taking exception to this recommendation:

"I do not recall that any enquiry or member of the judiciary in any capacity, has hitherto subscribed to a recommendation of this kind."[152]

The general recession which had set in from 1974 continued through 1975 and 1976. The accompanying budgetary situation and the necessity to conserve financial resources for priority capital works and the stimulation and maintenance of employment, precluded the development of detailed proposals for Government consideration and the commitment of financial resources to implementation of a scheme at that juncture.

Then, in May 1976, the Minister for Local Government, James Tully TD decided to defer the implementation of the Kenny majority proposals in view of the then prevailing economic and fiscal circumstances.[153]

In June 1976 the Royal Institute of Chartered Surveyors (RICS) submitted a detailed study entitled *"The Development Land Problem in Ireland"* in which they reviewed various attempts to find solutions to land acquisition, elaborated their objections to the Majority Report proposals and put forward alternative proposals. (The study was resubmitted in October 1979). A summary of the objections is as follows:

Mere ownership of land does not cause development to take place. Without the will to develop and without the expertise and financial resources, land will simply lie under-developed. One of the most valuable aspects of the system hitherto has been the vigilance of the entrepreneur regarding development opportunities and his vigour in pursuing them. That initiative would be lost. In

---

[151] *The Irish Times,* 8 February 1974
[152] National Archives file NA 2005/3/43
[153] National Archives file NA 2012/90/418 PD 76/33

its place identification of suitable land would depend on the foresight and skill of the already over-burdened local authorities whose structure did not lend itself to fulfilling the entrepreneurial role of the developer.

The proposals could not be brought into effect without overcoming the shortage of professional and technical manpower in local authorities. A further difficulty would be the very large financial outlay involved in acquisition of all land required for urban expansion. There would be a continuing burden on local authorities of paying for infrastructure and social facilities prior to the disposal of land for development. Administering the proposed system would involve high recurrent cost to local authorities, including the salaries and overheads of additional professional and administrative staff.

In addition, the study stated that the capability of attracting institutional funds and other private finance for development would be doubtful given that builders may have no adequate acceptable asset to offer by way of security for short-time finance for building and institutional investors would be reluctant to invest unless projects were both economically viable and offered an adequate share in future profits and unless they had an acceptable legal interest in the land. "The proposals put forward in the Kenny Report are not likely to directly bring about a reduction in the price of new housing," it concluded.

The alternative proposals put forward by the Institute envisaged a two-tier taxation system under which gains realised from market increases in land values attributable to causes other than betterment would be taxed at normal CGT rates, while those attributable to betterment (defined as the value increment resulting from planning decisions) should be taxable at a higher rate of tax.

However, the Revenue Commissioners criticised the form of taxation recommended in the Institute's Report on the grounds that

- It would require extremely complex legislation which would take years to "settle down".
- The system would be very difficult (and possibly very expensive) to administer as valuations of land would be required at certain stages of development.
- The concept of raising an assessment tax which did not become payable until certain events occurred in the future was an extremely

complex one and seemed to offer greater scope for avoidance than any of the existing provisions in relation to the other taxes.

- The transnational arrangements necessary for the introduction of such a tax on a basis that would be seen to be just would be very complex indeed.

The Revenue Commissioner felt that it would be unproductive to embark on a lengthy and detailed study of what would be required for the introduction of such a tax without knowing what was proposed in regard to the Majority Report of the Kenny Committee, pointing out that the Majority Report was opposed to taxation as a means of curbing the price of building land.

Chapter 10

Change of Government

The 1977 General Election

The Taoiseach Liam Cosgrave called a general election for June 1977, nine months before the expiry of the Dáil term. In the run-up to the election, most political commentators predicted the coalition would sweep back to victory.

But in the General Election, Fianna Fáil, again under leader Jack Lynch, but with a sleek, impressive campaign largely organised by its new general secretary Seamus Brennan, won a landslide majority of 84 seats on a manifesto that, among other promises, committed to the abolition of rates on houses and car tax and lump sum subsidies for first-time house buyers. The voting age had also been reduced to 18 for the first time. A number of high-profile ministers including Justice Minister Paddy Cooney and the Posts & Telegraphs Minister Conor Cruise O'Brien lost their seats while Local Government Minister Jimmy Tully just managed to get re-elected. Such was the shock of the election defeat that both Liam Cosgrave, still aged only 56 and Brendan Corish, aged only 58, both resigned their leaders' positions immediately.

There was no obvious successor to Corish as Labour leader but the spectacular backfiring of his constituency review ruled Jimmy Tully out of contention. Nobody blamed his performance as Minister for Local Government for contributing to the defeat. Writing in the *Sunday Independent*, political editor Joe O'Malley commented: "Had he (Tully) not refrained from taking precipitative, or indeed any, action on the Kenny report of 1973 which sought to impose restrictions on speculation in building land, which would have threatened a powerful pressure group?"[154]

Clare TD Sylvester Barrett was appointed the new minister for the renamed Department of the Environment, previously the Department of Local Government. In a draft Memorandum to Government, he proposed that the implementation of the Government's programme for the local

---

[154] *Sunday Independent, 14 November 1976*

government sector (which did not provide for the implementation of the Kenny Report) should have prior demand on the resources of his department and that further detailed action arising from the Government's previous decisions on the Kenny recommendations should not be taken. The Minister also proposed to keep the matter of house price (including the land element) under review.

Observations on the memorandum were received from a number of departments and various suggestions were put forward. For example, the Taoiseach's Department agreed with the approach set out in the Memorandum. The newly established Department of Economic Planning and Development (under Minister Martin O'Donoghue, a member of the Kenny Committee) in their first reply, understandably disagreed with the proposals in the draft memorandum and suggested that an inter-departmental study group be set up to examine the problems involved in implementing the Kenny Majority Report recommendations. More details observations were received from the Department of Economic Planning & Development early in 1978.

They pointed out that because the problems which led to the setting up of the Kenny Committee could recur, it was necessary to have proposals to deal with the problem.[155]

The Department of Finance forwarded their observations on the draft memorandum on the 9th of June, 1978. They suggested that proposals be prepared for the implementation of control of land prices based on the Kenny Majority Report proposals, or, if these were shown to be inoperable, the Department of the Environment should provide its own proposals. The Dept of Finance also pointed out in their observations that it would be unnecessary for the government, or local authorities, to undertake heavy financial input into land acquisition - local authorities should only purchase for their own needs as they arose and for private developers only when they produced satisfactory building plans and on condition that there would be immediate reimbursement.

The 1979 Memo to Government stated that while a committee such as that envisaged by the Minister for Economic Planning and Development (Martin O'Donoghue) might well be given the task of investigating the above questions but in the Minister's (Sylvester Barrett) view it would be premature

---

[155] National Archives file NA 2012/90/418 PD 76/33

for it to do so unless there was a firm indication by the government that it favoured the recommendations made in the Majority Report. "But there are serious objections to this," the Memo added.

Report of An Foras Forbartha

As a result of the ongoing discussions, in September 1978 *An Foras Forbartha* (the National Institute for Physical Planning and Construction Research) were requested "to examine in detail the changes that have occurred in the price of various types of building land and other land and to evaluate these price trends on a sound statistical bases". It was hoped that this study would provide reliable up-to-date information on the effect increases in land prices had on the cost of housing.

An Foras produced their report *"An Examination of Land Transactions and Prices, Dublin Area 1974 – 1978* at the end of May 1979. In all, 326 different transactions were examined. These transactions included land zoned for agriculture, or housing in development plans of the three local authorities (Dublin County, Dublin County Borough and the Borough of Dun Laoghaire).

During the period 1974 – 1978, the report showed overall agricultural land prices increased by about 140%. Prices for housing land in the new town areas to the west of Dublin County increased also by 140% whilst land prices in the north suburbs were estimated to have increased by 325% and in the south suburbs by about 360%.

The *Foras* report of May 1979 to Minister Barrett concluded with a recommendation that in view of the importance of both land and housing in national policy, there was need for a more extensive monitoring of land transactions and for the collection on a systematic basis of details of land costs in housing construction. However, the report indicated that the authors were unable to make any firm conclusion on the effect land prices had on house prices. The Minister noted in a memorandum to government that, according to the report, the increase in the price of housing land in the new town areas to the west of Dublin between 1974 and 1978 which *An Foras* estimated to be 140% was not unduly high.

Apart from the fact that it just kept pace with the increase in agricultural land during the same period, the memo noted that the rate of increase

126

compared favourably with the estimated increase in the earnings of adult male workers during the same period.

The 1979 memorandum to government noted that attempts in other countries at dealing with land prices were examined in the Department of the Environment and concluded that "it is not possible to find an example of a successful solution for circumstances such as those applying to Ireland with its constitutional restraints and limited availability of capital".[156]

The memorandum noted that under the terms of the Capital Gains Tax (Amendment) Act, the basic rate of Capital Gains Tax arising from the disposal of land increased from 25 to 30 per cent. It also noted that since the passing of the Housing (Miscellaneous Provisions) Act, 1979 the Minister had comprehensive powers to control house prices. For example, Section 18(4) of the 1979 Act empowered the Minister to refuse a Certification of Reasonable Value (CRV) if he was not satisfied with the amount of the cost, or value, of a site included in an application for a CRV.[157]

> Our society accepts free enterprise as a basic element in the economy. To this background it is inevitable that the price of building land, like that of any other commodity, will as a general rule be determined by the operation of supply and demand.... The eradication of speculation in land has proved very difficult because solutions that might succeed in this area also bring about the withholding of land from the market. It should be remembered that private building industry in Ireland produces output in housing in excess of £300m (€380m) annually. This is far greater than the public sector. In 1978 output in the private sector was an estimated £317m (€402m) whilst local authority housing output was an estimated £76m (€96.5m).[158]

---

[156] National Archives file NA 2012/90/418 PD 76/33

[157] The Certificate of Reasonable Value (CRV) was introduced in February 1973 for any new house for sale for which the purchasers wished to obtain a loan from a lending agency, a new house grant or exemption from payment of Stamp Duty. With the introduction of the £1,000 (€1,270) new house grant in 1977, the CRV scheme was extended to all new houses and apartments for sale.

[158] National Archives file 2012/90/418 PD 76/83

The memorandum concluded that there were substantial reasons for not implementing the Kenny proposals and also noted that local authorities did not have the staff to implement them.

Culture of Compensation

However, the compensation culture grew and expanded in the years that followed. Many developers benefitted hugely from a provision in the 1963 Planning Act that that allowed a developer, who had been refused planning permission after outline planning permission had been granted, to make a claim for compensation against the local authority at the full development value of the land. For example, in 1989, 16 years after the publication of the Kenny Report, Grange Developments, a property development company owned by developers Tom Brennan and Joe McGowan were awarded almost €1.9m in compensation following a decision by Dublin County Council to refuse planning permission at Montgorry near Swords, Co. Dublin. Dublin City and County Assistant Manager George Redmond - who was to feature prominently some years later in the Mahon Tribunal - signed off on the cheque.

In fact, as journalist Paul Cullen pointed out, for the builders it was a win-win situation as a refusal to grant permission could prove as profitable as a positive outcome.[159] It was only after this pay-out in 1989 that the loophole in the 1963 Act was closed.

The decade after the Kenny Report was published saw a remarkable growth in building output. Construction's share of total national output (GDP) increased from 12 per cent in 1970 to almost 17 per cent in 1981. However, it has been volatile with peaks and troughs reflecting the various economic up and down turns – house prices increased from 1970 – 73, took a downturn until 1976 and rapidly increased from 1976 – 78.

In their 1979 report, Baker and O'Brien noted that "at present the (Kenny) Report is still under official consideration and no indication is available as to whether or when its majority recommendation is likely to be implemented". They suggested that if the proposals were adopted, they would spread the

[159] Cullen, P. (2002) With A Little Help from My Friends: Planning Corruption in Ireland. Gill and Macmillan. P22

benefits accruing from developers more broadly and to make land available for local authority housing at a lower cost. But they added:

> We suspect that more radical and comprehensive measures than those recommended in the Report will prove necessary, and that they will need to cover all transaction involving a change in land use, wherever the land is situated.[160]

Baker and O'Brien pointed out that in order for a scheme such as the designated areas scheme or more radical proposals to be accepted, they would need to attract a broad spectrum of political support.

> Because the present system of land ownership is so obviously unfair it should prove possible to construct such a consensus for reform.....Unless society is prepared to endorse a fairly radical restriction of property disposal rights, with land prices essentially related to existing use, it is difficult to foresee any significant fall in land prices, or an end to the inequity of arbitrary windfall capital gains for those who happen to own suitable land near expanding towns.

The also pointed out that while land prices were a major cause for increased house prices rather than increases in building costs, both materials and labour, a halving of the average price of building land would have led to a reduction of £1,000 (€1,270) in the price of a standard new house. This would afford a minor but significant improvement in the opportunity for marginal households to enter the owner-occupied sector and would effect a worthwhile reduction in the public subsidy to new local authorities.

Land availability at low cost was, of course, just one part of the general problems faced by local authorities in the provision of housing. Other important matters include good physical planning, financial resources, technical skills and legal powers.

> The availability of cheap land is not a solution and, indeed, if the wider problems are not resolved, could serve only to exacerbate the situation if local authorities were thereby

---

[160] Baker, T.J. and O'Brien, L.M. (1979) The Irish Housing System: A Critical Review. Economic & Social Research Institute. Dublin. P.174

encouraged to reserve large tracts of land for development which they do not have the resources to undertake.[161]

Regular debates

Although never implemented, from its publication the Kenny Report and its recommendations continued to be raised regularly during debates in Dáil Éireann, almost always by Opposition deputies and with the government of the day generally kicking to touch. A typical example of this procrastination is the following Dáil exchange during Question Time on 22 May, 1980 - eight years after publication - on the Kenny Report between Fine Gael deputies Fergus O'Brien and Peter Barry, Labour's Ruairi Quinn and Minister of State at the Department of the Environment, Gerard (Ger) Connolly TD:

Deputy O'Brien asked the Minister for the Environment his proposals for the implementation of the Kenny Report on land.

Minister of State Connolly: Possible methods of dealing with outstanding problems on building land costs are under consideration in my Department in conjunction with other interested Departments. I will not be in a position to formulate my proposals until consideration of the complex problem involved is finalised.

Deputy O'Brien: I think this is typical of the Government. I am asking him if there are constitutional problems. He does not appear to be able to tell me. If there are, let him tell the House.

Minister of State Connolly : The Kenny Report has been around for quite a while. The former Government examined it too..... It may not be an answer in the Deputy's view, but before I make a decision, every aspect has to be carefully looked into.

Deputy Quinn : Is the Minister of State aware that the Minister for the Environment in November 1977 gave much the same answer, almost word for word, in relation to the complexity of the subject matter of the Kenny Report? Is it the view of the Department and the Minister of State that the matter has become any less or more complex since 1977?

---

[161] Report of the Joint Oireachtas Committee on Building Land, 1985: Para 1.8

Minister of State Connolly: The answer is as I said. The matter has been referred to a number of Departments and I hope we will be able to come to a decision on it in due course.

Deputy Quinn: If that is the case, can the Minister of State give any indication of what his Department did to reduce the degree of complexity since 1977?

Deputy Barry: The Minister of State appears to be saying that he was starting a whole cycle of examination again. Is that correct?

Minister of State Connolly: No. The Kenny Report has been around for some time. When I was given responsibility for housing, I decided to have a look at it.

Deputy Barry: There seems to be an attempt to put the Kenny Report on the long finger.

Minister of State Conolly: As Deputy Tully said yesterday, the Kenny Report is not the be all and the end all. The matter is complex, as everybody knows.[162]

Speaking in the Dáil during a debate on a Private Member's Bill in June 1980, Fianna Fáil Deputy Niall Andrews commented:

> .....the Kenny Report was passed from one side of the ideological chasm to the other, from one part of the Cabinet to the other part of the Cabinet, and no decision was made. The same Kenny Report gathered thick dust....

Deputy Andrews went on to blame ideological differences between Fine Gael and Labour as being the reason for the lack of action.

> ...In *the Irish Times* on Monday last, it was stated that after accepting the Kenny Report and announcing publicly that its proposals would be implemented with haste, the Coalition let it fade into oblivion. That is the crux of the matter. It is why coalitions have brought nothing but despair, gloom, disunity and a lack of harmony to our nation. In this context I am glad to note that for the first time the Leader of Fine Gael has accepted publicly

---

[162] https://www.oireachtas.ie/en/debates/debate/dail/1980-05-22/16/

that coalitions cannot work because of the ideological differences involved. These differences are immense.... [163]

Speaking in the Dáil in June 1980, Fine Gael Deputy Fergus O'Brien commented:

> There have been merely pious platitudes, with the Kenny Report being trotted out at regular intervals, taken out of cold storage, put back in again, the dust being blown off it from time to time. [164]

[163] https://www.oireachtas.ie/en/debates/debate/dail/1980-06-04/36/
[164] https://www.oireachtas.ie/en/debates/debate/dail/1980-06-10/30/

Chapter 11

Procrastination

Advice from Attorneys General

The fortunes of the Kenny Report were not helped by a period of political instability in the early 1980s. At the end of 1979, Jack Lynch was replaced as Fianna Fáil leader by Charles Haughey and Dr Garrett FitzGerald had succeeded Liam Cosgrave as leader of Fine Gael. Three general elections were held within a period of 18 months with a Fine Gael-Labour minority government in power from June 1981 to February 1982 when it was replaced by a Fianna Fáil minority government which, in turn, was replaced by a Fine Gael-Labour majority government in November 1982.

During this period advice on the Kenny Report from various attorneys general appears to have always been extremely cautious. In September 1981 for example, the then Fine Gael/Labour Government - with Peter Barry serving as Minister for the Environment having specifically requested this portfolio from FitzGerald - asked the AG's Office (Peter Sutherland SC, later appointed EU Commissioner and Director of the World Trade Organisation) for advice. In a preliminary note, the AG described the proposal to acquire land at existing use value plus 25% as "untenable".

> While as a matter of legal principle I think the scheme may well be defensible...from a practical point of view I think the risk of the Supreme Court finding the scheme unconstitutional on these grounds would be quite high.[165]

The AG's Office also advised that, in relation to the assessment of compensation by the High Court, if the compensation to be fixed was market value, less value attributable to public works, "there is no reason why the existing machinery or a variation thereof could not be used."

---

[165] National Archives file NA 2014/23/27, SR9/33

In the Fine Gael/Labour Government which returned to power in November 1982, Dr Garrett FitzGerald was Taoiseach while the Labour Party leader, Dick Spring, was appointed Tánaiste (Deputy PM) and Minister for the Environment. In January 1983 his department once again sought the advice of the Attorney General, Peter Sutherland SC. The AG was requested to advise generally "on the relevant constitutional constraints as he saw them and on the question of whether the scheme proposed in the Kenny Majority report would be likely to be held constitutional."

In addition, his opinion was requested on the following specific points arising from the Kenny Majority Report:

- Designating authority: would it be essential that the designating authority should be the High Court?
- Areas to be designated: would it be possible to extend the scope of the "designated area" as defined in the Majority Report, for example, to include all land designated for development in local authority plans?
- Basis of compensation: would it be acceptable to operate a scheme of compensation based on 125% (or some other arbitrarily selected proportion) of "existing use value"
- Applications to all and in designated areas: whether the omission of the proposed statutory obligation on local authorities to apply to the High Court to designate all land in their area falling within the definition of "designated area" could lead to further constitutional challenge on grounds of discriminatory and inequitable treatment of different land owners?
- Assessment of compensation: would it be essential that compensation for lands required by local authorities in designated areas should be fixed by the High Court rather than by means of existing arbitration system or a variation thereof?[166]

In response, Mr Sutherland replied that the answer to the questions whether it is essential that the High Court be the designating authority "is not capable of a simple answer".

> However, the alternative solutions with a designating authority other than the High Court are based on the assumption that

---

[166] National Archives file AGO File 2014/23/27

compensation would be paid on the basis of market value less betterment attributable to public works rather than existing use plus 25% as proposed by the Kenny Report. It may be that the Kenny Report would have reached a different conclusion on the question of judicial function had this been the basis of compensation considered by them. If the basis of compensation were to be that proposed by Kenny, the argument for regarding the designation function as judicial is greatly strengthened.

The Attorney General also advised that it would only be a court that could decide whether any, or all, of various aspects proposed in the Kenny Report could be unconstitutional.

In the absence of a court decision, one can only speculate about the direction the Court might take with the assistance of such Court decisions as are in point. Many of these decisions are quite old, or not directly in point. An example of the rapidity with which judicial thinking can develop is shown by the frequency with which Mr Justice Kenny, both in the Report and in the Central Dublin Development case, referred to the Rent Restrictions code as supporting his view that certain legislation would be, or was, constitutional and yet that code was found unconstitutional in Blake's case. In the four or five areas of major constitutional difficulty posed by the Kenny scheme, it is not, unfortunately possible to say with any degree of certainty how the Courts would decide the constitutional questions involved.

Another Memo to government from the Department of the Environment in September 1983 shows the cautious approach of the Attorney General, Peter Sutherland SC, partly arising from the decision in the *Blake v the AG* [1982] I.R. 117 where the Supreme Court held (*inter alia*) that Part 2 of the Rent Restrictions Act, 1960, which restricted the amounts of the rents payable to their landlords by tenants of controlled dwellings, was invalid having regard to the Constitution in that those provisions constituted an unjust attack on the property rights of certain landlords contrary to Article 40.3.2° since those provisions restricted the exercise of the property rights of one group of citizens for the benefit of another group in a manner which failed to provide compensation for the first group and which disregarded the financial capacity or needs of the members of the groups.

The 1983 Memo states the AG's advice emphasised the speculative nature of any views expressed on the constitutionality of proposals affecting private property rights in the absence of a detailed body of law since the case of *Blake v the AG* regarding the Rent Restrictions Act.

The very conservative and cautious attitude adopted by successive attorneys general has been identified as a key reason - or an excuse - for the non-implementation of the Kenny Report. According to Mike Allen, who served as Labour Party General Secretary under three party leaders from 2000 to 2008 there appeared to be a tendency in opposition to maximise the possibility of change but when the party entered government, the Attorney General took the most risk-averse position. "When I was there, it was probably an emotional thing but to pass a motion to implement the Kenny Report was an absolute staple at every conference that took place......What that (Kenny) report is about is the constitutionality of the issue and it never gets tested because people keep saying a case could be made that it is not constitutional and so it never gets tested."

Former *Irish Times* political editor Stephen Collins says Labour's failure to act on the Kenny Report while in government is "inexplicable" given the party's rhetoric in Opposition. "Labour was in government in the 70s, 80s and 90s and could have made the implementation of the Kenny report a condition of entering government but never did so. The party obviously came up against resistance from Fine Gael and Fianna Fáil but clearly did not regard the issue as a priority."[167]

Collins also says the reluctance of attorneys general was often used as an excuse for the lack of action. "The possibility that the Bill might represent an unconstitutional infringement of the rights of private property was the standard reason given by successive governments for not acting on the Kenny report. It does seem that some of the attorneys general over the period did advise that it could be unconstitutional but as far as successive governments were concerned, that was simply a convenient excuse to avoid taking action. If they were determined to act, they could have passed a law implementing Kenny and allowed the Supreme Court to decide if it was, or was not, constitutional."

---

[167] Interview with Stephen Collins 2019

Eithne FitzGerald is an economist who served as a Labour Party deputy and minister of state at the Department of Finance from 1993 to 1994 and at the Department of Enterprise & Employment from 1994 to 1997 where she introduced a number of pieces of progressive legislation, including the Ethics in Public Office Act, 1995.

> I think the Department (Environment) was always very wary of it (Kenny Report) from a legal perspective. And I think one of the killer judgments was the Paddy Madigan case as well as the Blake case. (In 1981, Dublin solicitor Paddy Madigan was successful in challenging the constitutionality of the Rent Restrictions Act, 1960 and freeing landlords significantly from the constraints of rent control)...... I think that spooked everybody in the Department of the Environment because effectively that judgement said basically, in interpreting the Constitutional provision that the rights of private property are subject to the exigencies of the common good, that if you want to elevate the common good above the rights of private property, you have to pay for it at market prices.[168]

According to FitzGerald, the role of the attorney general is critical in any government. "They are," she said, "the person with the veto at the Cabinet table".

> I would have found that on a piece of the Ethics legislation. We were looking for one particular measure and Dermot Gleeson SC was Attorney General at the time. And he just said no, this is not possible under the Constitution, this is as far as you can go in the Act and no further. It was to do with Article 15.10 of the Constitution, which states the Dáil regulates its own affairs. Dermot, I know, took a particular view on it that the Oireachtas could not legislate to give away any of its powers to a third party such as the Standards in Public Offices Commission. Even if I disagreed legally with the interpretation - I'm not a lawyer - Dermot Gleeson is a very eminent lawyer and once he took that view that was it. It was no. But even if you disagreed with the interpretation, that was it - the AG's word was the final say on

---

[168] Interview with Eithne FitzGerald 2020

anything at the Cabinet table that could have possible Constitutional implications.

An unusual feature of the Irish system, possibly due to the relatively small scale of the country, is a high reliance on this centralised source of legal advice rather than on internal legal advisers within agencies or departments. The manner in which this advice on constitutional questions is settled on is not very clear, as the workings of the AG's office are not publicly disclosed and its processes are relatively secret. For example, it is unclear what standard the AG applies when assessing constitutionality.

Writing in the *Sunday Independent* newspaper, barrister, author and former legal advisor to the Department of Foreign Affairs Charles Lysaght highlighted an important question on whether the opinion of an attorney general on any prospective legislation should enjoy finality in the processes of government.

> Opinions - whether they are given by the attorney general, or any other lawyer - on whether legislation is constitutional are no more than predictions as to how the courts, ultimately the Supreme Court, will interpret the Constitution..... Assessment of the merits of a legal opinion is impossible without sight of its reasoning..[169]

According to Lysaght, when denying the Oireachtas, or others, sight of the reasons supporting an opinion of the attorney general, government ministers are wont to rely on the general privilege of clients not to reveal the advice of their lawyer. This ancient privilege, he wrote, is one related to the exigencies of litigation enabling prospective and actual litigants to be frank with their legal advisers and to get honest advice in return. But, significantly, he added that the practice has no rationale for legal advice given to government on the constitutionality of contemplated legislation.

> The invocation of the privilege in such cases impoverishes public debate and is anomalous in an era of open government and freedom of information. Legal professional privilege, as it is sometimes called, has allowed successive governments to hide behind the advice of attorneys general - without revealing

---

[169] Sunday *Independent, 17 January 2021*

in most cases the reasons for that advice - as justification for not proceeding with a host of desirable measures. A long-standing casualty was the legislation recommended by the Kenny Report in the 1970s that would have reduced the price of land for building.

Lysaght noted that it has been remarked in criticism of the practice that it gives an excessive power of veto over legislation to the attorney general, who is not even a member of the government.

> They may find themselves under pressure from the Taoiseach or other ministers to provide "helpful advice" enabling the government to cite legal advice to avoid responsibility when, for political reasons, they do not want to promote legislation. One needs strong attorneys general not beholden to the government they advise, to resist the devaluation of their office by being used as a sort of mudguard for members of that government.

Since the Supreme Court rulings of the late 1980s, economist Eithne FitzGerald said the courts have softened their interpretation around what the private property clauses in the Constitution requires.

> Subsequent rulings have become much more nuanced, and give much more balance to the public good aspect of the Constitutional clause, however after that apparent change of mind, or more positive interpretation of the Constitution, the Kenny Report still hasn't travelled.[170]

In fact, FitzGerald said the closest the Department of the Environment ever got to Kenny was the legislation that former Minister of State Noel Ahern (brother of Taoiseach Bertie Ahern) put through with the Part V of the Planning and Development Act, 2000.

> That was the nearest thing to Kenny that was legislated for in terms of requiring developers, or landowners to take a hit for the common good. But Kenny really hasn't been revisited, and

---

[170] Interview with Eithne FitzGerald 2020

I think one of the inhibitions was that the Department of Environment was always nervous about its constitutionally.

Former Attorney General Dermot Gleeson argued that contentious matters with Constitutional implications rarely get to Cabinet and are argued out in advance. "There are some very good lawyers on the staff of the AG's office and usually contentious issues are sent to one of them for analysis, he said. "There are very differing styles of attorneys general but a key aspect in my view is a good working relationship with the Taoiseach and the other party leader if it is a coalition.[171].

In the 1993- 97 Government Dermot Gleeson was a former schoolmate of the Taoiseach John Bruton and knew the Tánaiste Dick Spring from his court work. His time as AG was noteworthy for the setting up of the Criminal Assets Bureau and the digitising of statutes. Gleeson pointed out that the Irish system differs to the British system where the AG is called into Cabinet when required whereas he/she is a permanent fixture at the Irish Cabinet.

In fact, another Attorney General, Declan Costello, who held the position in the National Coalition Government of 1973 – 77, expressed his disillusionment when he learned how limited his powers were..[172]

Private Members' Bills

The Labour Party and, in particular, Ruairi Quinn, an architect by profession, regularly championed the Kenny Report, though almost always from the Opposition benches.

On 3 June 1980, Deputy Quinn used Dáil Private Members' Time (when opposition deputies are allowed to table a motion or a Bill) to introduce his own Local Government (Building Land) Bill. In his opening remarks, he said he had spent almost a year drafting it and he believed that political consensus had now been reached on the need to regulate the price of urban building land. He said he had attempted to "bring in a Bill which meets the first test of

[171] Interview with Dermot Gleeson SC 2020
[172] Collins, S. & Meehan, C. (2020) *Saving the State: Fine Gael from Collins to Varadkar.* Gill Books P. 140

being workable, both in terms of meeting the requirements of the Constitution and of being feasible for operation when it becomes law".

> Under our Constitution and our present legal system, the added community value created by the growth and expansion of the urban community can be captured by an individual land-owner who, by accident of location, is in a position to benefit from it. That individual landowner can subsequently resell back to the community land at that increased price and retain the profit.[173]

Deputy Quinn said it had become "effectively impossible" for the local authorities, as planning bodies, to meet the housing needs of the increased urban population and some mechanism was urgently needed to regulate the cost and supply of development land to the market "in order to maintain some degree of social justice in our society".

While he said the traditional reluctance to interfere with land rights was understandable and, to an extent, was embodied in the 1937 Constitution, the recent increases in land prices could not be justified.

He even quoted some of the examples contained in the Kenny Report itself. He added that he did not believe the Constitution of 1937 was "ever designed either by Dr. McQuaid[174] or by the late Eamon de Valera to enable fortuitous and accidental landowners on the periphery of urban areas to capture for themselves the community created value of urban growth".

Deputy Quinn said he regretted that the Kenny Report had dealt only with new land coming onto the market and not with the even more critical problem of the redevelopment of inner-city land which had ceased to be used for its original purpose and was in the process of transition.

> I share the view that the Kenny Report was inadequate and I regret that successive governments have not brought forward a legislative proposal which, in part, would meet the positive aspects of the findings in that report and add to them a measure which would enable the local authority to respond to

---

[173] https://www.oireachtas.ie/en/debates/debate/dail/1980-06-03/34/
[174] Dr John Charles McQuaid served as Archbishop of Dublin from 1940 - 1972

the question of existing development land coming on to the market for the second, third or subsequent time.

He said his new Bill addressed that absence along with allowing for a process of public participation and consultation. Ultimately, it would be up to the local authority to define the designated area and the local authority would be the only body entitled to purchase the land in that area. In the absence of agreement on price, a "Lands Tribunal" would be established to arbitrate on the price for those who wished to continue farming to the extent that the cost of re-location, in addition to the acquisition of a new farm, would be provided.

> I do not see in any clause of the Constitution that the inalienable right to private property confers on the citizens of this State the inalienable right to the maximum market price they can screw out of the community. I have read the Constitution and all the arguments surrounding this and I have yet to come across that particular clause.

The Bill was opposed by the Fianna Fáil Minister for the Environment, Sylvester Barrett, who said it illustrated "the pitfalls for those who opt for an easy, ready-made solution without taking account of the constitutional, administrative and financial problems which beset the question of building land prices".

The Minister argued that with this basis of compensation, land owners would not be willing to sell their lands and the Bill then obliged the local authority to proceed to acquire the property by compulsory acquisition. But on compulsory acquisition, he said the basis of compensation is not market value but existing use value.

> Here again it requires no stretch of the imagination to be certain that owners of affected property would resist compulsory acquisition by every means in their power, including recourse to the courts. The acquisition of every plot of ground in designated areas would be fought out long and bitterly.

Minister Barrett referred to a similar type of legislation which was introduced by the Attlee Government in 1947, the Town and Country Planning Act, which provided that all development rights in undeveloped land should rest in the

State. This Act had failed to provide the land and was rescinded by the next Government in 1953.

The Minister's colleague, Deputy Niall Andrews told the same debate that "our society accepts the concept of free enterprise as a basic element of the democratic structure. This being so, it is inevitable that the price of building land will be determined in general by the operation of the principle of supply and demand".

Speaking on behalf of Fine Gael, Deputy Tom Fitzpatrick said his party could not support Deputy Quinn's Bill because it would require "genuine landowners of all categories, big and small, throughout the country to become public benefactors".[175]

Also speaking during this debate, the former Labour Minister for the Environment, James Tully, who was in office when the Kenny Report was published in March 1973, significantly remarked that he did not, in fact, see it until the end of that year.

> I took office in the Department of Local Government on 14 March 1973. The Kenny Report was not made available to me; it was made available to my predecessor (Robert Molloy) and did not come into my hands until almost the end of the year. To suggest that it was in my possession from March, 1973 - as indeed was suggested a few days ago in the newspapers - is something I should like to kill here and now.

As outlined earlier in this chapter, the Minister said a great deal of work had been done on the report. But it had weaknesses including it did not deal with all urban sites.

The Quinn Bill was defeated during its first debate at Second Stage by 59 votes to 15 with Fianna Fáil voting against it and Fine Gael abstaining.

Having been out of power for seven months from June 1981, Fianna Fáil returned to government in February 1982 and the new Minister for the Environment, Ray Burke, wrote to the Attorney General Patrick, Connolly

---

[175] https://www.oireachtas.ie/en/debates/debate/dail/1980-06-04/36/

SC.[176] and to his successor John Murray SC.[177] on 24 May, 30 July and 4 October respectively, seeking their advice on the Kenny Report but no reply was received to any of the three letters before that government collapsed on 4 November, 1982.

In the summer of 1982, Labour deputy Ruairi Quinn published a second Private Member's Bill, the Local Government (Building Land) Bill, 1982. The purpose of this Bill was to enable local authorities to designate land required for development and to enable a local authority to acquire land at existing use value in the forthcoming five years.

However, a note from the Secretary to the Government, Dermot Nally, on 11 May 1982 shows the Government decided to oppose it on the following grounds:

- In view of the probability that its provisions are repugnant to the Constitution
- Because of the actions which the Government have taken in the Budget to ensure that a major part of the increased value of development land will accrue to the public through the substantially increased capital gains taxes on disposal of such land and
- Because the Government intends to take whatever additional measures may be necessary to ensure that land is made available to local authorities for development free of any element of speculative gains, in line with the aims of the Kenny Report and to review the provisions of the Local Government (Planning and Development) Acts 1963 and 1976 in regard to the zoning of land by local authorities and the operation of Section 4 of the City and County Management (Amendment) Act 1955 in relation to planning decisions.[178]

Opening the debate, Deputy Quinn noted there was "a certain sense of *déjà vu* about this" in that "almost two years to the day, the House had an opportunity of debating for a similar length of time a Bill exactly like this one."

---

[176] Patrick Connolly SC served as Attorney General from 10 March 1982 – 16 August 1982

[177] John Murray SC served as Attorney General from 17 August 1982 – 14 December 1982 and from 11 March 1987 to 25 September 1991

[178] National Archives file NA 2012/90/418

I, perhaps more than any other Deputy - and I am not taking any personal credit for this - asked every six months to the day as to what the Government were doing in regard to the Kenny Report. As the Minister's files will show, the stock answer was dusted down and wheeled out on each occasion with monotonous precision, that was that the Government were reviewing legislation with a view to implementing the Kenny Report. When any of us asked how soon that would be, we were told that it would be "in the near future" or in the "foreseeable future". During all of that time the price of building land was soaring in real terms relative to the cost of house prices.[179]

Opposing the Bill, the Minister for the Environment, Ray Burke said the Labour Bill "even contains the same minor printing errors as the 1980 Bill and the only differences that I can see between the two Bills are that the date and price are different."

He added that while the new Attorney General (Patrick Connolly SC) was undertaking a review "I can only say that the advice available at present is that there are serious doubts about the constitutionality of the Kenny scheme".

In his contribution Minister of State Gerard Brady (Dublin South-East) offered the following observation:

> Several attorneys general have been asked for their views on this problem right back to the mid-sixties and all of them have said that, while there was no constitutional bar to the compulsory acquisition of land, in the interests of the common good it would be very difficult to acquire any such land at anything less than the full market value, plus adequate allowances for disturbance etc.[180]

In his contribution, giving a strong hint at the close association between many politicians and developers, the then Galway Labour Deputy Michael D. Higgins (later elected President of Ireland in 2011) said he had thought, for example, "of looking around the House and listing the names of all those I know to have benefited from speculation, or who had contacts with different

[179] https://www.oireachtas.ie/en/debates/debate/dail/1982-05-11/16/
[180] https://www.oireachtas.ie/en/debates/debate/dail/1982-05-19/15/

people who benefited from the sale of land but I decided that to proceed in that manner would occupy most of my time."[181]

Following a commitment from the Government to establish an All-Party Committee to examine "all aspects of building land", including the Labour Bill, Deputy Quinn withdrew the Bill but said it was remaining on the Dáil Order Paper pending developments.

In July 1982, the Report of the First Commission on Taxation, chaired by Miriam Hederman O'Brien, was published and it echoed calls for the recommendation in the Kenny Report to be implemented, particularly in relation to betterment.

The Report noted that under the Capital Gains Tax (Amendment) Act, 1978 gains arising on the despoil of development land were to be charged at a rate of 30 per cent. Proposals to change these arrangements were announced in the Budget of 25 March 1982. These included an increase in the rate of tax on development land to 50 per cent, except in compulsory acquisition cases where the proposed rate was 40 per cent. Levies were also imposed on developers for the provision of services and in County Dublin the contribution levy was £4,000 (€5,078) per acre. In its conclusions, it totally re-echoed the Kenny Report's principle:

> Where an increase in the price of development land is attributable to community action or decision or to the anticipation of such actin of decision, then, in principle, the whole of that increase should accrue to the community.[182]

Joint Oireachtas Committee on Building Land

In September 1982, a new Joint Oireachtas Committee on Building Land was established consisting of 13 members of the Dáil and seven members of the Seanad.[183] The first chairman was Labour Deputy Ruairi Quinn, then in

---

[181] https://www.oireachtas.ie/en/debates/debate/dail/1982-05-12/23/

[182] Commission on Taxation, 1982. P. 226

[183] The members of the Committee were Deputies Michael Begley, Hugh Coveney, Avril Doyle, Jim Fitzsimons, Michael Keating, Ray MacSharry, Robert Molloy, Ruairi Quinn, Albert Reynolds, Alan Shatter, Liam Skelly, Seán Walsh and Pearse Wyse and Senators Katherine Bulbulia, Denis Cregan, Patrick Durkan, Seán Fallon, Michael Ferris, Jack Fitzsimons and Brendan Ryan.

Opposition. It had, in fact, a far wider remit than that of the 1971 Committee on the Price of Building Land (Judge Kenny's Committee) and was asked to make recommendations in relation to the supply of building land and to have regard to a number of items, including the 1973 Kenny Report. Speaking in the Seanad Fine Gael Senator Katherine Bulbulia said the terms of reference of the Joint Committee permitted a wider approach to an evaluation of all issues connected with the supply of land and the cost of land. It was, in a way, a reflection of the wider appreciation which had grown up with the passage of time, and an awareness of the range and complexity of the issues which are connected with building land.[184]

The Committee held its first meeting in September 1982 and sought submissions from the public. It eventually reported in 1985 when the Government had again changed to a Fine Gael/Labour coalition and the Chairman was now Fianna Fail's Robert Molloy, who as Minister for Local Government, had originally commissioned the Kenny Report back in 1971. The political wheel had, in many ways, come full circle.

Replying to a debate on the Report in the Seanad on 6 May, 1986 the Labour Party Minister for the Environment, Liam Kavanagh[185], said the Government would bring forward proposals "this year" to deal with the recommendations in the report and "perhaps, also taking a look at what was in Kenny and seeing if we can include some of the thoughts and recommendations of that report without offending the Constitution".

Both the Kenny Majority and Minority Reports emphasised the "inadequate investment in the sanitary services programme in the 1960s which was not sufficient to meet the increased demands for serviced land for housing, industry and other purposes". However, in the aftermath of the Kenny Report there was a vast improvement. Investment in sanitary services doubled between 1970 and 1974 as housing completions also doubled (Dept of the Environment). The 1985 Joint Oireachtas Committee concluded that "it is likely that the supply of serviced land is now on a much-improved footing compared with the early 70s, at least where water and sewerage are concerned".

---

[184] https://www.oireachtas.ie/en/debates/debate/seanad/1986-02-06/6
[185] Liam Kavanagh served as Minister for Environment from 1983 - 1986

The supply of privately services land appears in most cases to respond fairly readily to market demand except in cases of topographical difficulties, or similar unusual circumstances.[186]

The 1985 Committee did point out that changes in housing markets can stop a building project happening or delay it significantly. "In effect, builders or developers may pay too much for land and find themselves unable to develop and dispose of it without incurring loss".

The 1985 Committee also noted that the more rapid increase in land prices gives an incentive to landowners, speculators and non-building interests to purchase zoned land. This, it said, resulted in a severe distortion in the price of land relative to its development potential which appeared to happen in 1972/3 and 1978/79.

However, the 1985 Oireachtas Committee rejected the Kenny Report on the basis that its approach was too narrow "and its conclusions are, in some instances, at variance with its analysis" (Paragraph 7.8). The Committee concluded that the land market was but one part of a general market in property. It argued that it is almost inevitable that if market values are suppressed in one sector of the market, they will re-emerge elsewhere.

> Therefore, a proposal to supplant the land market must recognise that its implications and effects are more far reaching than this market sector alone and have to be dealt with in a much wider context.[187]

The 1985 Committee concluded that the Kenny Report is "unduly hasty in virtually condemning a market in land" (1985 Building Land Report: ParA8. 14). The Report went on to quote the legal advisor to the Minister (James Tully) stating that it was probably unconstitutional.

> The rights of Article 40 are very strongly stated and I am satisfied that this proposal of the Kenny Report would have little chance of surviving a Constitutional challenge in the

---

[186] Report of the Joint Oireachtas Committee on Building Land 1985: Par 3.46
[187] Ibid Par A8.10

Courts based on the argument that it would amount to an unjust attack on landowners' property rights.[188]

That Committee made a number of recommendations including an examination "of the liabilities incurred, and tax receipts from, transactions in building land to establish a basis for evaluation effectiveness of taxes". It also recommended that Stamp Duty be made a liability of the vendor rather than the purchaser.

New lease of life

After the dismissing of the recommendations of the Kenny Report in the 1985 Report, it was quietly shelved although on 7 October, 2003 the Labour Party leader Eamon Gilmore, (then in Opposition) introduced the Planning and Development (Acquisition of Development Land) (Assessment of Compensation) Bill, 2003. He told the Dáil that the rights of property owners must be regulated by the principles of social justice and the common good as set out in the Constitution.

> Our advice is that any constitutional challenge to legislation along the lines proposed by Kenny would fail. In the present circumstances, in particular, where we face a severe housing shortage, social justice and the common good must surely dictate that land owners should not accrue huge gains purely as a result of land rezoning or planning permission.[189]

However, the Bill was opposed by the Minister for the Environment, Heritage and Local Government, Progressive Democrat Deputy Martin Cullen and it was defeated in a Dáil division by 63 votes to 38 on 8 October, 2003.

The Kenny Report does not appear to have been given any serious consideration again until the publication of the 1996 Review of the Constitution and the Ninth Progress Report (Private Property) by the All-Party Oireachtas Committee in April 2004 which concluded the Kenny Report recommendations were not repugnant to the 1937 Constitution (See Chapter

---

[188] Ibid Par Par A8.18
[189] https://www.oireachtas.ie/en/debates/debate/dail/2003-10-07/19/

7). This was to give a new lease of life to the Report's recommendations which continue to be debated to this very day.

Once again, the implementation of the recommendations of the Report were raised in Dáil debates. For example, on 4 July, 2006, Green Party leader Trevor Sargent raised the issue of house prices with the Taoiseach Bertie Ahern. Deputy Sargent said that given the average house price was €300,000 and one third of that price comprised the site price, he asked the Taoiseach to acknowledge that if that house was built on a site priced as agricultural land, that is, approximately €10,000, rather than the inflated price currently allowed, the price of the house would be approximately €210,000.

He continued:

Does the Taoiseach accept that by not acting on the report on building land by Mr. Justice Kenny of 1973, his government is standing over a kick-back for the builder for every house built of about €90,000?

The Taoiseach: I will answer Deputy Sargent directly on this issue. I was in favour of the Kenny report many years ago. I am still in favour of it.... I am in favour of the conclusions of the report of the All-Party Committee. The report of the All-Party Committee states that we should be able to deal with the fundamental issues by legislative means.

Mr. Sargent: Where is the legislation?

The Taoiseach: It is being drafted. I am pressing to get on with it and I do not disagree with what Deputy Sargent stated in that regard.

But Mr Ahern again urged caution on the Constitutional question:

A significant number of people state that such legislation, on which I hope we will come to a conclusion over the summer, could well be challenged. If that is the case, we would need a constitutional referendum ...of which I also would be in favour of trying.

It was put forward by the committee - we debated the matter many times in the House - that we should try the legislative route and we are trying it. The Attorney General[190] has not given me a final version of the report, but I hope we can do it by legislation and we will try to do it by legislation. I will

---

[190] Rory Brady served as Attorney General from 7 July 2002 until 16 June 2007

try to address it over the summer. Deputy Sargent has asked me a serious question for once and I am trying to give him a serious answer.[191]

The year 2004 saw a major report on housing published by NESC. Entitled *'Housing in Ireland: Performance and Policy'* it examined many aspects of housing and land management and made a number of recommendations.

It noted the two traditional assumptions in the economic analysis of land and the housing market. The first was that the supply of land is fixed and the second is that the owner of land will use it in the most profitable way available. These two assumptions "underpinned the dominant ideas on how the price of land was determined by the demand for housing and the effects of taxation of development gains".[192]

The report noted many of the problematic issues in the Irish planning system, notably that the type of planning undertaken in Ireland does not ensure that the land allocated for development is actually built upon.

> The uncertainty and variability of land supply and the planning system shape the business practice of developers and others in the market. They prompt them to invest in land-banks to ensure they have an ongoing supply of suitably located sites. Planning and perceived land scarcity give particular land-owners the power to influence the timing and location of development.[193]

The Report proposed that in order to have an effective policy on land, a combination of four approaches were required:

-   A land-use strategy over a long horizon, including zoning and servicing of land
-   Land for enhanced social and affordable housing programmes
-   Sufficient active land management to ensure delivery of housing
-   Betterment-sharing measures, designed in a way that does not damage supply.[194]

---

[191] https://www.oireachtas.ie/en/debates/debate/dail/2006-07-04/14/
[192] National Economic & Social Council (2004) Housing in Ireland: Performance and Policy (No. 112 2004). NESC. Dublin. P.188
[193] Ibid. P. 9
[194] Ibid P. 9

Chapter 12

Consequences of Non-Implementation

Tribunal of Inquiry

The issue of speculative gain was to be a constant thorn in the area of housing policy for decades to follow, finally erupting in the costly and drawn-out Tribunal of Inquiry in the 1990s.

Details of the 'Tribunal of Inquiry into Certain Planning Matters and Payments', commonly known as the Mahon Tribunal, after the name of its last chairman, Judge Alan Mahon, have been widely published. In summary, the Tribunal was a public inquiry in Ireland established by Dáil Éireann in 1997 to investigate allegations of corrupt payments to politicians regarding political decisions taken. It mostly investigated planning permissions and land rezoning issues in the 1990s in the Dublin County Council area. Using investigations to collect evidence and public hearings with witnesses, it investigated allegations made in the media prior to its establishment and allegations subsequently made to the Tribunal itself.

The Tribunal ran from November 1997 to March 2012 and was the most expensive public inquiry held in the Republic of Ireland at the time. Public hearings concluded in September 2008, and following several delays due to legal challenges, the Tribunal began preparing its final report. It published four interim reports and the final report was published on 22 March 2012. The reports had far-reaching effects and consequences, including the following:

- On 2 April 2008, then-Taoiseach Bertie Ahern resigned due to continuing controversy over payments he had received.
- Findings of corruption were made against 11 councillors.
- Former Assistant City Manager George Redmond (RIP) and former Environment Minister Ray Burke both served prison sentences for tax evasion.

- Former Fianna Fáil TD Liam Lawlor (RIP) served three separate prison sentences for non-co-operation.

The Final Report contained a total of 64 recommendations for further consideration in relation to a range of policy areas including: Planning; Conflict of Interest; Political Finance; Lobbying; Bribery, Corruption in Office, Money Laundering and the Misuse of Confidential Information and Asset Recovery.

The Tribunal hearings led to a plethora of new legislation including the Ethics in Public Office Act, 1995, the Freedom of Information Act, 1997, the Standards in Public Office Act, 2001, the Local Government Act, 2001, the Electoral Act 2012, all of which impose strict codes of conduct on politicians, civil and public servants.

In 2015 the Houses of the Oireachtas passed the Regulation of Lobbying Act which requires all persons and organisations involved in lobbying to make regular transparent returns on the public register www.lobbying.ie.

Under the Act, "lobbying" is described as the initiation, development or modification of any public policy or programme; the preparation of amendment of any legislation; the award of any grant, loan or contract and specifically, the development or zoning of land (other than people's homes).

As outlined previously, the Planning and Development Act, 2000 finally allowed local authorities to acquire up to 10% - previously 20% - of land at existing use value. It was referred to the Supreme Court by President Mary McAleese and found not to be in contravention of the Constitution. Almost 27 years later, Judge John Kenny's recommendations were proved correct. Speaking in the Dáil in 2016, the Minister for Housing, Planning and the Environment, Simon Coveney described the Bill as "a serious and well directed intervention in this area".

In relation to planning, one of the most significant recommendations considered by the Government was the establishment of an Independent Planning Regulator, who could assume some of the Minister for the Environment, Community and Local Government's planning oversight functions and who could also be charged with carrying out investigations into systematic problems in the planning system.

The Office of the Planning Regulator was established in January 2019 and has a range of functions, including:

- independent assessment of all local authority and regional assembly forward planning, including the zoning decisions of local authority members in local area and development plans.
- conducting reviews of the organisation, systems and procedures used by any planning authority or An Bord Pleanála in the performance of any of their planning functions under the Planning and Development Act 2000 (as amended), including risks of corruption and on foot of individual complaints from members of the public and
- driving national research, education and public information programmes to highlight the role and benefit of planning.

As mentioned earlier, the 2004 All-Party Committee on the Constitution proved a turning point when it found the Kenny Report to be constitutional. The Report found that the Designated Area Scheme was more practicable than the ambitious national scheme proposed by the Uthwatt Report in the 1940s which had a considerable influence on the Kenny Committee. Also as mentioned previously, the decision by the Supreme Court in relation to Part V of the Planning & Development Act, 2000, whereby local authorities could acquire 10 per cent of a development for social housing at existing use value had, in effect, already validated the main recommendation of the Kenny Report.

Meanwhile, the uncertainty and volatility in the development land market continued unabated. For example, in a report on housing published in 2000 economist Peter Bacon and architect Fergal MacCabe wrote:

> At present there is considerable uncertainty in the housing market in relation to when and where significant amounts of additional serviced land will become available in Dublin city and county. As a result, demand is being fuelled for development land and speculative elements of demand are persisting, including the artificially bringing forward of demand for housing.[195]

[195195] Bacon, P & MacCabe, F. (2000) *The Housing Market in Ireland: An Economic Evaluation of Trends & Prospects*. Government Publications Office. Dublin. P. 2

Social and Affordable Housing Bill 2016

Implementation of the Kenny Report continued to be championed, notably by the Labour Party, though mostly from the Opposition benches. In November 2016, for example, Labour's Spokesperson on Housing, Jan O'Sullivan TD introduced a new Private Member's Bill, the Social & Affordable Housing Bill, 2016 which proposed a number of measures including one regarding the amount of compensation made in the compulsory acquisition of land. It proposed the implementation of the recommendations in the Kenny report of 1973, "following on from the All-Party Oireachtas Committee on the Constitution, which examined the proposals in 2004 and found that they did not contravene the Constitution regarding the balance between private property rights and social good". [196]

Deputy O'Sullivan said the Kenny Report was about controlling the price of building land so that when land is required for building as cities develop, it did not result in such huge profits and what happened in the tribunals.

> I was a member of the All-Party Committee on the Constitution that met to discuss the implementation of the Kenny report. Chaired by a very good Fianna Fáil person (Denis O'Donovan TD), the Committee agreed that the Kenny report was not unconstitutional because it struck the correct balance between the social and community good and the rights of private property, which are protected in the Constitution.

The Constitution was not an obstacle, Deputy O'Sullivan argued and was never meant to protect private property at the expense of the common good.

Labour Party leader Brendan Howlin told the House:

> The Kenny report predates any of us coming into this House. It was a solution that was put forward then to ensure that someone would not make an unconscionable killing because they owned land that was simply zoned for development. We have seen people becoming multimillionaires on the basis of a decision by a council to zone land.

---

[196] https://www.oireachtas.ie/en/debates/debate/dail/2016-11-15/6/

However, the measure was not supported by the Minister for Housing, Planning, Community & Local Government, Simon Coveney TD who said there appeared to be "practical shortcomings with the proposals in terms of its operation and legal shortcomings which put in question its constitutionality". The Bill, he said, would discriminate arbitrarily between a landowner who could sell development land at open market prices and those affected by a particular decision of a local authority to acquire their land at the much lower current use value.

Fianna Fail's Spokesman Barry Cowen also opposed the Bill stating "there is no logical reason why this assessment system, which covers the multitude of circumstances in which CPOs take place, should be replaced by a simplistic rule specifying 125% of the pre-zoned current value. This would be unimplementable and, without doubt, would breach individuals' rights to fair compensation."

However, Solidarity-People Before Profit Deputy Bríd Smith launched an attack on the Labour Party for not implementing the recommendations of the Kenny Report when in government.

> It is ironic that the Labour Party Bill is finally seeking to implement the Kenny Report which, as Deputy Jan O'Sullivan stated, was issued 40 years ago when the State was immersed in corruption and appalling planning scandals. In how many Administrations has the Labour Party been directly involved since the Kenny Report was issued? It could have addressed this issue before we reached the worst housing crisis in the history of the State...............

Four years later, when Taoiseach Leo Varadkar called a General Election for February 2020, the Kenny Report featured yet again in both the manifestos of the Labour Party and the Social Democrats.

Following the formation of the new government in July 2020, newly elected deputy and Social Democrats spokesperson on housing, Deputy Cian O'Callaghan raised the Kenny Report during a debate on a Sinn Féin housing motion on 7 July.

> ....There is no reason we should be gifting that uplift in land values to private developers. In effect we are using public resources to make landowners rich while, at the same time,

making housing unaffordable for people. That is something we need to tackle and, if we are serious about affordability, it is something we should be doing. One of the arguments often raised against that relates to constitutionality. When the 2004 Oireachtas All-Party group, which included representatives from the Government parties, examined the Constitution, its recommendation was that the Kenny report would be constitutional to implement. It noted that the Supreme Court had found that Part V provisions were constitutional and that the Kenny report had argued strongly that the legislation should be passed and referred to the Supreme Court in order that it could be tested beyond doubt. That would have an impact on housing affordability.[197]

According to Deputy O'Callaghan there are a number of reasons why the Kenny Report was never implemented, including political representation, closeness between mainstream political parties and developers and speculators and finally, ideology.

Firstly, the Dáil and indeed the Cabinet has had a much higher concentration of landlords, landowners and estate agents, than for example tenants in either the private residential rented sector or social housing sector. Secondly, a deeply embedded conservative and in later years neo-liberal ideology has guided thinking at both a political level and within the Customs House and local authorities. This combined with an almost deference to developer interests has resulted in political decisions which have benefited private speculation over and above the provision of housing needs.[198]

Property Cycles

In recent decades the history of the housing market in Ireland has mirrored that of the economy, periods of expansion followed by periods of contraction. The Irish economy is relatively small and open and therefore the various economic

---

[197] https://www.oireachtas.ie/en/debates/debate/dail/2020-07-07/16/
[198] Interview with Cian O'Callaghan TD, 2021

cycles are amplified to a higher degree than would be the case with a larger economy. This, in turn, is reflected in the property market which follows the economic cycle curves. In effect, the booms and busts of the economic cycles are reflected in the property cycles.

Former government advisor Aidan Culhane argued that the boom-and-bust pattern of Irish housing has its roots in the tenure pattern, financing and government spending policies, and perhaps above all in the political environment around housing.

Because owner-occupation has been the clear preference of public policy since the foundation of the State, most housing has been built speculatively by private developers: that activity is entirely dependent on the economic cycle..... Because of the public policy preference for owner-occupation, there has been no alternative apart from a residualised social housing sector. Households have therefore, rushed to purchase at times of plenty and retreated from the market in worse times. [199]

'Stability' is very difficult to achieve in housing development, according to Dr Lorcan Sirr of TU Dublin. There is, he says, typically a delay between demand being identified and demand being met by the delivery of housing.

> Even when demand is satisfied, there is typically still a lot of housing in the pipeline for delivery, which cannot afford to be abandoned. On the other side of the roller coaster, even as prices are falling, there may still be new housing coming onto the market. This is known as 'development lag'. Supply and demand are never in equilibrium given housebuilding takes a number of years. The production of widgets or cars or many other industrial products can be increased overnight, but housing cannot. [200]

According to Sirr, there have also been a series of sometimes random policy changes that supercharge housing output without having regard to issues of credit, household indebtedness, spatial impact and so on. "There has never been a serious attempt by policymakers to control the price of land and hence the cost of housing".

---

[199] Interview with Aidan Culhane 2020
[200] Interview with Dr Lorcan Sirr, 2020

According to Tom Dunne, former head of the School of Real Estate at TU Dublin, when the economy rebounds in an economic upturn, the property market is slower to respond and the government usually does not allow it enough time. Instead, they generally accelerate the response by introducing incentives of various kinds to increase demand but are not so good at increasing supply.

> They control the housing market by controlling the demand for property and usually that creates this uplift before the system is able to respond to it and you get higher prices. Then, they don't withdraw those incentives quickly enough in the property cycle and they end up withdrawing when it's too late. That's what makes the property market so volatile in Ireland.[201]

As pointed out previously, for historical reasons, Ireland very much operates an Anglo-Saxon model of housing which is much more volatile than many countries in Europe which have a very different approach. Says Dunne:

> It is more volatile whereas on the Continent the Germans and the Danes have a very different view of the world. It's not that Anglo-Saxon boom-and-bust, free-enterprise driven market. It's much more socially democratic in the true sense, so they try as best they can to moderate the boom-and-bust cycles and they built in systems that seem to moderate the downflows and the increases.

Advocate for the homeless and founder of the McVerry Trust, Fr Peter McVerry says successive Irish governments have never handled boom-and-bust very well.

> In the boom times when the government has plenty of money they go in for building, an approach that promotes the economy but the economy doesn't need to be promoted in the boom times and then when in austerity, when the economy should be promoted and we should be building because it creates employment, it boosts the economy and it gives badly needed employment, the government does not build. So, I

---

[201] Interview with Tom Dunne, 2019

think we go on a merry-go-round. When the merry-go-round is going fast, we make it go faster and when the merry-go-round is going slow, we slow it down further. [202]

In addition, the thorny issue of how to acquire land for development and how to deal with the "compensation betterment" problem was never properly addressed. The problem traces its roots back to the Local Government (Planning and Development) Act, 1963 where the issue was not addressed. Judge Kenny and his Committee struggled with the existing legislation and tried to bring forward a solution. To date it has been rejected by successive governments although the main principle - that of acquiring land at existing use value - was established as in full compliance with the Constitution in the Supreme Court decision on the Planning & Development Act, 2000.

In regard to compensation, according to Dr Rachael Walsh, Assistant Professor of Law at Trinity College, the position on compensation has not changed much at all in Irish law over the last one hundred years.

> The overall structure has always been, and continues to be, rooted in the English legislation, the 1919 Act and these are still the basic principles that we apply now. Added on to that have been bits and pieces of legislation that create distinctive compensation rules for a particular issue so the planning context was one where a discreet set of rules were developed for compensation, but very much drawing on the 1919 principles. Similarly, your more recent examples, the NAMA Act in 2009 has its own compensation principles but also linking back to the 1919 Act. [203]

As a result, the whole issue of compensation has become a very complex patchwork of legislation in contrast to many European countries where there is one statute which deals with the rules applicable for compensation determination across the board. Says Walsh:

> I suppose an advantage of the system that we do have is that, because the roots are there in the 1919 legislation, there's quite a lot of caseload built up over time, English case law, but also

---

[202] Interview with Fr Peter McVerry, 2019
[203] Interview with Dr. Rachael Walsh, 2020

Irish case law, that can be drawn upon when looking at questions of valuation and compensation. The disadvantage is that there is this patchwork-like nature to the compensation landscape, so giving an answer to the question on the compensation rules in Ireland is a very complicated and long answer as opposed to a straightforward answer like it might be in some other jurisdictions.

The Constitution

Elsewhere, this book examines the Constitutional implications for the recommendations of the Kenny Report. Articles 40.3.2° and Article 43.2 were fundamental to the analysis carried out by the Kenny Committee. According to *Kelly: The Irish Constitution*, judicial attempts to clarify the relationship between these Articles "have taken a number of twists and turns".

> ...the older case looked to Article 43 as the principal guarantee of the individual's right to a specific item of property. Then for a brief period during the early 1980s, Article 43.1 and 43.2 were relegated to the role of protecting the institution of private property, while Article 40.3 protected the rights of the individual. However, since the latter half of the 1980s, the courts have invoked the concepts of social justice and the exigencies of the common good, mentioned in Article 43, when considering whether restrictions on specific property rights constitute an unjust attack for the purposes of Article 40.3..[204]

UCC Law lecturer Gwynn Morgan concurred, saying there was "a judicial mood-swing over time" and among individual judges, as to how protective towards constitutional property right it is necessary to be and, in consequence, how stringent towards legislation that interferes with it.

> These views have naturally affected the choices available to the Oireachtas and, in the decades after the Kenny Report, the courts decided a number of constitutional cases in which they took a strongly pro-protection of property rights line. That

---

[204]Hogan GW et al (2018) *The Irish Constitution, 2018*. Bloomsbury Publishing. 7.8.05

was undoubtedly one reason why the report was never implemented.[205]

Indeed, this restrictive approach was noted by former Taoiseach Dr Garret FitzGerald when he remarked: "I can testify from personal experience in government that concern about possible restrictive interpretations of the Articles on private property has been a major impediment to legislation required in the public interest...for example in relation to treatment of windfall profits from development land.[206]

In a Thomas Davis lecture in 1988 entitled *Property in the Constitution and the Courts*, Judge Ronan Keane cast some doubt as to whether the Kenny Report would survive a constitutional challenge. In particular, he singled out part of Paragraph 88 of the Report which dealt with the Constitution.

> ...The Constitution does not give to each citizen the right to get the full market price for any of his property which he decides to sell. If it did, then all price controls would be repugnant to the Constitution and we are convinced that this is not the law. Moreover, if each citizen has the right to get the full market price for any part of his property which he decides to sell, each owner of house property must have the right to get the full market rent for it when he lets it. But if this is the law, the Rent Restrictions Acts and the Landlord and Tenant Acts, both of which regulate the amount of rent which a landlord may lawfully get for some types of property and which, in effect, prevent him from realising the full market price on sale of the property by giving privileges to tenants, are repugnant to the Constitution. Nobody has ever suggested this in the thousands of cases under those Acts which have come before the Courts.[207]

[205] Gwynn Morgan, D. (2012) Government and the Courts. In *Governing Ireland: From Cabinet Government to Delegated Government* (O'Malley, E. & MacCarthaigh M. eds) IPA. pp. 232 -233
[206] FitzGerald, G. (1998) The Irish Constitution in its historical context. In *Ireland's Evolving Constitution 1937 – 1997* (Murphy, T. & Twomey, P.M. eds). Oxford: Harte. P. 36
[207] The Kenny Report, Par. 88

Speaking in hindsight, Judge Keane pointed out that the Rent Restrictions Act, 1960, was subsequently held unconstitutional, precisely because it deprived the landlords of the market rent from their property without compensation. A similar fate befell the Housing (Private Rented Dwellings) Bill, 1981, which was intended to replace compensation. "It must be at least doubtful, in these circumstances that the Kenny Committee would survive a constitutional challenge", he added.

Judge Keane did, however, suggest the legislative route as an option.

> If existing legislation is tilting the balance unfairly in favour of the private speculator and against the public interest, then it should be perfectly possible for the legislature to design a scheme that further delimits the property rights of the people concerned, in the interests of the common good. This would probably be a more rewarding approach to the problem than judicial creativity: recent suggestions that substantial awards of compensation may themselves be constitutionally frail, as being an unwarranted diversion of public funds into the pockets of speculators, while they have an attractively rhetorical ring, may not withstand closer scrutiny.

He continued:

> It is of the nature of a society that favours the promotion of private enterprise-and, under the directive principles of social policy, the state is required to favour such enterprise that it will occasionally award windfalls to some. The legislature should be capable of deciding at what point social justice, or the common good, requires that individuals should sacrifice the gains they have made from their shrewdness, foresight, hard work or good fortune to the greater welfare of the community. Provided the statutory framework they establish for so doing is not flawed by a basic unfairness, there hardly seems occasion for the courts to intervene.

Dr Rachel Walsh of Trinity College agrees there has been both legal and political confusion over the Articles relating to property in the Constitution.

Now, it seems pretty clear that the view of the courts is you read the two provisions together, and the Constitution protects ownership, as an institution, and it also protects individual property rights, but that the protection for those rights is subject to the common good, social justice, and that the idea of unjust attack that's in 43.2 is read subject to those more specific provisions in Article 43. So, having two articles, possibly can be criticized as being a bit cumbersome and clunky but I don't think from a legal perspective it is now unclear what the Constitution means.

The All-Party Oireachtas Committee in their 2004 Report examined the issue at length. While noting it was impossible to be definite on the question, it nonetheless concluded:

Judged by contemporary case-law, it is nevertheless very difficult to see why the recommendations contained in the Kenny Report would not survive constitutional scrutiny. In the *Planning and Development Bill* the Supreme Court held that the Oireachtas was entitled to conclude that 'the provision of affordable housing and housing for persons in special categories and of integrated housing was rationally connected to an objective of sufficient importance to warrant interference with a constitutionally protected right and, given the serious social problems which they are designed to meet, they undoubtedly relate to concerns which, in a free and democratic society, should be regarded as pressing and substantial.' By extension, therefore, the imposition of price controls on building land would be regarded as an objective of social importance which would warrant interfering with a constitutional right.[208]

Homelessness advocate Fr. Peter McVerry dismisses the notion that the Kenny Report recommendations were in any way repugnant to the Constitution.

---

[208] The All-Party Oireachtas Committee on the Constitution. *Ninth Progress Report: Private Property* (2004). Government Publications Office. P. 39

The Committee was chaired by a high court judge. So clearly, it was not obviously unconstitutional. And if the politicians saw it as constitutional, they should have gone straight to the Supreme Court and declared it to be constitutional. But they didn't bother doing that. And I think we've seen the consequences in the continuing planning corruptions ever since.

Former Housing Minister Jan O'Sullivan, who was a member of the All Party Oireachtas Committee, believes the Constitutional argument was "firmly put to bed" by the 2004 report.

I am of the view that the reluctance to implement the recommendations stems more from motivation to protect land-owners' interests. If it had been implemented in advance of the huge expansion in construction during the Celtic Tiger era, I believe it would have considerably dampened down the cost of building land and, as a result, protected to some extend from the rapidly escalating cost of homes during those years and the economic collapse of those who were building and those who were buying those houses. But I would not in any way exonerate the disgraceful behaviour of banks and other lending institutions and their reckless lending.[209]

However, there have been frequent calls to give clarity to this issue by way of a Constitutional referendum. In particular, this thesis noted the strong recommendations of the 1996 comprehensive review of the Constitution that a referendum be held to bring clarity to the confusion that often surrounds Articles 40.3 and 43.3.2°.

While this suggestion has been largely side-lined in recent times, it found favour again in the run-up to, and aftermath of, the February 2020 general election debate and was specifically mentioned in a number of documents. For example, the manifesto of the Social Democrats stated:

Article 43 of the Constitution seeks to balance private property rights with the common good. The problem is that, too often, the common good loses out. This holds us back on issues such as

---

[209] Interview with Jan O'Sullivan, 2019

nationwide rent caps, rent certainty and addressing upward only rent reviews. Successive governments hid behind a conservative interpretation of this provision to avoid taking the radical steps needed to deal with our dysfunctional housing sector. If we are to put the common good at the heart of our efforts to bring the housing crisis to an end, we need certainty around Article 43. In the absence of a challenge through legal action, we would favour bringing forward a referendum to let the people decide if the balance should be weighted more towards the common good..[210]

In its housing section, the Labour Party gave a very specific commitment: "Labour will legislate for the compulsory purchase of lands at existing use value, building on the 1973 Kenny Report proposals"..[211]

After the February 2020 General Election, the first Fianna Fáil/Fine Gael agreed document stated: "Reduce the cost of land to improve the affordability of housing, employing all measures up to and including referenda." (Fianna Fáil-Fine Gael mission document, 2020, *Housing for All*). When the final Programme for Government *Our Shared Future* was published following negotiations between Fianna Fáil, Fine Gael and the Green Party, it contained a very broad sentence in the section of Political and Public Service Reform, coupled in with a possible referendum on voting rights for Irish citizens abroad, which sated: "We will hold referendums on housing and the extension of the franchise at presidential elections to Irish citizens living outside the State". Oddly, the six-page section on housing entitled *Housing for All* made no mention of a referendum. The closest the programme got to any reference to the principles of the Kenny Report was a sentence which read: "Review how community gain can be captured through a review of the development levy process, rezoning system and planning permission conditions". No further detail or timeframe was given.

Indeed, Dr. Lorcan Sirr of TU Dublin was very critical of the programme or its potential to control the price of development land.

> Mostly, any housing content in it is meaningless: vague, un-costed, no points on delivery; nothing on bringing down the price of land. Most of the housing points were a) either already

[210] *Homes within Reach, 2020*. Social Democrats
[211] *Affordable Housing for All,* the Labour Party, 2020

in legislation b) in train anyway; or c) never going to happen/kicked down the road....The Kenny Report in the Programme for Government was conspicuous by its absence.

Writing in the *Business Post*, Political Editor Michael Brennan said that during the negotiations with the Green Party, the Fianna Fáil/Fine Gael framework document survived largely intact.

> But one key element was dropped. There had been an agreement between the two parties to hold a referendum on capping land prices, as a way of reducing the high cost of housing. But Fine Gael was spooked when there was a backlash from developers and farmers, who faced the prospect of getting lower prices for land sold for housing. The commitment to have such a referendum is no longer in the new *Programme for Government*. There is a separate commitment to have a referendum on the right to housing to satisfy the Green party demand. [212]

The Green Party's housing negotiators were Deputy Neasa Hourigan, architect Patrick Duffy and barrister and South Dublin Green Party councillor Deirdre Ní Fhloinn while the Fine Gael housing team was led by Housing Minister Eoghan Murphy and advisor Paul Melia. The omission of the Committee on the Kenny Report is odd given party leader Eamon Ryan's public call for the implementation of the report during the election campaign. The main emphasis of the Green Party negotiators appears to have been on planning regulations, fire and safety issues and related matters.

According to one source close to the negotiations, the notion of a referendum to cap land prices in certain cases was pushed for by Fianna Fáil. The notion of a referendum had been included in the framework document on the expectation that talks might begin with parties such as Labour or the Social Democrats who had such a commitment in their manifestos. In the event such talks never got off the ground. The general commitment to hold a referendum on housing was a very broad one but was hoped to instigate a major debate on the whole area of housing, including land acquisition, as was the establishment of the new Housing Commission.

---

[212] *Business Post, 21/06/2020*

Chapter 13

Ongoing Efforts

Acquisition of Development Land (Assessment of Compensation) Bill 2021

On Wednesday, 16 June, 2021, the Labour Party during Private Member's Time, introduced the Acquisition of Development Land (Assessment of Compensation) Bill 2021. The Bill, if implemented would, in effect, implement the main recommendation of the Kenny Report.

Introducing the Bill, party leader Alan Kelly said the report contained a set of radical recommendations to help solve Ireland's housing problems and should be commended. It was a report, he said, that had been talked about ever since but despite all of the chaos and disaster which property had created for Irish people in the time since 1973, it had never been implemented.

> ... In the time since 1973, we have had housing crisis after housing crisis, including a calamitous economic collapse in which property development and speculation, facilitated by multiple Fianna Fáil governments and not regulated by the banks, bankrupted the country. We have had numerous tribunals and scandals, costing hundreds of millions of euro, and all too many criminal cases about corruption and rezoning in the planning process. They have all passed and the Kenny Report still has not been implemented. [213]

Deputy Kelly told the Dail that many of the problems the country now faced could have been avoided if the Kenny report had been implemented.

> This measure, he said, which had been opposed by Fianna Fáil and Fine Gael for generations, would immediately have ended the ability of land hoarders and speculators to make enormous

---

[213] https://www.oireachtas.ie/en/debates/debate/dail/2021-06-16/8/

profits at the expense of first-time buyers. It would have effectively ended land hoarding as a practice. If it had been implemented, there may never have been a property bubble and collapse, nor a housing crisis or anything like the scale of the crisis that exists today.

Taking into account current planning density guidelines of between 35 and 50 units per hectare, Deputy Kelly said he estimated that, if implemented, the Bill would reduce the cost of a new-build, three-bedroom semi-detached house built on a greenfield site in the greater Dublin area by approximately €30,000. The Party, he said, had also seen a senior counsel's legal opinion, which it commissioned, that the legislation was completely constitutional.

> I know it is completely constitutional. It also needs to be said that the Ninth Report of the All-Party Oireachtas Committee on the Constitution in 2003 also found that implementation of the Kenny report was constitutional. Let us not hear any of that rubbish today... To paraphrase a Chinese proverb on the best time to plant a tree, the best time to implement the Kenny report was 1973. The second-best time is now.)

In preparing the legislation the Labour Party had commissioned senior counsel Feichín McDonagh to look at the constitutionality of the Kenny Report. He concluded:

> Developments in case law since 1973 and more particularly since the All-Party Committee issued their 9th Report do not serve to undermine the recommendation made in the Kenny Report to the effect that land required for development by local authorities could be compulsorily acquired at existing use values plus an additional percentage at the figure of 25% and that this would not offend the Constitution. Whereas of course one cannot rule out the possibility that ultimately the balance which the Supreme Court might strike could be against such a proposal, there is certainly in the case law nothing to suggest that the courts will adopt a level of deference towards the policies deemed appropriate by the Oireachtas. In the context of any such proposals, the courts acknowledge that the Oireachtas is the primary body to determine issues of social

justice and that the balance might be struck in the context of a pressing social need. [214]

Deputy Kelly also quoted the Taoiseach, Micheál Martin who in 2018 had stated:

> I think implementing Kenny is morally the right thing to do - I don't think there should be windfall profits once land is rezoned but it would also undoubtedly reduce the cost of housing because the price of land at the moment is a significant factor in increasing the price of houses.

However, when the Minister of State for Housing, Local Government & Heritage, Green Party, Deputy Malcolm Noonan rose to speak, he said that while he agreed in principle with the aims of the Bill and acknowledged it was well intended, he was proposing an amendment to defer debate on the Bill for 12 months "to allow sufficient time to consider the work of the Law Reform Commission and finalise proposals currently being formulated by the Government, in line with the Programme for Government commitment."

Minister of State Noonan said the Bill was premature with regard to the final report of the Law Reform Commission on the reform and consolidation of compulsory purchase order laws, which was expected before the end of 2021 and which, he understood, would include a draft Compulsory Acquisition of Land (Consolidation and Reform) Bill. This will would, he said, be the culmination of an extensive process that had been ongoing for almost five years. It would be substantive work that would need to be considered.

> The Bill is also premature with regard to alternative Government proposals. In this regard, the Programme for Government includes a commitment to bring forward proposals for reform in the area of community gain at the land zoning stage of the planning process, work which is now advanced. This will take the form key flagship measures arising from the forthcoming housing for all strategy and directly related legislative proposals being concurrently formulated as a general scheme of a new legislative proposal.

---

[214] Opinion of Feichín McDonagh SC to the Labour Party 2021 Par. 83

Minister Noonan said a weakness of the Bill was that it would apply only to such land transacted after 3 June 2021, meaning the development lands that do not change hands at any stage after that date would not be affected. The Bill would, therefore, exclude any benefit in respect of land on which there is an extant permission as full development and improvement value plus investment return would remain payable.

He also advanced arguments that had been put forward by many opponents of the Kenny Report in the past including it would be a disincentive to buy, or sell, development land for the delivery of residential development that could impact housing supply in the short to medium term. It would, he argued, create uncertainty in the development sector; be disproportionate and discriminate against new entrants to the market and not provide a mechanism for fair or equitable application and be impractical to apply. The Bill as drafted, he said, would risk the immediate creation of a two-tier land market as it would give rise to motivation to cease all land transactions in the short to medium term.

In his contribution, Sinn Féin's Spokesperson on Housing Eoin Ó Broin said while he was very grateful to Deputy Kelly to give him this opportunity to support the legislation, "many of us can agree that it would have been better if the Labour Party had sought to introduce this legislation when in government rather than just from the Opposition benches". The idea, for example, that a Law Reform Commission report was a reason to delay was laughable, he said, given how often Fianna Fáil and Fine Gael-led Governments ignore those reports and leave them sitting on the shelf. The fact that the Government has other, similar proposals, somehow means that another good proposal cannot be progressed was, again, disingenuous.)

In his contribution, the Social Democrat's Housing Spokesperson Cian O'Callaghan said it was 48 years since the Kenny report was introduced. For 21 of those years, the Labour Party was in government over six Governments, from 1973 to 1977, 1981 to 1982, 1982 to 1987, 1992 to 1994, 1994 to 1997 and 2011 to 2016.

> During most of the times the Labour Party was in government, the Ministers with responsibility for the environment and housing were Labour Party Ministers. It rings hollow to hear the Labour Party talk about the implementation of the Kenny Report when it has had so many opportunities to implement it.

No Fianna Fáil deputy contributed to the debate and the only Fine Gael contributor was Minister of State Peter Burke who re-iterated the Government's position on the Bill.

When the vote was taken on the Government's Amendment, it was accepted by 79 votes to 58. Accordingly, the Labour Party Bill was deferred for one year. Yet again, the Kenny Report had been kicked to touch although significantly, not rejected outright.

In April 2022, a report by the independent think-tank agency TASC endorsed the Bill.

This report endorsed the proposed Acquisition of Development Land Bill, 2021 which aims to modernise the central recommendation of the Kenny Report as it proposes that LAs should be enabled to compulsorily acquire land as it proposed that Local Authorities should be enables to compulsorily acquire land.

Housing for All

On 2 September, 2021 the Government published its long-awaited *Housing for All – A new Housing Plan for Ireland*. In a jointly-written Foreword the three-party leaders, Taoiseach Micheál Martin, Tánaiste Leo Varadkar and Green Party leader Eamon Ryan said the programme set out the Government's mission to tackle the housing crisis. Described as "the most ambitious housing plan in the history of the State" the three leaders stated their objective was "that everybody should have access to sustainable, good quality housing to purchase or rent at an affordable price, built to high standard and located close to essential services, offering a high quality of life".

The plan was to be overseen by a Cabinet Committee on Housing to be chaired by the Taoiseach. In the chapter titled "Pathway to Increasing New Housing Supply" the document promised to introduce "updated Kenny Report style powers to ensure sharing of the increase in land values resulting from zoning decisions and more community gain".[215]

The document explained that the new concept of Land Value Sharing (LVS) was a fundamental transformation to the planning and land value system that had been identified since the 1973 Kenny Report. The document

---

[215] *Housing for All (2021) A new Housing Plan for Ireland.* Government of Ireland. P.23

promised that the additional value of zoned land would be "shared in a fairer way with the State and the community will benefit as a result".

> The concept involves securing a proportion of the value uplift of a development site, tracked from a point of zoning or designation, to a point of planning permission. These proposals reflect the very significant increase in market value derived from re-zoning and State investment and will ensure that the community benefits as a result.

However, as pointed out in this thesis, the Kenny Report rejected any such levy. Specifically, in Chapter 6 he said the notion of a "betterment levy" on the difference between the price realised on the disposal of land after planning permission had been granted and the market price based on its existing use would only increase the price of serviced and potential development land and therefore an increase in the price of all buildings on the land. [216]

As pointed out elsewhere, the question as to how you compensate people for land suitable for development was never really resolved in the UK. That question was never answered properly in the original British Town & Country Planning Act, 1954 which formed the basis for the 1963 Planning Act in Ireland. As a result, the problem continued in Ireland. Indeed, the system, as examined in detail by the Uthwatt Committee in Britain, failed to resolve the issue. While on the face of it, the system of a levy may initially have seemed very attractive, it did not work out well in practice when tried in Britain and showed in time that, inevitably, the purchaser had to increase the price of the houses to recover the price of the levy. The system was ended the by the Conservative government in the 1954 Town and Country Planning Act.

The failure of a development charge, or levy, in Britain appears to have lain in the inevitable resistance to it from landowners who faced binding restrictions on how they could use their land and could no longer profit when their schemes were approved.

The view that *Housing for All* does not represent the Kenny Report was supported in a Dáil debate on *Housing for All* on 28 September 2021 by Sinn Fein Deputy Eoin Ó Broin who stated nothing in the plan resembled the Kenny Report's recommendations on land.

---

[216] The Kenny Report, Par. 57 E.

On the contrary, Mr. Justice Kenny was against the kind of measure the Government has outlined in the plan because it will do nothing to tackle land price inflation, but why let the facts get in the way of a good sound bite? [217]

Social Democrat Spokesperson on Housing, Deputy Cian O'Callaghan concurred:

On the land value sharing measures in this report, let us be very clear this does not amount to the implementation of the Kenny report.

Because it was not resolved in Ireland, of course when the economy took off finally in 1964/65 land prices went up because house prices went up and there was immense speculation in land. The concentration was on getting land rezoned, the local authority had an obligation to service the zoned land and speculators made a lot of money. They continue to do so up to the writing of this book.

According to Dr Lorcan Sirr, the continuing housing crisis means that governments can now no longer totally ignore the Kenny Report.

Despite the shift in political focus to the pandemic of 2020, housing issues were brought further into stark relief by the state of emergency, and particularly household preference for security and ownership. The Pandemic allowed potential purchasers an unforeseen opportunity to accelerate their savings plans, so that by mid-August 2020 house prices were again beginning to rise due to the increased numbers of households chasing a limited supply of housing for sale. Households' limited ability to buy new housing shifted the spotlight to who exactly was buying up new homes and attention focused on institutional investors and even the State's role in buying up new housing from under the noses of potential purchasers and especially first-time buyers.

This, combined with the advancement of the newly-constituted Land Development Agency and public unrest at not just the

217 https://www.oireachtas.ie/en/debates/debate/dail/2021-09-28/15/

limited supply of housing, but a supply of new housing being limited by the actions and policies of the State, has brought up once again the spectre (for political parties) of the Kenny Report as government struggles to keep all sides happy (institutional investors, first-time buyers, voters, lobbyists, and so on). Traditionally, governments want nothing to do with the Kenny Report, but by 2021 pressure was mounting to the degree that it could no longer be ignored (which is not the same thing as saying its recommendations will actually be implemented).[218]

Zoned Land Tax

In Budget 2022, delivered in the Dáil on Tuesday, 12 October 2021, the Minister for Finance Paschal Donohoe announced the introduction of a new zoned land tax. The tax, which would not be introduced for a two-year period, would replace the existing vacant site levy, which had proved a major failure. (In July of 2020 only €21,000 had been paid in respect of the 2020 levy, leaving a total outstanding bill of €14m).

> The new tax was to target any unused land zoned and serviced for housing, regardless of its size. The tax was to be based on the market value of the land at a rate of 3 per cent, the same starting point for the vacant site levy when it was first introduced. According to the Minister the reason for the lead-in time was to "give scope to review the workings of the tax, to listen to stakeholders and ensure it is both effective and equitable".[219]

The idea of such a tax system was rejected in the Kenny Report for the reason that such a tax could not be applied on lands which were not serviced. In Judge Kenny's view the area of land which would be liable for such a tax would be small and the assessment procedure would likely lead to prolonged litigation.

---

[218] Interview with Dr Lorcan Sirr, 2021
[219] (https://www.oireachtas.ie/en/debates/debate/dail/2021-10-12/4/

We think it probable that if such a tax were introduced, the yield from it would be very small and that the cost of its assessment might well exceed the ultimate proceeds..[220]

---

[220] The Kenny Report, Par. 64

Chapter 14

Identifying the Issues

The Price of Land

A key consideration to any study of the Kenny Report is the importance of the price of land in influencing house prices. Many commentators would argue that land prices tend to be residual and they are not the cause of high prices but rather the result of high house prices. Thus, the price of development land tends to be volatile because the price of houses is volatile. In an upswing in house prices, people tend to invest in land because they are confident the price will go up, at least in the short term. To this extent, the price of land induces speculation.

> There are some perverse incentives when you talk about land because as soon as land prices start going up, people invest in it because it is going up. The very fact that land is going up draws people into buying it whereas, in normal economics, if the price of something goes up, it deters purchasers. Land can work the other way and be attractive when it is going up in price. [221]

Economist Kieran McQuinn argues that international literature suggests that markets that have relatively stable periods of inflation are generally markets where land is fairly freely available and that do not have any great restrictions on land.

> In Ireland, because we have never tried to attack the speculative element of land and because development land can become so expensive, because people can essentially hold on to it without any great cost that leads to the price of land becoming very expensive. As a result, that land is less likely to come on stream as freely as it would in other jurisdictions. When you have that restricted nature of the land and restricted in not being available

---

[221] Interview with Tom Dunne 2019

for development, that then causes big booms and busts generally in the market.[222]

McQuinn says the Kenny Report got at the point that we need to take the speculative element out of land and land values because that is causing land to be restricted in its availability which, in turn, causes bigger booms and busts.

Social Democrats housing spokesperson Deputy Cian O'Callaghan said the price of development land is both a key component of current house prices and also a key potential driver for halting of construction at any point in the future where house prices fall significantly.

> As house prices increase, the price of development land increases – meaning that once house prices fall, many sites become unviable as the builder can no longer make a sufficient return on the price of the development land that they purchased. Access to development land – or rather lack of access – is a key barrier to many smaller builders – and helps maintain local monopolies by larger developers who can control all of the development land in an area.[223]

Planning Regulator Niall Cussen said he has long held the view that for planning aims and objectives to be fully and properly implemented, a planning process has to have appropriate leverage over the land management process and it has to be able to deal with the distortions, or the pressures, that can be placed on the achievement of planning objectives by its impacts on land values and so forth.

> So, in the classical sense if you have an area identified in your development plan that is of strategic importance for regeneration, or housing delivery purposes and it's split between 10 different owners and they are of 10 different minds in the context of how they should reap the rewards of the land value increase they have certainly received as a result of this objective in the development plan, unless you have a mechanism to capture that land value for public good and unless you have effective mechanisms to bring those 10

---

[222] Interview with Kieran McQuinn, 2019
[223] Interview with Cian O'Callaghan TD, 2021

different landowners into some sort of co-ordinated approach to the development of those lands, achievement of that objective in the development plan will be very difficult. [224]

One of the problems facing researchers is that there is not a huge amount of data available on the effect of land prices on house prices. The quality of the data is quite poor, says Kieran McQuinn. Getting decent, reliable data to be able to track costs is difficult. He said:

> It is closed and sheltered from competition unlike many other sectors in the Irish economy. Productivity probably could be improved which ultimately would reduce costs. But the cost of land is still probably the main one that is inhibiting supply.

Sinn Féin's Eoin Ó Broin said land is the second biggest factor after the cost of construction. As an example, he cited in Dublin in 2019 the land purchase price for a standard 3-bed house, or apartment, in Dublin was between €75,000 and €100,00.

> Land value and the speculative element is having a detrimental impact on the provision of residential accommodation in both the provision of private and social housing. Land is key and is the biggest inhibitor of the private sector to bring genuinely affordable home-to-rent, or to buy, certainly in the bigger urban centres. [225]

Developer Michael O'Flynn believes the basic problem in the Republic of Ireland is that house prices are too expensive. There is no easy solution to that, he said but a lot of the expense goes back to land.

> We don't have strategic land management plans in this country. We went down the road in the crazy days of everyone getting a bit of zoning everywhere, regardless of whether it was a good or a bad idea and once they got zoning, they got planning and infrastructure. It was just not the builder made a mistake, or the funder. It was made by the policy-makers as well. They like to forget this. The reality is planners were involved in rezonings, they

---

[224] Interview with Niall Cussen, 2021
[225] Interview with Eoin Ó Broin TD, 2019

were involved in planning permissions. That could not happen without public service input [226].

According to O'Flynn, when "things went crazy", the cost of land could be anything up to 40pc of the overall house price. While since then it has come back to somewhere around 25pc to 30pc now [227] and more in places but the huge variation is because of no proper planning.

O'Flynn is critical of the prices some companies have paid for land even in recent years. This arises when there is insufficient land zoned in the right place and people take a view that prices will continue to rise and they can pay more. He instanced the price paid for the RTE site in Donnybrook where he says a price was bid which would only work for one of two reasons, a planning gain, or an escalation of prices.

> Where are we going in this country if people are going to overpay in the hope of getting an escalation of price? I'm one of the old-fashioned developer/builder types who makes his profit out of building the house but now we have a lot of people into financial engineering. They are into speculation. People will only speculate where there is a money opportunity. You don't have people speculating in potatoes or hay or straw. We have a land management system in this country that has failed us completely and until we deal with that management system we are not going to deal with the problem.

Former Minister of State Eithne FitzGerald concurred, arguing that in the current regime, developers may often find other activities more profitable than actual house-building, such as influencing the authorities to increase, or vary, the zoning on land to increase the number of units to be built on it, or to reduce public obligations like minimum size or wheelchair accessibility and then, when the value of the land is enhanced, they may flip it. "The return from such activities may be quicker, cheaper and less risky to achieve than embarking on building an estate or apartment block, and selling them on in two years' time when some unknown may have altered selling prices," she said.

---

[226] Interview with Michael O'Flynn, 2019
[227] The interview with Michael O'Flynn was conducted in December 2019

She also cautions that in the event of a Kenny-style mechanism being introduced, some kind of mechanism would be needed to avoid profiteering.

> If land is suddenly made cheaper via Kenny-style reforms, and the developer gets his/her sites in Dublin at €200,000 each instead of €400,000, in principle they could sell the houses for €200,000 less. However, if people are still willing to pay €500,000 for a finished house, until new developers move in and bid down the price, current developers could decide to take most of the value of the cheaper sites as extra profit.

Long-time Labour councillor and former Lord Mayor of Dublin Dermot Lacey believes there must be some control over development land.

> There has to be an easier compulsory purchase scheme. A constitutional amendment isn't about implementing the Kenny report. A constitutional amendment is about dealing with property rights in the Constitution. And that has to be dealt with and it has to be tackled because it's a huge barrier. [228]

However, former Taoiseach John Bruton dismisses the notion of a Kenny-type solution to Ireland's housing problem.

> As to the Kenny Report, I think the view was that it required a constitutional change to diminish property rights in a fairly substantial way. The problem is that we have plenty of houses, but not where people want to live (in cities). It is a cyclical problem. If you depress land prices artificially by the exercise of state power, people will be unwilling to sell, and compulsion will have to be resorted to. By the time you get through CPOs, the housing crisis will be over. [229]

Control of Finance

Finance and its availability is central to house-building. Councillor Dermot Lacey says Dublin City Council probably has enough land on which to build for the present. A big problem is the supply of money and the flexibility to

[228] Interview with Councillor Dermot Lacey 2020
[229] Interview with former Taoiseach John Bruton, 2019

181

deliver housing in a sustainable manner. He instanced the Irish Glass Bottle site in Dublin's Poolbeg area as an example. Before a spade could be put in the ground, the land had to be assessed on the open market place and NAMA had to get back its value which, in turn, pushed up the price of the houses to be built. "My own strong view," he said "is that something along the lines of the Kenny Report - and I'm open enough for it to be varied - needs to be examined with existing use value being paid plus a small compensatory amount for not being able to enhance the value to yourself way down into the future. That has to be done."

The abolition rates in 1977 Lacey sees as a watershed in limiting the ability of local authorities to build houses.

> I've calculated based on two figures that if you set the amount of rates that would have been collected in 1977, using only the number of houses in Dublin City in 1977, set that against the Rates Support Grant we got *in lieu* of domestic rates. Add to that the decision in 1982 to abolish rates and government properties. The loss to Dublin City Council since 1977 has been in the region of €10 billion. Now that would build a huge number of houses. And that's not just forgone in house building, that's money gone in democratic spending, the expenditure by the people elected by the people of Dublin on the priorities that they would determine. So instead, we have priorities determined by the civil service and, in my view, that is not good.

Developer Michael O'Flynn is also hugely critical of the role of the Central Bank in controlling house prices.

> The Central Bank is now involved in controlling house prices. That is not their function. Their function is to control the financial industry. Where were they when we needed them most back in the noughties when there were 100 per cent plus mortgages? And now we are over-correcting, as we do always in this country. There is now an affordability problem that is really serious.

Clearly the capital requirements to build houses and apartments today are far more onerous than those required by small builders in the past to build four or six houses who were often brick-layers or carpenters turned builders. They often sold the houses on and used the cash received to start the next phase of a housing estate. However, building today's A-rated homes may also require new skills, techniques and materials that traditional small builders lack.

The wipe-out of so many builders in the crash and the reluctance of the banks to lend the same proportion of development funds has contributed significantly to the reduction of the supply of builders/developers.

Vested Interests

Vested interests were, without doubt, one of the key reasons for the non-implementation of the Kenny Report. Economist Kieran McQuinn believes that at any time when there are huge returns to be made from something there are obviously people about who oppose any change to the *status quo*:

> You would have hoped that the scale of the housing crisis, the scale of the knock-on implications that it had for the country and for society in general that it would have enabled people to say we really need to do something significant and substantial here. The introduction of the vacant site levy is an improvement in that regard but it is a shame that we never implemented the spirit of Kenny.

Labour Senator Marie Sherlock said it is important not to underestimate the scale of the opposition within the centre right parties of Fianna Fail and Fine Gael to the proposals within the Kenny Report and just as importantly the fear of the opposition that would be mobilized by farming groups and business were any attempt be made to implement its recommendations.

> The Kenny report has typically been viewed by such groups as akin to "appropriation" of land from private landowners and of course was to be resisted in any shape or form. [230]

Deputy Cian O'Callaghan agrees pointing to the closeness between mainstream political parties and developers and speculators:

---

[230] Interview with Senator Marie Sherlock, 2020

For several decades the relationship between mainstream political parties and large builders and developers was too close. This has been documented in the planning tribunal reports. Political donations and personal monetary gifts were given to some elected representatives in return for land re-zonings which conferred considerable wealth to individual landowners and land speculators.

Farming organisations have always opposed selling land at anything less than full market value, a principle that continues to the present day. In the negotiations following the February 2020 General Election, a report appeared in the *Farming Independent* on the 10th of March 2020 under the headline "Farmland price cap on coalition talks agenda" suggesting the principles of the Kenny Report might be dusted down and implemented. Immediately the farm lobby swung into action with the IFA issuing a press release headed: "IFA will oppose any land grab by the next government". The release quoted the new IFA President Tim Cullinan stating that any attempt to "take private property from the citizens and pay less than the market value will be strongly resisted by IFA, farm families and property owners".

This was followed by an editorial in *The Irish Farmers Journal* on the 25th of March 2020 which stated the plans to include a referendum to facilitate an artificial cap on the value of land had angered farmers. "The suggestion that land - unlike all other assets - could be acquired at below its market value should not be allowed pass under the radar," it added.

Lorcan Sirr argues that the Kenny Report, had it been implemented, would have affected the price people would have got for their land, would have thus precluded land speculation and for landowners who already held land with planning permission for increased value uses, it would have affected their wealth. "In fact," he said, "the effect on wealth/value is the prime reason it has never been implemented. Those with land of value, or potential value, are also a powerful lobby group."

Political reasons

Reluctance of political leaders and the power of pressure groups have emerged as key factors in suppressing the Kenny Report for several decades.

A majority of interviewees quoted in a Master's thesis by Stephen McDonagh cited a lack of leadership and powerful vested interests as the main contributing factors for the Kenny Report not being implemented. [231]

Campaigner Fr Peter McVerry has no doubt but the decision not to implement Kenny was due to "pure corruption" on the part of politicians.

> My view is that many people were going to make money out of the rezoning of their land. They were going to become millionaires. Not by doing a day's work, but by watching the grass growing on their field, which was about to be rezoned, and many of those landowners were friends of politicians and the politicians, basically I think were corrupt. I think we've seen a lot of corruption in the whole planning process and I think this was pure and simple corruption. If we had implemented that report housing today in Ireland would look very, very different...... The problem with our political system is that our politicians are people who play golf with and know a lot of developers, a lot of builders, a lot of people who own land, and I'm quite sure that a large part of the reason was that they were quite happy to see their friends making a lot of money out of this.

According to McVerry, the cost of up to 50% of housing can consist the cost of land. And if the Kenny report had been implemented, the cost of housing would have been stabilized and would not be able to reach the peaks that it has in the decades since the Kenny Report.

According to property expert Frank Ryan the risk with politics and housing is the desire in politics for short-term or immediate dividends which collides with a complex system that is slow, long-term and dependent on continuity. He also points out that leadership is required in ancillary institutions, in the market suppliers and in the lobby groups. "Strong leadership in any of these organisations can influence politics and distort policy", he said.

---

[231] McDonagh, S. (2018) *Better Land Use Management: Evaluation the Appropriateness of the Kenny Report for 2018.* Unpublished MSc thesis in Dept. of Real Estate, TU Dublin. P.66

According to Ryan, no action followed the Kenny Report "primarily for political and leadership lethargy reasons". While there were suggestions of potential legal difficulties, the objective of the common good and a balanced housing objective suggest "there is a sound constitutional support for policy away from a market system."

While the Labour Party had always favoured the implementation of the Kenny Report, when in government, they were always very much the minority partner and issues had to be prioritised. Former General Secretary, the late Brendan Halligan believed the plethora of problems that beset the 1973 National Coalition problem, notably the Northern Troubles, were a major constraint. "If it hadn't been for the North, it would have been implemented," he told this writer. "I think so. But I can't prove that any more than anybody else."

Senator Marie Sherlock says that for the Labour Party, the context for the negotiations for the programme for government since the 1980's has also been extremely important. Mass unemployment was the single greatest challenge for each of the periods that Labour entered Government. In 1981, it was just above 6% but was on course to rapidly doubling within two years. In 1993 it was 15.7% and in 2011 it was 14.5%. "The mission to afford people a dignified and decent livelihood set the context for the prioritisation of resources and energies in the programme for government negotiations."

However, she added:

> The recommendations of the Kenny report are even more relevant today than when it was first published, both for local authorities and for development of housing. The experience of the last 30 years of development in Ireland has demonstrated what happens in the absence of a co-ordinated approach to land management in this country. However, it would be a mistake to believe that the Kenny report is panacea to the State's housing problems. Its full potential could only be realised in tandem with significant changes to the decision-making powers for local authorities and their capacity to access finance.

Former Labour Party General Secretary Mike Allen believes failure to implement the Kenny Report is felt internally in the Labour Party.

When the party is in opposition, motions get passed and probably exaggerate claims are made of what can be achieved and then they go into government and nothing happens. There is a failure to explain even to itself. The minister who did not do it should explain why and then forget about it and move on to something else. At this stage to hang onto a notion, or a fundamental idea and rather than make the case for that idea - we are going back now to an almost mythical report - in terms of getting this done you would be better to make the case afresh as opposed to try to implement a report that is very old. It is better now to take it out of the row over the majority and minority reports and let's look at the issue.

Aidan Culhane, who advised a number of Labour housing ministers says each housing crisis has had its own particular character. For example, the 2011 government faced a housing crisis largely focused on unfinished housing estates, negative equity, and so on. There was oversupply of housing everywhere.

Similarly, 1992 was a relatively benign housing environment in terms of house prices and availability. I imagine - though I can't be sure - that this has been why the matter hasn't been pushed. At the time of the 2011 negotiations, the windfall tax was in place and most of the "profiteers" were bankrupt. I guess it is subject to the same immediacy issues that beleaguer programmes for governments. Also, in this context, I would assume that the priority accorded to it, relative to the resistance from conservative parties/officialdom, has meant it hasn't been pushed.

The 2018 NESC Report concluded there were many reasons why the Kenny recommendations for active land management were not adapted at the time, or subsequently. At the time, it noted that housing affordability was promoted through extensive mortgage interest relief and substantial construction of social housing.

Indeed, even though these policy approaches were greatly reined back, there seems to have remained a faith, not supported by experience – or, indeed, by housing and urban economics – that speculative development of owner-occupied housing might deliver housing affordability and a sustainable pattern of urban development. Subsequently, there may also have been a lack of confidence that Ireland has an institution capable of undertaking the land development role. In addition, one tool of active land management internationally, credible powers of compulsory purchase, has not been seen as practical.[232] (NESC, 2018: 53).

Builder/developer Michael O'Flynn believes the Kenny Report failed because "it was a blunt instrument".

We are now in a situation where that failed and advantage has been taken of it since. For good or bad, the Kenny Report got rejected we now need to look at what is the right solution. How do we fix that without breaching the Constitution and being so complicated that it goes on forever......We have to figure out where do we need development, what quantum do we need, what house types do we need and we must then zone enough land to fit those requirements. Zoning in places where it is not wanted puts more pressure on places where it is wanted. We have plenty of land zoned but we don't have enough land zoned where land is needed.

O'Flynn argued the reason governments are not fixing the housing thing is because "it is too complicated".

They'd love to say the figures are coming right because they know by the time the election comes nothing will have happened anyway to prove them right or wrong. They throw the ball up in the air and that is all they are doing. There is nothing concrete being done to say this thing is going to come right. It's not coming right and in fact it is getting worse. I have always said until it affects jobs it won't get fixed.

He also blamed the Irish political system as a large part of the problem.

---

[232] National Economic & Social Council (2018) *Urban Development Land, Housing and Infrastructure: Fixing Ireland's Broken System* (No 145 2018). P.53

No minister or politician should be in government for more than 10 years. The current system enables politicians or even dictates them to do nothing because they always think about one thing, re-election. They are totally and utterly obsessed with re-election. If you know you are out in 10 years, you can do things. You can't have the same people involved forever. The structure of politics is flawed. People would also be slower going in if it was not a lifetime job and you need people with experience, people with gey hair - or no hair!

Councillor Dermot Lacey said the policy of successive governments over the years allowed housing to move from being a home to being a commodity.

Then it moved into the marketplace. And then in the early 80s, the Department of Local Government placed far more reliance on building housing through the private sector, than in local authorities. And it's not that I believe we only need local authority houses, we need both. But what happened was that the supply of housing to local councils that used to come through the local government sector dried up totally, so that the houses that used to be previously available for people who were going to buy their own house were sucked away from them. So, the waiting list and the value and the price for houses shot up.

Lacey is a long-time critic of the now Department of Housing, Local Government & Heritage through all its name changes.

I have absolutely no doubt that they have an agenda, which is to remove local councils away from house-building. They want to move the housing supply into the private sector. And that was aided and abetted by a Fianna Fáil party that was heavily linked to the building sector during the 80s and 90s, and a Fine Gael party which is quite ideologically hostile to the building of local authority houses. So, you had a perfect storm. Politically it suited the party in government, to protect the building sector. Ideologically Fine Gael was not going to oppose it. And on top of that, the department which wanted to take responsibility for delivering housing off its workload was happy to see that happening..... He who pays the piper calls the tune. And not alone does the Department call the tune, but they write the music, they control the copyright, and they insist on when it can be played.

Fr Peter McVerry also believes there is an ideology that the private sector should provide housing and the private sector should offer accommodation to low-income people with a subsidy like the HAP payment from the government. "I think there's an ideological bias against local authorities owning and controlling their own property," he argued.

He feels there is a huge reluctance to go down the route of local authorities building houses but he believes it is the only route out of a housing crisis.

> Most people on low incomes do not want to move into the private rented sector because they don't have any security there. They want housing that is owned and controlled by government, either through the local authority or through approved housing bodies. And I think we have got to go back to providing that. In 1975 this country built 8,500 council houses, in 1985 and we were in a recession so we didn't have a lot of money we still built 6,900 council houses. In 2015 we built 75 council houses. A big jump in 2016 to about 250 and it has been increasing since. But it's still far too slow and far too inadequate a pace..... I find it very hard to be optimistic until we have a commitment to going back to building social housing on a large scale. I am not optimistic.

According to Frank Ryan, any policy change must deliver an adequate supply of land at a price that is complimentary, and proportional to a balanced/viable housing supply for all sectors. In summary for market prudential purposes, any policy must achieve the following objectives:

- Pay the land owner sufficient compensation to comfortably dislodge the current use of the lands and cater for its relocation and disturbance
- If the land owner is to be paid, in addition, some dividend for the zoning/development potential, it should relate to the specific user type of housing envisaged for the land (the current bland residential zoning approach defeats this purpose.
- The development value payment at (2) should only arise – and be paid – at the time of the completion and sale of each house.

Chapter 15

Compulsory Purchase, the Constitution and Vested Interests

Compulsory Purchase

The basic rules of compensation in Ireland have not changed in over 100 years. The current law emanates from many different pieces of legislation and different rules apply depending on the type of compulsory purchase order (CPO) involved, whether for electricity, railways, roads or other matters. In addition, much of the relevant legislation predates the foundation of the State, including the Lands Clauses Consolidation Act 1845, the Railways Clauses Consolidation Act 1845 and the Acquisition of Land (Assessment of Compensation) Act 1919.[233]

The Kenny Report analysed them and came up with its own unique set of recommendations. This approach was re-iterated to a large extent in the 2004 Ninth Progress Report of the All-Party Oireachtas Committee on the Constitution.

According to Hibernia REIT founder, Dr Bill Nowlan, compulsory purchase has been badly administered but it need not be as bad as it is made out to be. "That is due to bad management and bad administration," he said. "Most people don't actually go the full route to the court. The building of the motorways up and down the country is an example of how the CPO process was well managed by the NRA. But once you let the politicians get involved in the process you get derailed." The 2004 NESC Report recommended that local authorities use their compulsory powers to acquire lands before they are zoned for residential development. Such an approach seems long overdue.

Such a measure to give the LDA compulsory powers was contained in a new Bill brought before Cabinet in July 2020 by the new Minister for Housing Darragh O'Brien. But he indicated that there was sufficient public land

---

[233] https://www.lawreform.ie/press-room/6-family-law.429.html

available for the present at any rate. "We have enough land ourselves initially".[234] This was strongly disputed, however, by builder/developer Michael O'Flynn in an Irish Times article on the 3rd of July 2020 where he stated: "We should develop a strategy to deliver land that is both zoned and services for home-building. Notwithstanding the views of those who are on the frontline, there is, in fact, a shortage of such available land.

According to Planning Regulator Niall Cussen, there is a sense that the LDA should have powers to compel, or resolve, land ownership issues.

> Take the example of where the LDA was tasked by government to develop a major State land bank and say, access to it was, was blocked because of a ransom strip and there was no mechanism whereby the LDA could CPO that to sort that out. Access to CPO powers by the LDA to deal with obstacles to bringing lands that come within its remit into production would seem reasonable.

On the other hand, Cussen pointed out that a very wide-ranging power or scope for the LDA to buy just about anything anywhere, may give rise to the concerns about having an unfair advantage in the market place for land.

> CPO legislation is something of a "policy Cinderella" where it has no clear Departmental "owner" and because of the vastness of the consolidation and reform project that would be bringing CPO legislation into the 21st century, it is no surprise that the issue has been somewhat long-fingered.

In March 2023 proposals to speed up, clarify and improve the fairness of the system for the compulsory purchase of private land were published by the Law Reform Commission.[235]

A new system that would involve deadlines for authorities that have been granted an order to compulsory purchase land was proposed as was an immediate payment of no less than 90 per cent of the estimated value of the land to the owner, with the payment to be made when the land is vested in the acquiring authority.

---

[234] *Business Post, 26 July 2020*
[235] https://publications.lawreform.ie/Portal/External/en-GB/RecordView/Index/62559

In the report, the Commission noted that its recommendations were focused on the law in relation to compulsory acquisition rather than on policy issues. "Nonetheless, the consolidation and reform proposals in this report would, in the commission's view, streamline the use of compulsory purchase to achieve public policy objectives in general," it stated.

The report dealt solely with the issue of what happens after a compulsory acquisition order has become operative. The steps up to the making of an order are not covered by the report as they were the subject of a Government Bill. The Commission recommended the replacement of the current "notice to treat" system, whereby a landowner is instructed to deal with an authority in relation to the ordered acquisition of land, with a "vesting order" procedure, where the steps involved in the ownership of the land being vested in the new owner are laid out and include timelines and rules in relation to early compensation.

Under the proposed scheme, the acquiring authority would have a year within which it has to decide if it is going to proceed with an order it has been granted. This would replace the current situation where landowners can have a potential compulsory purchase order hanging over them for an extended period. Under the new proposal, if the authority did not serve a vesting order on the landowner within a year, then the compulsory purchase order would lapse. An owner would be given at least three months' notice before an authority proceeds with an acquisition, and the vesting order has to be effected within six months from the date it is served.

Under the existing system, an acquiring authority does not get ownership until compensation is agreed and determined, and the owner proves their title. Under the proposed new system, ownership would be vested in the acquiring authority regardless of any title complications that might exist.

The Commission proposed that a payment of not less than 90 per cent of the value of the land would be given to the owner at the time of the vesting of ownership in the acquiring authority, and that a new, more transparent system be put in place for resolving subsequent disputes over valuations. At the moment a landowner can be waiting years for payment if the valuation of the land is disputed.

The Commission also proposed that the Valuation Tribunal, which currently deals with valuations of property for the purposes of levying rates, be charged with resolving disputes over valuations in compulsory acquisitions, with reasoned decisions to be published on its website to increase transparency and aid consistency. Currently there are about 50-100 requests every year for disputes to go to an arbitration hearing, with many being settled before the hearing takes place.

The Commission did not consider whether the law should provide for the assessment of land at a value below market value. "The question of whether a social good should be achieved by way of obliging owners to sell their property to the State at below market value... is a question of policy more properly addressed by the executive and the legislature," the report stated. It did not express a view but did recommend that policymakers consider the idea that people who are displaced from their homes by way of compulsory purchase orders be given an additional payment over and above the value of the property involved.

The Constitution

'It can't be done; the Attorney General has advised it may be unconstitutional,' is quite a familiar refrain in Irish political discourse for shutting down further discussion on an issue in need of resolution.

There is now little, if any doubt among lawyers, but that the recommendations of the Kenny Report were not repugnant to the Irish Constitution. According to Dr Rachel Walsh of Trinity College, for a period after the introduction of the 1963 planning legislation and indeed into the 1970s people struggled with understanding planning as anything other than a restriction of property rights but over time they came to appreciate free power to develop land as you see fit is not in any way a natural feature of anybody's rights in respect of land. With the benefit of hindsight, it is relatively easy to see how the Kenny Report was controversial because planning law was a much newer feature of the legislative landscape.

> Planning is an aspect of social policy to be worked out in balancing rights in the public interest and the Constitution absolutely provides for that. It says that the State can delimit the exercise of property rights to secure social justice in the common good. As I would see it, it was always abundantly clear that planning law was very much at the centre of securing the common good and social

194

justice, so restrictions imposed on property rights, provided they
are reasonable and proportionate, are legitimate.

Barrister and former legal advisor Charles Lysaght has pointed out that it would
seem that the constitutional issue was often used purely as an excuse for lack of
action although the very cautious approach by successive attorneys general
gave such objectors a level of political cover. Writing in the *Sunday
Independent* on the 17th of January 2021 he stated: "Ultimately, responsibility
for legislation rests with the Taoiseach and other ministers. If they are
convinced that a particular item of legislation would be in the public interest,
they should not be inhibited by doubts whether it is constitutional. They should
leave that to the courts that, alone, have the authority to give definitive rulings
on the Constitution. There is provision in the Constitution itself for referring
bills to the Supreme Court to rule on their constitutionality.

In cases where there is genuine doubt, that is the proper way to proceed."

ESRI economist Kieran McQuinn is one of the many people sceptical of
such objections.

> I worked in the Central Bank and I did a lot of work on mortgage
> arrears and we heard a lot of talk about constitutional rights. I
> was always sceptical about that. Change the law if needs be.
> These things are thrown around as a reason not to do things and
> very often if we hold them up to scrutiny, they do not stand up.
> It seems logical that at some point an end needs to be brought to
> this confusion which inevitably will result in yet more cases
> being tested in the higher courts, or future attorneys general
> being reluctant to approve draft legislation as has happened
> heretofore.

Sinn Fein Deputy Eoin Ó Broin says because something may be constitutionally
problematic is not a reason for not doing it. "Sometimes forcing the matter into
the courts is a way of resolving something that would otherwise be left undone."

Writing in *thejournal.ie* in December 2019 David Kenny, Assistant
Professor of Law at Trinity College, wrote that the potency of property rights
in the Constitution is often exaggerated. The courts, he said, particularly in
recent decades, have given the Oireachtas a lot of leeway in restricting
property rights in the common good.

Courts give deference to legislative judgement on what is needed to achieve the common good, as the Oireachtas has particular expertise and a unique perspective on the needs of social justice.... When assessing if a restriction on property rights is unconstitutional, the courts apply a proportionality test: they assess if the benefit of the law in advancing the common good is outweighed by the harm to personal rights. In assessing this, context is king: the courts have to consider the particular objectives of the law and the current social problems it is designed to address.

Vested Interests

It has been widely argued that the dismissal of the Kenny Report was due to vested parties protecting their own interests along with political cowardice. There was an onslaught of objections from vested interests to the implementation of the Report when the National Coalition Government sought submissions in the wake of its publication in 1973. Apart from the reservations by the Department's own legal advisor, there were strenuous objections from the farming organisations, the Incorporated Law Society, the Royal Institute of Chartered Surveyors (RICS), building, auctioneering and other professional bodies.

Developers and farmers have always been fiercely opposed to selling land at anything less than market value. We have already seen how farmers objected during the discussion on a Programme for Government in the aftermath of the February 2020 general election. These concerns have also been raised by farmer representatives on NESC.

> The members of the farming pilar entered reservation on some of the policy ideas in the report, particularly around their potential impact on the property rights of citizens and have conveyed these to the rest of the Council. [236]

The introduction of a plethora of ethics legislation following the Tribunals of Enquiry has at least provided a level of transparency to lobbying by these

---

[236] National Economic & Social Council (2004) *Housing in Ireland: Performance and Policy* (No. 112 2004). NESC. Dublin V.

vested interests. Under the terms of the Regulation of Lobbying Act, 2015, all lobbyists must enter a record of lobbying activities on the lobbying.ie register three times each year.

As pointed out earlier, politicians very often hid under the excuse of conservative court rulings to explain their lack of action.

Corruption

A particular feature of Irish society has been the almost total lack of any social sanctions and stigma against entrepreneurs and other private agents involved in corruption, or people who make vast profits at the expense of the wider community. While the widespread speculation on land was not, and is still not illegal, in the past the vast profits that could be made led to corruption of politicians and officials resulting in the Tribunals of Enquiry. In fact, until the 1990s following a number of Tribunals of Investigation, virtually no ani-corruption legislation existed. Making enormous profits through pure land speculation for residential housing, is intrinsically undemocratic because it seeks to bestow unfair and unjust advantage to the few which is contrary to the beliefs in liberty, equality and fraternity. Barrister and author Elaine Byrne wrote:

> The courage to adhere to high standards of probity is eroded when the definition of public interest is distorted by those who that seek to promote the interests of vested individuals. This perception of corruption within political leadership ultimately reduces loyalty towards a sense of state by its citizens.[237]

Change of Approach

In its 2018 Report, NESC concluded that the dramatic experience of boom, bust and prolonged stasis makes it clear that the problem with the housing system is largely systemic. According to the Report, it is a mistake to see the post-recession shortage crisis as simply a legacy of the crash, which, as it fades, would yield a return to 'normality'.

---

[237] Byrne, E. (2012) *Political Corruption in Ireland 1922-2010: A crooked harp?* Manchester University Press. P. 238

It is the system that shapes the interaction of the different elements and actors. Dysfunctional patterns, interactions and outcomes are hard-wired into our approach. Without a change in the system, we are condemned to an endless sequence of isolated measures. Reforms should be based on a coherent, evidenced-based view of what an effective and inclusive system of urban development, land management and housing affordability looks like.

According to NESC, international experience suggests that cost-rental is the most effective and fiscally sustainable way of achieving permanent affordability. As regards, land use, NESC argued that it is vital that the land be put in the hands of actors who will develop it in a timely and appropriate manner, rather than seeking to maximise state revenue by selling it outright, without regard to when and how the land will be developed. This, it stated, would constitute a change from the approach adopted by many public bodies, including NAMA.

Restating this aim from the 2018 Report, the NESC 2020 Report noted such an approach is implied in both the National Planning Framework (NPF) and the National Development Plan (NDP) and many of the elements for achieving it are touched on in these documents.

However, system change necessitates not only recognition and articulation of need, but overt articulation of the method to deliver on it. There must be a follow-through from accepted principles to explicit supporting actions…. The Council has highlighted the need for public institutions with a strong developmental mandate to have the political authorisation and executive capacity to take the necessary action and drive sustainable urban development, including the increased provision of affordable housing.

The NESC Report added that the legislation establishing the LDA on a statutory footing presented an opportunity to ensure it has the required ambition, mandate and power.

The "right actors" in the mind of Labour Councillor Dermot Lacey are without doubt the local authorities. Here, he favours the Labour Party notion of councils grouping together and sharing resources.

198

The challenge to tackle our housing problem can only be resolved at council-wide level or national level. And I think, in fact, the proposal in the Labour Party manifesto to group local authorities together so that they could share resources, such as architects and quantity surveyors and so on was not a bad compromise between those who believe there is only the State that can do it and those people who believe only the local councils can do it.

Property journalist Donal Buckley believes there is now some certainty as to height and densities that will be allowed in cities which should provide some stability in the price of development land. But he sees the need for a new approach, much of which will depend on the operation of the Land Development Agency.

The State needs a whole approach to planning and joining up the dots in terms of its own land and in terms of urban development to encourage the provision of housing within urban areas. I think it is sad to see so much agricultural land, particularly in fertile counties like Meath and North Dublin being diverted into housing, particularly low-density housing. More development needs to focus closer to rail and bus stations to ensure that there is a better use of it.[238]

In addition, as Dr William Nowlan has argued the proposed Dutch Partnership Model has the potential to significantly increase supply and achieve economies of scale in housing delivery. Separately, he said the Vienna Cost-Rental Model for supplying affordable rental homes to key workers by non-governmental agencies is compatible with the Dutch Partnership Model and both models are readily achievable in Ireland given governmental supports. The Vienna Model, he said, relies on funding supplied by capital markets and which would also be available in Ireland. Such support structures, he said, would cost the taxpayer very little and, in any case, significantly less than the billions the current Housing Assistance Programme and RAS type leasing systems are costing the Exchequer.

---

[238] Interview with Donal Buckley, 2019

It could be argued that Minister Robert Molloy appointed the Committee on Building Land to merely kick a thorny issue down the road (a well-known political method of avoiding making a decision), or to seek a viable solution. The evidence points to the latter but from his own comments in various Dáil debates, it would appear that he was himself not in favour of the final report. That so much time and effort was put into something which was effectively shelved is not something new in Irish politics. What is striking is the vehemence of the opposition to it, both from within the commissioning department and from the vested interests. This opposition has continued to this day.

Chapter 16

Conclusions

Report still relevant

Judge John Kenny was known to be extremely disappointed at the manner in which successive governments during his lifetime treated the report into which he committed so much time and effort. According to the Cambridge Dictionary of Irish Biography, the Kenny Report was "a model of its kind" but the failure on the part of successive governments to implement it – in which he had invested so much energy and so many resources – "always rankled with him."[239]

According to former Attorney General Dermot Gleeson, there is probably little doubt that the Kenny Report was constitutional but it almost certainly would have been challenged in court by the farming community had any government tried to implement it.

The arguments as to the failure to implement it and the reasons put forward on both sides are many and complex. Writing in *The Irish Times* in July 2018, Dermot O'Leary, chief economist with Goodbody, suggested one of the reasons perhaps was the benefits of implementing such a policy would not accrue to the minister that implemented them given the length of time such a policy takes for the results to be seen. Ministers, he said, are normally in need of quick fixes for problems. In housing there are few of these.[240]

Housing Minister Darragh O'Brien said the Kenny approach would be quite reliant on a strong role for the State in acquiring lands through compulsory purchase.

> Whether local authorities would have had the capacity to fund the level of CPO and interaction in the housing market which belies the Kenny approach is open to question when one considers the significant recessions and constrained public

---

[239] *Cambridge Dictionary of Irish Biography*, 2009. P.132
[240] *The Irish Times, 25 July 2018*

resourcing in periods following on from the Kenny Report.... The Kenny report is set in the context of housing delivery which was largely on greenfield development, and indeed the 1970s and 1980s probably marks the significant expansion of suburban Ireland. From the perspective of today, we know the impacts of urban sprawl on climate change and wellbeing, and are more acutely aware of the need to develop brownfield site. Therefore, our perspectives on land use much reflect this consideration. Our policy interventions need to reflect the particular challenges we face in this decade. For example, I believe that the approach in Part V of the Planning and Development Act 2000 through which social housing is provided as part of private development is an important shift in policy since the Kenny Report.

The Kenny Report was of its time and any judgement of its findings and recommendations must bear this in mind. For example, it very much reflected the relative paucity of legislation at the time, something that has been tackled in the intervening years, most notably with the Planning and Development Act, 2000.

Many of its concerns have now been overtaken by time but it is still remarkable how many of its recommendations continue to be relevant 50 years later and continue to feature in national housing debates. [241]

Planning Regulator Niall Cussen believed the fact that the Kenny report was not implemented in full denied Irish people a very interesting chapter on how any legislation on housing policy could be implemented in this country. By not implementing the Kenny report, he said the country fell back on a two-pronged approach with the State building housing for those that could not provide housing for themselves and leaving the market to provide all other housing - deciding when and where and how much it would charge for housing and cherry-picking the relevant lands for development and so on.

It would have certainly been an intriguing prospect to have seen Kenny implemented. Maybe it would have been subject to

[241] Interview with Minister Darragh O'Brien, 2021

legal challenge. Maybe that might have succeeded, maybe it might not have succeeded and we might be into a different situation than what prevails today. But I think the key thing was that we ended up moving from potentially a very public policy-driven approach to a developer-driven one to when and where housing would be delivered in our cities and towns and rural areas.[242]

Cussen believes the Kenny Report is still relevant today.

Planning objectives require effective land management mechanisms. Public policy-making that confers significant land and property value increases can sometimes create distortions in the achievement of long-term planning objectives....There are good examples in and around many of our cities of blocks of land that have been held for 30 years or more in high demand locations close to rail lines water services and roads and that instead of being developed, see their value increase every year. Land use zoning objectives confer a private advantage out of public policy that needs balancing mechanisms to ensure those public policy objectives are achieved.

As stated in the Introduction, the 2020 NESC Report stated that the core principle of the Kenny Report is as relevant today as it was 50 years ago.

The State must empower itself in the medium term to acquire land in designated development areas at existing use value plus some premium......The State must update the compulsory purchase process and implement a mechanism to capture betterment in order to control land costs and ensure affordable housing for future generations. These enhanced policy instruments would also have the potential to transform areas of major urban centres where land is sub-optimally used, thus contributing to the NPF goals of more compact and sustainable urban development.

---

[242] Interview with Niall Cussen, 2020

Dysfunctional system

The Irish housing system has not always been dysfunctional. Indeed, it is arguable that it functioned very effectively in the late 1950s and the early 1960s.

House building was one of the major success stories, for example, of the 1948-51 coalition government where the construction of local authority units jumped massively from 744 units in 1947 to 8,117 by 1950.

According to Dr Bill Nowlan, founder of Hibernia Reit and Urbeo Residential, the Irish Republic once had a "world class system".

> We were the envy of the British Empire and we blew it all for short-term political gain. We had a stock of 400,000 social housing and we blew it apart by two means, one was differential rents because that meant there was not sufficient rental income coming in to actually manage the portfolio and the second was by giving away the houses via tenant purchase which meant they just disappeared. [243] (Nowlan 2021)

According to Nowlan, there was a clear change in government housing policy.

> It encouraged owner-occupation and made it affordable through grants and subsidies, including tax concessions to depositors in building societies. It also provided enough new council housing to meet the real needs of those who could not afford to house themselves.

However, as Nowlan also pointed out, this policy was costly for the State in lost mortgage interest relief, rates relief, new council builds and direct cash grants to new home buyers. This approach clearly changed in the 1970s and later years when State capital was directed more towards new schools, hospitals and roads. This new policy of reduced spending on housing clearly led to a housing crisis when the economic recession of 2006 – 2011 hit.

According to Sinn Féin's Eoin Ó Broin, while governments never got it completely right, there was a period between the late 1940s and the mid-80s when the housing issue was handled much better. But then two fundamental issues happened. Firstly, the almost complete withdrawal of the State from

---

[243] Interview with Dr Bill Nowlan 2021

social housing from 7,000 or 8,000 in one year in the 80s to 700 in the following year. There was also a shift in council housing from being good quality housing for working people to what was often seen as welfare housing for the very poor.

> The second problem was what the academics call the "financialisation" of home ownership so there was a shift from local authority loans and grants and a small amount of building society loan finance to its replacement by high street bank finance. Those two policy drivers have since 1991 underpinned every government housing policy. They underpinned *Building Sustainable Communities* in 2007, Alan Kelly's *Social Housing Strategy 2014* and *Rebuilding Ireland.* They shifted responsibility for underpinning the supply of social housing to working people from the public sector to the private sector with all the social consequences we saw in the crash. It has also pushed ever increasing numbers of social housing tenants into the private rented sector who have to be subsidised by the State. So, while I don't think we can go back to the 60s and 70s, the notion of State support for affordable homes means there needs to be more build by local authorities. [244]

However, Housing Minister Darragh O'Brien (2020 -) said it was somewhat sweeping to suggest that policy was successful pre-1960s and unsuccessful thereafter.

> This period has been marked by different approaches to economic policy, periods of population growth and increased urbanisation, different economic cycles with particular impacts on migration patterns and on the availability of funding for public housing.... The period post mid-1960s' is characterised by the reversal of Ireland's economic fortunes, largely based on industrial and education policy.

> Ireland's population has increased by two-thirds or 2m people, from 3m to 5m people since then. Probably, the greatest levels of direct state intervention in housing were in the 1970's into the

---

[244] Interview with Eoin Ó Broin TD, 2019

1980's, while the period of greatest output in housing delivery was in the 2000's.

Public policy systems in Ireland do not generally appear robust enough to flatten out house prices and so, instead, there is a cycle of high house prices, people needing to borrow money to pay the higher prices which leads to over-heating in the market and inevitably a crash.

There is, however, already a large supply of vacant and derelict property in urban areas in Ireland which are very slow in development. The register of vacant land for the Dublin City Council area as of January 2020 showed a total of 380 vacant sites nationwide. Since the introduction of the new vacant site levy in January 2019 building had commenced on less than 80 sites by January 2020.[245]

The 2018 NESC Report noted that after the 2006 – 2011 recession much development land came under the control of NAMA but according to its 2016 Annual Report just 6% of land sold by NAMA had been built on. The CEO of NAMA highlighted land hoarding as a major problem. While housing figures have since improved the planning and development levy system continues to be a major impediment to increasing housing supply. Until real change is introduced to the system, there will be just minor shifts in various directions. Indeed, as has been frequently pointed out by various commentators in the past, one piece of government action often cancelled another.

NESC identified effective solutions to the provision of housing as a combination of:

- Active land management by highly skilled and respected public authorities
- Active urban development, including both planning and infrastructure
- Housing policies that focus on achieving permanent affordability, and
- The emergence of a building industry that has the organisations, financial and technical resources to work effectively within these approaches

---

[245] *The Irish Times, 13 January 2020*

Advocate for the homeless Fr Peter McVerry believes there is far too much bureaucracy which must be eliminated.

> There's a huge bureaucracy and actually in the 2020 Budget, there was a commitment to reducing that bureaucracy. And I thought that was the best thing in the Budget as I didn't think there was much else. There were no details and we haven't seen any of it since. But the local authorities do complain it can take three years from putting an application into the department to actually getting a shovel in the ground, which is ridiculous.

Social Democrats Deputy Cian O'Callaghan said the current situation where land can be zoned on an arbitrary basis by lobbying councillors can be disastrous in terms of leap-frogging, or housing estates popping up in areas which are not served by infrastructure.

> I have very direct experience from my 10 years as a councillor seeing how this diminishes quality of life, increases car dependency and congestion and pollution. The current delivery of Part V social housing where the state pays multiples of the build cost for a new social home makes no sense – when the state has conferred the value of the land by putting in infrastructure and re-zoning it.

According to Planning Regulator Niall Cussen, the Irish planning process would significantly benefit from the introduction of a mechanism that can tackle the issue of lands not coming forward for development that instead enable the local authority to bring them into production.

> I think it is fair to say that given everything we know now about the importance of planning, in terms of creating sustainable communities and all its many laudable objectives, addressing climate change, delivering housing, I think we're well past the point where the planning system could be very substantially and beneficially bolstered by land management and acquisition measures.

Also as pointed out by Frank Ryan, the Department of Finance has no direct interest in housing, or housing policy - as a net funding flow to government finances. Outside of the Taoiseach, it is the strongest element of government and apart from external monitoring and analysis, it is not a participator in dialogue on housing with market suppliers. It is clearly the case that a more direct involvement of the Department in the drafting and implementation of housing policy would be beneficial.

Inconsistent land supply

From previous analysis in this book, it is clear that uncertainty and inconsistency of a sustainable land supply is one of the key factors in shaping the practices of the property market and those who work in it. As pointed out previously, the biggest risk undertaken by developers is the purchase of land. If the developers and builders are to maintain continuity and sustainability, they need to be sure of ongoing supply of suitable land. The prices they can pay depends on the price they expect to be able to charge for the finished houses, less the construction costs, development levies and a profit margin. As margins can often be tight, a sudden drop in house prices can see the developer go out of business and large amounts of land lie undeveloped.

According to the 2020 NESC Report one reason why construction is an underused delivery mechanism for social housing is access to land for social housing. This, it said, applies particularly to AHBs.

> Borrowing money to acquire land for social housing is a risky proposition, as is the case for private development. The availability of land suitable for social housing varies by local authorities. Some local authorities have land but are not able to use it for social housing on account of the high debts on the land. There is a need for a scheme to alleviate local authority land debt that is constraining social housing output. Under the EU fiscal rules, the repayment of debt by government does not count as government expenditure, or add to the deficit but is treated as a financial transaction.[246]

Rebuilding Ireland pointed out that access to land at a reasonable price remained a key barrier for developers:

---

[246] National Economic & Social Council (2020) *Housing Policy: Actions to Deliver Change* (No 150 2020). NESC Dublin. P.42

As this Plan has been developed, a consistent message that has come through from many local authorities, housing providers and funders is that one of the best ways to ensure availability of reasonably priced housing is ensuring that there is a good supply of "ready-to-go" development land that is available at a cost that reflects the realistic value of what can be developed on those lands, taking account of all the usual input costs. Despite a large reserve of zoned land across all our planning authorities, not all of that land would appear to be readily available to the broad range of housing providers. It is often reported that landowners may not sell their lands to housing providers until prices match their expectations, regardless of what may be a realistic land price in terms of the overall price of housing that it is economically viable to provide on those lands.[247]

According to Kieran McQuinn the cost of land is still probably the main reason that is inhibiting supply. If there are to be changes, they have to be on the supply side, notably in reducing inputs such as the cost of land. The Kenny Report tried to provide a solution by allowing local authorities a means of acquiring and providing a stable supply of development land.

Today the need to acquire private land is not as urgent as in the 1970s. According to the 2018 NESC Report, there was then at least 1,900 hectares of state-owned land (made up of 1,700 hectares owned by local authorities and the Housing Agency along with 200 hectares in the ownership of state and semi-state bodies). This has the potential to provide at least 50,000 housing units. However, it is clear that it could take a considerable period of time to get these lands developed. Publicly-owned sites now have a central role in addressing the housing crisis and starting the transition to a new system of active land management and urban development, according to the report.

Property journalist Donal Buckley said developers still largely purchase land on a speculating basis. He gave as an example, the sale of a 188-acre farm next to Ashbourne town, Co. Meath in 2019 for between four and a half and €5 million, or about €25,000 per acre. Only 25 acres was zoned and that was for amenity and not for residential development, but effectively the price was about double the price of agricultural land. "So, obviously, the investors

---

[247] *Rebuilding Ireland* (2016) Action Plan for Housing and Homelessness. Government of Ireland.

bought it in the prospect that this would be developed at some future date so effectively the hope value of that land was double the agricultural value of the land," he concluded.

Builder/developer Michael O'Flynn, however, questioned the notion of the viability of such an approach to state and semi-state bodies.

> They are now busy doing an audit of everything around the country but I have met no State body yet to say they have surplus land that they don't need. They all have their own plans.

> How long would it take them to move from A to B and start compensation and all that goes with it. Brownfield development is not viable. Brownfield development is expensive development. There are an awful lot of extra costs with brownfield development.

Councillor Dermot Lacey believed that as land is finite, its development must be carefully managed.

> We have to use land properly, and people who own the land, have an entitlement to get some value for their land, but they don't have an entitlement, in my view, to get extortionist rates because the lands have been rezoned. They are entitled to a fair payment, plus a little bit of extra compensation and I think by and large Kenny got it right. And the sooner a new government implements it, the better.

Direct procurement on public land, is critical for the future of housing in Ireland according to Dr Lorcan Sirr. "Half the price, twice the number of houses, control of what goes where along with oversight of standards. Some of this housing for social uses, some for affordable sale. In cities, develop a cost-rental model, based on average rent of €700 per month. It can be done. The cost of construction is a red herring in narratives around why housing has to be so expensive. Unit ceiling costs from local authorities shows just how cheaply good housing and apartments can be delivered," he said.

Housing Minister Darragh O'Brien agreed that development land is a key factor and the aforementioned NESC report highlights the role it plays in the housing market.

There is an important role for local authorities and the State in ensuring that sufficient land is zoned and serviced to meet our development needs. Obviously, the planning system is the key means of ensuring this and a number of measures have been put in place to move to a plan-led rather than developer-led approach. Critically, *Project Ireland 2040* now ensures that our National Planning Framework and National Development Plan act in concert, to ensure that investment is spatially aligned. This underpins the type of active land management which NESC has promoted over a number of years.

Price breakdown and a Land Price Register

Developer Michael O'Flynn recalled that when he first built houses in the late 1970s, the land element was never more than 10pc of the cost of a house. The house had 3pc VAT not 13.5 pc as now.

> You did not carry the funding cost as land was bought subject to planning and it was bought in phases. But there was a bit of certainty around it as well that if you bought zoned land, you would get planning and it would take a certain amount of time. But now planning takes forever. Every time you add time onto planning you are adding cost. People don't fully realise that because when you buy a house, you just want an overall price not the constituent costs.

Given the confusion as to exact make-up of costs of a new housing unit, there is clearly merit in the suggestion that the price of a house should be broken down and the constituent parts clearly identified, including the land element and VAT. The Society of Chartered Surveyors Ireland (SCSI) carried out studies on the cost of delivering three-bedroom semi-detached houses in the Greater Dublin Area in 2016 and 2020.

In 2016, their "Real Cost of New House Delivery" research reported that it cost €330,000 to deliver a three-bedroom semi-detached home to the market. Four years on in 2020, their research showed that this delivery cost had increased to €371,000 which is an increase of €40,818, or 12%. The so-called "soft costs" – land, development levies, professional fees, VAT and developers' margin – increased by seven per cent or €12,000. Land and acquisition costs of €61,000 (16%), VAT of €44,000 and a developers' margin of €44,000 made up the main elements of soft costs, underscoring the argument that high land values are a key driver of property prices even though in this instance the figure of 16% was at the lower end of the scale.

However, in figures obtained from the Department of Housing, Local Government and Heritage in September 2020 by Orla Hegarty of UCD, it was shown that local authorities can build homes for considerably less than they are paying private developers for social housing.

Writing in *The Irish Times,* she said when procured directly by local councils, the "all in" cost for a typical three-bedroom house was on average less than €300,000 and in some areas less than €250,000. "Where land is available, actual construction, de-risked from speculative markets and high-cost finance, is affordable.....If you want to build affordable housing in Ireland, how you go about it is really important. What we've got at the moment is a system whereby we rely very heavily on developers, which is just one way of buying housing and their way of building housing is largely to do with maximising the land value."

The SCSI report highlighted that the cost saving differential in the delivery of private housing compared to social housing can be within a range of €140,000-€160,000 due to the nil cost attributed to land, levies, finance, developer's margin and sales and marketing costs. A lack of available data for the cost of land for housing is an issue that was identified in the report.[248]

If any government is serious about tackling the housing crisis and building the 30,000 to 35,000 homes which are required in the early 2020s, it is clear that it needs to tackle the significant increases which have occurred in housing delivery costs as a matter of urgency. One of the obvious ways of assessing the importance of the price of development would be the creation of a land sales' register which formed one of the recommendations in the SCSI report. Lack of information on land prices was one of the issues that bedevilled the work of Judge Kenny in the early 1970s and the problem still continues. Said Dr Lorcan Sirr of TU Dublin:

> A database of land prices would help us understand and assess
> the importance of location, revealing the relationship between
> urban and rural locations - and where the two meet is often the

---

[248] https://www.scsi.ie/documents/get_lob?id=1551&field=file

most interesting and important - and across regions. A land price register would also allow governments to make better and more efficient land use allocation decisions, deciding what land should be used for and where.

Given all this, it is astounding that we have to rely on second and third-hand information on land prices, often provided by the market itself.

Many countries around the world already have such a database, often tied in with a *cadastre* system of land registration. A *cadastre* is an up-to-date legal record of all documentation for a parcel of land, including a parcel identifier and boundaries. Italy, Japan, Germany and Spain are just some examples.

The EU's statistics agency, Eurostat, produces land price data but at too high a scale to provide any meaningful geographical detail at local level. Here, Lorcan Sirr argued, a land price register should include not only the price of the land, but also its location, current use and any planning permission it has.

More informed decisions can be made when there is more information. For example, in housing, there are three main components that determine the final purchase price. These are the hard and soft costs of construction, the price paid for the land and the developer's profit. We know the first component as local authorities and others have been building houses and apartments on free land without any profit. From their figures, across the country, an average two-bedroom apartment or three-bedroomed house costs €250,000-270,000 including VAT to build. For housing built and sold by the private sector, if the cost of land was available on a public register, then knowing two of the three main elements of the sales price, we could determine the third. This would help us make sense of developer claims that apartments or houses cannot be built for less than €400,000, or whatever the claim of the day is (Sirr, 2020).

From 'Betterment' to 'Location Value'

The definition of "betterment" has caused problems in relation to the acquisition of development land over many decades. Attempts at its definition were attempted as far back as the Uthwatt Report in Britain in the 1940s which heavily influenced the thinking in the Kenny Report in the 1970s. A number of attempts have been made to define it and it was often intended to describe the increase in land value arising from the investment by the local authority in infrastructure such as roads, water and sewerage and sometimes to describe the increase in price brought about by all the economic and social forces, including planning decisions and actions.

In fact, it could be argued that the Kenny Report arose because when the Government introduced the Planning Act in 1963, it never attempted to resolve what they did not resolve in the UK what is loosely called the "compensation betterment" problem.

The 2018 NESC Report noted that in recent times the terms 'land value' and 'land value capture' are now used and these relate to the windfall profits that arise from the provision of services. However, as noted by the report, these terms also have caused some confusion and lacked total clarity. The NESC Report favoured the term 'locational value' and the use of such a term or similar, which would relate to windfall profits arising from zoning and the provision of services, should be introduced and given widespread usage.

The "Apostles of Inertia"

There is no question but the Kenny Report fell victim to being one of the projects that received lip service from successive governments, but with no clear intention to implement it.

In the words of former *Sunday Independent* political editor Joseph O'Malley: "Like draining the Shannon and a few other projects, the Kenny Report was lauded by successive taoisigh and ministers, all of whom seemed to have no intention whatever of implementing it."[249]

For the past 50 years, successive governments have played a political game with the Kenny Report, on the one hand acknowledging its merits and worthiness but at the same time, expressing worry about its constitutional

---

[249] Interview with Joseph O'Malley 2020

implications without ever taking the obvious step of introducing legislation and/or testing it in the courts.

Speaking at a seminar organised by the Institute of Professional Auctioneers & Valuers in Dublin on 7 November, 2019, economist David McWilliams claimed that inequality in Ireland is driven by land ownership and not by education. He said it was incumbent on society to look at the property industry and identify the problems where often just a handful of people benefitted. His advice to the estate agents was "to think a little bit more as a poet and less as an economist".

He quoted some lines from W.B Yeats' poem *The* Second Coming, written after the First World War:

Things fall apart; the centre cannot hold;

Mere anarchy is loosed upon the world,

The blood-dimmed tide is loosed, and everywhere

The ceremony of innocence is drowned;

The best lack all conviction, while the worst

Are full of passionate intensity.

After 50 years of debate, the merits of the 1973 Kenny Report continue to be debated. At time of writing, there have been 13 general elections and 14 governments since the report was published in 1973 and none has sought to implement it. Never was so much political commitment given to the implementation of something which was never actually implemented.

The Constitutional aspects having been finally laid to rest, the report's main recommendation that local authorities could acquire land at existing use value was finally vindicated in the Supreme Court decision on the 2000 Planning & Development Act.

Former Housing Minister Jan O'Sullivan believes the report still has relevance and should be implemented.

> Implementing it now would also provide the opportunity for Local Authorities to acquire land for the construction of state-led social and affordable housing on a planned basis and in conjunction with the targets in the *National Development*

Plan, Ireland 2040. Reform that included implementing the recommendations of the Kenny Report now, can put Ireland's future provision of homes in accordance with the needs of our current and projected population, on a secure footing.

Lorcan Sirr of TU Dublin strongly argues that there is no need for a referendum to bring in the Kenny Report's proposals. "We just need political leadership to get on with it. We have a Supreme Court to decide on its legality".

Former ministerial advisor Aidan Culhane believes the relevance of the Kenny Report today may be in spirit more than in letter. "The Land Development Agency is in the Kenny mode and could, if configured correctly, act to regulate the supply of land".

But as Judge Keane wrote:

> It is an unhappy fact, however, that there will always be ministers, legislators and civil servants who prefer leaving things as they are on the basis that this will cause them less trouble in the long run. And it is unfortunately the case that the tangled undergrowth of the constitutional provisions on private property has given the apostles of inertia a plausible excuse for their restful attitudes. [250]

---

[250] Keane, R. (1988) Property in the Constitution and the Courts. In De Valera's Constitution and Ours (Thomas Davis Lecture). Gill & Macmillan. Pp. 146 – 149

References

Books & Journals

Aalen, F.A. (1992). *Ireland. In C. Pooley (Ed.) Housing strategies in Europe 1880 – 1930* (pp 132 – 164). Leicester University Press.

An Foras Forbartha (1979) *An Examination of Land Transactions and Prices.* Government Publications Office, Dublin.

Bacon, P. (1998) *An Economic Assessment of Recent House Price Developments.* Government Publications Office.

Bacon, P. & MacCabe F. (1999) *The Housing Market: An Economic Review and Assessment.* Government Publications Office.

Bacon, P & MacCabe, F. (2000) *The Housing Market in Ireland: An Economic Evaluation of Trends & Prospects.* Government Publications Office. Dublin.

Baker, T.J. and O'Brien, L.M. (1979) *The Irish Housing System: A Critical Review.* Economic & Social Research Institute. Dublin.

Bannon, M.J. (2004) 'Forty years of Irish planning: An overview', Centre for Urban and Regional Studies. In *Journal of Irish Urban Studies,* Vol.3 (Issue 1), 2004. Centre for Urban and Regional Studies, Trinity College Dublin & the Faculty of the Built Environment, Dublin Institute of Technology, Bolton Street.

Bentley, D. (2017) *The Land Question: Fixing the Dysfunction at the root of the housing crisis.* Civitas. London.

Blackwell, J. (1988) *A Review of Housing Policy (National Social and Economic Council).* Government Publications Office. Dublin.

Breen, D. (1924). *My Fight for Irish Freedom.* Mercier Press.

Budget 2022 (2021) Department of Finance, Dublin

Byrne, E. (2012) *Political Corruption in Ireland 1922-2010: A crooked harp?* Manchester University Press.

Cahill, N. (2018) *International Approaches to Land Use, Housing and Urban Development.* NESC Dublin.

Collins, S. (1996) *The Cosgrave Legacy.* Blackwater Press. Dublin

Collins, S. & Meehan, C. (2020) *Saving the State: Fine Gael from Collins to Varadkar*. Gill Books

Connaughton, B. (2012) Minister and their Departments: Inside the 'Black Box' of the Public Policy Process. In *Governing Ireland: From Cabinet Government to Delegated Government* (O'Malley, E. & MacCarthaigh M. (eds) IPA. Dublin. pp. 61 – 87.

Cooney, J. (1999) *John Charles McQuaid, Ruler of the Catholic Church*. O'Brien Press.

Committee on the Price of Building Land (Kenny Report) (1973). The Stationery Office. Dublin.

Commission on Taxation, First Report, Direct Taxation (1982). The Stationery Office. Dublin.

Constitution of Ireland (1937) (Bunreacht Na hÉireann). Government Publications Office.

Cullen, P. (2002) *With A Little Help From My Friends: Planning Corruption in Ireland*. Gill and Macmillan.

Cunningham, G. (1963) Policy and Practice. *Administration*. 41. pp 229 – 38.

Daly, M. (1984). *A Social and Economic History 1860 – 1914*.

David, M. and Sutton, C. (2011) *Social Research: An Introduction*. Sage Publications.

Davies, B., Turner, E. & Snelling C. (2016) *German Model Homes? A Comparison of UK and German Housing Markets*. Institute of Public Policy Research. London.

Dean, H. (2005) *Social Policy*. Polity Press, MA, USA.

Denzin, N.K. & Lincoln, Y.S. (Eds) (2003). *Collecting and interpreting qualitative materials*. Thousand Oaks, CA: Sage

Dictionary of Irish Biography https://dib.cambridge.org/ Cambridge University Press

Dooley, T. (2004a). *Land Politics in Independent Ireland, 1923- 1948: The case for re-appraisal*. Irish Historical Studies, 34(134), 175 – 195.

Dooley, T. (2004b) *The Land for the People. The Land Question in Independent Ireland*. UCD Press.

Dunphy, R. (2005) *The Making of Fianna Fáil Power in Ireland, 1923 – 1948*. Oxford University Press.

Easton, D. (1965) *A Systems Analysis of Political Life*. John Wiley. New York

Edgeworth, B. (2007) 2007) *Rural Radicalism Restrained: The Irish Land Commission and the Courts* (1933 – 39), 42 Irish Jurist (N.S.) 1

Edmonds W. Alex & Kennedy, T. (2013) *An Applied Reference Guide to Research Designs*. London: Sage Publications.

Expert Committee on Compensation and Betterment (Uthwatt Committee) (1942) https://discovery.nationalarchives.gov.uk/details/r/C8776

Fahey, T. (2002) The Family Economy in the Development of Welfare Regimes: A Case Study. *In European Sociological Review*, Vol 18 No. 1. Oxford University Press.

Farrell, C. (2016) Kenny Report (1973) – Four Decades on the Shelf. *Policy.ie*

Ferris, T. (2015) Reflections on the Public Policy Process in Ireland in *Administration* Vol 62, No 4. IPA. pp 87 – 106

FitzGerald, G. (1998) The Irish Constitution in its historical context. In *Ireland's Evolving Constitution 1937 – 1997* (Murphy, T. & Twomey, P.M. eds). Oxford: Harte. Pp 29 – 40

Fraser, M. (1996). *John Bull's Other Homes. State Housing and British policy in Ireland, 1803 – 1922*. Liverpool University Press.

Friedrich, C. J. (1941) *Constitutional Government and Democracy: Theory and practice in Europe and America*. Little, Brown & Co. Boston.

Galligan, E. and McGrath, M. (2013) *Compulsory Purchase and Compensation in Ireland: Law and Practice*. Bloomsbury London.

Gaughan, J.A. (1992) *Alfred O'Rahilly. Part III Controversialist.* Kingdom Books.

Gwynn Morgan, D. (2012) Government and the Courts. In *Governing Ireland: From Cabinet Government to Delegated Government* (O'Malley, E. & MacCarthaigh M. eds) IPA. pp. 232 -233

Haffner, M., Hoekstra, J., Oxley, M & van der Heijden, H. (2009) *Bridging the Gap between Social and Market Rented Housing in Six European Countries?* IOS Press BV

Hall, P. (2014) *Good Cities, Better Lives: How Europe Discovered the Lost Art of Urbanism* Routledge. New York

Harvey, W.S. (2010) *Strategies for conducting elite interviews* qrj.sagepub.com

Hill, M. (1997) *The Public Policy Process*. Routledge. New York.

Hogan, G. (2009) 'Kenny, John Joseph' in *Dictionary of Irish Biography* (McGuire and Quinn eds). Royal Irish Academy and Cambridge University Press

Hogan, G.W., Whyte, G.F., Kenny, D.,Walsh, R. (2018) *Kelly: The Irish Constitution*. Bloomsbury

Holeywell, R. (2013) *Vienna Offers Affordable and Luxurious Accommodation* http://www.governing.com/topics/health-human-services/gov-affordable-luxurious-housing-in-vienna.html

Honohan, P. (1992) *Fiscal adjustments in Ireland in the 1980s. Economic and Social Review,* 23(3) 258 – 314

Horgan, J. (1986) *Labour: The Price of Power*. Gill and Macmillan. Dublin

Housing for All (2021) A new Housing Plan for Ireland. Government of Ireland

Housing, Town Planning Act, 1909 http://www.irishstatutebook.ie/eli/1909/act/44/enacted/en/html

Howlett, M., Ramesh M., Perl, A. (2009) *A Studying Public Policy: Policy Cycles & Policy Subsystems*. Oxford University Press.

Jenkins, W.I. (1978) *Policy Analysis: A Political and Organisational Perspective*. Martin Robinson London.

Jennings, R. (1980) *Land Transactions and Prices in the Dublin area 1974 – 1978*, An Foras Forbartha.

Jones, C. and Stephens, M. (2020) 'Challenge of capturing socially generated land values' In *Town and Planning Review* Vol 91 (6) p.621 - 642. Liverpool University Press

Jones, D. (2001) *Divisions within the Irish Government over land distribution policy, 1940 – 70*. Eire-Ireland, XXXVI, 83 – 109.

Keane, J.B. (1966) *The Field*. Mercier Press

Keane, R. (1983) *Land Use, Compensation and the Community*, 18 Irish Jurist (N.S.) 23

Keane, R. (1988) Property in the Constitution and the Courts. In *De Valera's Constitution and Ours* (Thomas Davis Lecture). Gill & Macmillan.

Kenna, P. (2006) *Housing Law and Policy in Ireland*. Clarus Press Ltd.

Kingdon, J.W. (2014) *Agendas, Alternatives and Public Policies*. Pearson Education Ltd.

Labour Party (2020) *Affordable Housing for All: Labour's Proposals for State-led Action to Fix the Housing System* www.labour.ie

Law Reform Commission (2017) *Compulsory Acquisition of Land*. (LRC IP13 – 2017). Law Reform Commission.

Lawson, J. (2009) '*European Housing Strategies, Financing Mechanisms and Outcomes*'. Conference Paper, OTB Research Institute for Housing, Urban and Mobility Studies, Delft. Delft University of Technology, The Netherlands.

Lee, J. (1989) *Ireland 1912 – 1985*. Cambridge University Press

Lindblom, C.E. (1979) Still Muddling, not yet through. *Public Administration Review*, 39. IPA.

Litton, F. (2012) An Overview of the Irish System of Government. In *Governing Ireland: From Cabinet Government to Delegated Government* (O'Malley, E. & MacCarthaigh M. eds) IPA. pp15 – 34.

Local Government (Planning and Development) Act, 1963 http://www.irishstatutebook.ie/eli/1963/act/28/enacted/en/html

Mac Cormaic, R. (2017) *The Supreme Court*. Penguin Ireland.

McDonagh, S. (2018) *Better Land Use Management: Evaluation the Appropriateness of the Kenny Report for 2018*. Unpublished MSc thesis in Dept. of Real Estate, TU Dublin

MacLaran, A. (2001) Middle-class Social Housing? Insanity or Progress? Dublin: *Economic and Social Trends*. (3) Dublin: Centre for Regional and Urban Studies, Trinity College.

MacLaran, A. (2003) *Making Space: Property Development and Urban Planning*. Arnold. London.

McGuire, J and Quinn, J. (2009) *Cambridge Dictionary of Irish Biography*. Cambridge University Press.

McVerry, P. (2019) *A Dose of Reality*. Redemptorist Communications. Dublin.

Malloy, R.P. (1986) Equating Human Rights and Property Rights – The Need for Moral Judgement in an Economic Analysis of Law and Social Policy. Ohio State Law Journal, Ohio State University. Vol 47, No 1 (1986), pp163 -177

Mansergh, N. (1934) *The Irish Fee State: Its Government and Politics.* George Allen & Unwin Ltd.

Mills & Reeve LLP (2010) The Uthwatt Report https://www.lexology.com/library/detail.aspx?g=468f4538-0bda-47b0-9c2a-1676acc185b0

Mullins, D. and Murie, A. (2006) *Housing Policy in the UK.* Palgrave macmillan

Murphy, G. (2010) Interest Groups in the Policy-Making Process. In *Politics in the Republic of Ireland.* (Coakley, J. & Gallagher, M. eds). Routledge, New York pp. 327 – 358.

National Economic & Social Council (2020) *Housing Policy: Actions to Deliver Change* (No 150 2020). NESC Dublin

National Economic & Social Council (2018) *Urban Development Land, Housing and Infrastructure: Fixing Ireland's Broken System* (No 145 2018). NESC. Dublin.

National Economic and Social Council (2015) *Ireland's Rental Sector: Pathways to Secure Occupancy and Affordable Supply* NESC (No. 141 2015). Dublin

National Economic and Social Council (2015) *Housing Supply and Land: Driving Public Action for the Common Good* (No. 142 2015) NESC. Dublin

National Economic and Social Council (2014) *Social Housing at the Crossroads: Possibilities for Investment, Provision and Cost Rental. (No 138 2014)* NESC Dublin

National Economic and Social Council (2014) *Home Ownership or Rental: What Road is Ireland on?* (No. 140 2014) NESC. Dublin

National Economic & Social Council (2004) *Housing in Ireland: Performance and Policy* (No. 112 2004). NESC. Dublin

Needham, B. (2012) *Institutions for Housing Supply* in Smith, S.J. (Ed.) *International Encyclopaedia of Housing and Home.* Elsevier, Amsterdam

Nolan, W. (2015) *The Migration Policy of the Irish Land Commission in County Meath: Theory and Practice, In: Crampsie, A. and Ludlow, F. (eds.), Meath History & Society: Interdisciplinary Essays on the History of an Irish County.* Dublin: Geography Publications.

Norris, M. (2016). *Property, Family and the Irish Welfare State.* Palgrave macmillan.

Norris, M. and Byrne, M. (2021) *The Political Economy of Housing in Ireland* in *The Oxford Handbook of Irish Politics* (Farrell D. and Hardiman, N. eds). Oxford University Press.

Ostrander S.A. (1993) Surely, you're not in this this just to be helpful. Access, rapport and interviews in three studies of elites. *Journal of Contemporary Ethnography* 22(1): 7 - 27

O'Brien, J.V. (1982). *Dear Dirty Dublin: A city in Distress, 1899 – 1916.*

Ó Tuathaigh, G. (1986) *Before the Famine 1798 – 1848.* Gill.

Pope John XXIII (1963) *Pacem in Terris* (Peace on Earth) http://www.vatican.va/content/john-xxiii/en/encyclicals/documents/hf_j-xxiii_enc_11041963_pacem.html

Planning and Development Act, 2000 http://www.irishstatutebook.ie/eli/2000/act/30/enacted/en/html

Portéir, Cathal (1995) *The Great Irish Famine.* Mercier Press.

Priemus, H. & Louw, E. (2003) 'Changes in Dutch Land Policy: from Monopoly Towards Competition in the Building Market' *Environment and Planning B*: Planning and Design, 30: 369 – 78.

Programme for Government (2020 - 2025) *Our Shared Future* https://static.rasset.ie/documents/news/2020/06/draft-programme-for-govt.pdf

Rebuilding Ireland (2016) Action Plan for Housing and Homelessness. Government of Ireland.

Report of the Constitution Review Group (1996). Government Publications Office.

Report of the Joint Oireachtas Committee on Building Land (1985). Government Publications Office.

Report of the Tribunal of Inquiry into Certain Planning Matters and Payments https://planningtribunal.ie/wp-content/uploads/2016/11/sitecontent_1257.pdf

Ryan, F.P. (2019) *Lessons in Irish Housing.* Oaktree Press.

Ryan, T. (1992) *Mara, PJ.* Blackwater Press.

Sanders, P. and Wilkins, P. (2010) *First Steps in Practitioner Research.* Ross-On-Wye: PCCS Books.

Sammon, P. J. (1997). *In the Land Commission: A Memoir 1933 – 1978.* Blackhall Publishing Ltd.

Sheehan, J.T. (1993). *Land Purchase Policy in Ireland 1917 – 1923: From the Irish Convention to the 1923 Land Act.* (MA thesis, NUI The Maynooth, 1993)

Social Democrats (2020) *Homes with Reach: Making housing available, making housing affordable* www.socialdemocrats.ie

Solow, B.L. (1971) *The Land Question and the Irish Economy 1870 – 1903.* Harvard University Press.

Sturge J.E. and Hanrahan K.J. (2004) Comparing telephone and face-to-face interviews: a research note. *Qualitative Research* 4(1): 107 – 118.

The All-Party Oireachtas Committee on the Constitution. Ninth Progress Report: Private Property (2004). Government Publications Office.

TASC (2022) *Trading Places: TASC Report on Land and Housing.* TASC

Threshold (various) (1987) *Policy Consequences: A Study of the £5,000 Surrender Grant in the Dublin Housing Area.* Threshold

Tobin, F. (1984) *The Best of Decades: Ireland in the 1960s.* Gill and Macmillan.

Town and Regional Planning Act, 1934 http://www.irishstatutebook.ie/eli/1934/act/22/enacted/en/html

Walsh, R., Fox O'Mahony, L. (2018) *Land Law, property ideologies and the British-Irish relationship.* Common Law World Review. Sage Journals. https://doi.org/10.1177/1473779518773641

Whitaker, T.K. (1956). *Capital formation, saving and economic progress. Journal of the statistical and Social Inquiry Society of Ireland , XV (1955/1956), 184 – 209*

Wilson, G.K. (1991) *Interest Groups.* Basil Blackwell

Wylie, J.C.W. (1975) *Irish Land Law.* Professional Books Ltd. London

Appendix 1

Planning and Compulsory Purchase

Planning

Two areas of major interest to the Kenny Committee were the planning system, as operated in the late 1960s/early 1970s following the passage of the 1963 Local Government (Planning and Development) Act and the whole area of compensation which had bedevilled successive governments in trying to control building land prices.

According to Planning Regulator Niall Cussen when a government gets its housing policies right, it tends to get its planning policies right as well. "Planning objectives are very difficult to achieve unless you have access to fiscal or land management mechanisms to correct, or address market behaviour that may not be in the interests of the common good," he said.

During the last part of the 19th and early 20th Centuries many of the problems of dealing with planning and compensation had been experienced in Britain where a number of solutions had been offered. However, in its review of British legislation, the Kenny Report (Par. 34) warned that while many of the changes suggested were attractive in principle, they involved "such complicated and administrative detail that they are unworkable".

The traditional way of describing the highest possible level of ownership that can be held in real property land is "Fee Simple". Under Fee Simple, the owner has the right to use it, exclusively possess it, dispose of it and take its fruits.

A fee simple represents absolute ownership of land, and therefore the owner may do whatever he/she chooses with the land. An often-quoted Latin maxim, generally credited to the Roman jurist Accursius in the 13th Century, is: "*Cuius est solum, eius est usque ad coelum et ad inferos*" which translates: "*whoever owns the soil, holds title all the way up to the heavens and down to the depths of hell*".

However, while the definition suggests wide-ranging rights, these are always subjected to extensive state control, particularly in large urban areas.

Relevant issues include rights of neighbouring owners, zoning, infrastructure requirements and so on.

Development rights, which form part of legal property rights, are regulated through the planning system. Irish planning legislation dates back to the various Town Improvement Acts passed in the mid-19th Century. Comprehensive legislation covering both town and country was not introduced until well into Ireland's independence in the Town and Regional Planning Act, 1934 and amended in 1939. Under this Act local authorities were authorised, but not required, to engage in planning but no time limit was set for the preparation of the planning schemes.

By the 1960s the urgent need for physical planning became very apparent. In Ireland the growth in urban population had a major influence on the demand for housing. The 1961 Census recorded Ireland's population figures at its lowest since records began at just under three million (www.cso.ie). However, for the first time, more people were living in urban than in rural Ireland. But the 1960s were also a turning point in the modernisation of Ireland. A new more confident and progressive Ireland was emerging.

In the words of one writer: "The blinds were let up, the windows were thrown open, the doors were unlocked and good, bad or indifferent, the modern world came in among us at last." [251]

The failure of the 1934 and 1939 Town and Regional Planning Acts, a growing population and new political mindset towards economic planning provided the underlying rationale for the 92 lengthy sections of the 1963 Planning Act. From now on planning permission was dependent on the availability of serviced land and, where such land was not available, the local authority had the power to zone agricultural land for residential and commercial purposes.

The 1963 Act

The 1963 Local Government (Planning & Development) Act is generally regarded as a turning point in Irish planning and was spearheaded by a far-seeing and innovative Donegal Fianna Fáil TD and Minister for Local Government, Neil Blaney. Niall Cussen, the first Planning Regulator in

---

[251] Tobin, F. (1984) *The Best of Decades: Ireland in the 1960s*. Gill and Macmillan. P.8

Ireland described the Act as "a pretty revolutionary or innovative piece of legislation in the Irish public policy context. So, it didn't have any great antecedents and predecessors, or indeed competitors, even in a broader or European context. ...it was more that you are dealing with a very innovative area of public policy". Speaking in the Dáil on 3 June 1980, some 17 years after the 1963 Act was introduced, Labour Deputy Ruairí Quinn described it as "one of the most radical pieces of legislation of this House".

The Report of the 2004 All-Paty Oireachtas Committee on Property stated that since the introduction of the 1963 Planning Act, development rights were no longer inherent in the right of ownership of property. "Indeed," it added, "the planning system is constructed on the principle that the State has the right and the need to alter the bundle of legal rights that relate to property.

Examples of the Irish State restricting, or removing, property rights include the control of airspace, the granting of security of tenure to tenants and, of course, the development of property under the various Planning Acts.

Introducing the Bill to the Dáil on 22 November, 1962, Minister Blaney, who had embarked on a study tour of the United States and Canada to see first-hand how planning issues were handled there, said its purpose was "to make provision, in the interests of the common good, for the proper planning and developing of cities, towns and other areas, whether urban or rural (including the preservation and improvement of the amenities thereof)." The Bill proposed to repeal the Town and Regional Planning Acts, 1934 and 1939, together with certain other statutory provisions which related to the control of building and development.

> A community's needs and expectations are not static: they are growing and changing all the time. It is one of the tasks of planning to secure that current developments make allowance for this growth and for keeping up with changing or improving standards. Thus, we must plan not alone for the community's present needs but also for its future needs in the light of prospective growth in demand. [252]

Blaney said the Town and Regional Planning Act, 1934 had only been partially successful because it was dependent on a local authority adopting "a planning

---

[252] https://www.oireachtas.ie/en/debates/debate/dail/1962-11-22/113/

scheme". However, twenty-eight years after the passing of the Act only one planning scheme, Dublin City, had been submitted for confirmation. In regard to the collection of "betterment" from land-owners, he said it depended on a planning scheme being brought into force under the Act. The new Act ended any future liability for betterment charges.

In his view, Minister Blaney said the revenue from betterment charges payable to the planning authority by those whose property was increased in value arising from the planning scheme would be "impossible to determine or collect". He also noted that during the period of 15 years when similar provisions to the 1934 Act were in operation in England, only three instances of the collection of betterment were recorded. The principal purpose of the 1939 Act was to try to overcome some of the major defects of the 1934 Act insofar as those defects had then come to light but in retrospect it had little overall impact. Section 19 of the innovative 1963 Act required every planning authority to devise a Development Plan within three years in which land would be zoned for "particular purposes whether residential, commercial, industrial, agricultural or otherwise".

In his Dáil speech, Minister Blaney defined planning as simply "making the best of what you've got" and the first step then was "to find out what you've got".

The 1963 Act provided that all planning authorities must make development plans and exercise planning controls over both structural works and material changes in the use of structures and other land. Significantly, provision was also made for an equitable system of compensation in respect of both future and past planning restrictions. The 1934 Act had provided for the payment of compensation in respect of Town Planning soon after the making of a planning scheme. This provision had caused problems for local authorities as they were at risk of receiving compensation claims beyond their means if a plan was made. Part VI of the Bill tried to remove this uncertainty.

Section 55 of the Bill also provided for compensation in respect of planning restrictions when a planning authority refused planning permission, or imposed conditions. This was to give rise to huge claims in later years when developers were refused planning permission. The basis of compensation, Minister Blaney told the Dáil "was the reduction in value of the claimant's estate or interest in the property and, in the case of an occupier of such property, the damage (if any) to his trade, business or profession, occasioned by such restriction."

Under Section 11 of the Local Government (No. 2) Act, 1960, planning authorities had the power to acquire land either by agreement, or compulsorily for the purposes of any of their functions. Without prejudice to that power, Section 72 of the 1963 Act set out a number of purposes for which land could be acquired by a planning authority. The purpose of the section was to make explicit the right of planning authorities to engage in the development, or re-development of land in the interests of orderly and economic development.

Minister Blaney told the Dáil he was satisfied the new provisions of the Bill would enable planning authorities to undertake urban renewal. "Re-planning and re-building on modern lines requires the assembly of sites, and this can often be achieved only if the planning authority acquires the area," he said.

Under the terms of the 1963 Act, the then 87 local authorities were committed to planning, with the minister having overall responsibility to ensure conformity. In effect, the minister of the day had the power to sanction, or refuse, any particular planning request.

Fourteen years later, following criticism of this power, the Fine Gael/ Labour Coalition government introduced the 1976 Local Government (Planning & Development) Act, one of which terms transferred this power to the newly established Bord Pleanála (Planning Board). From then on, the rejection of planning applications could be - and still are - appealed to An Bord Pleanála.

Unintended consequences

In 2004 the All-Party Oireachtas Committee pointed out that scarce assets always attract high prices. In the case of building land, if properly regulated, the market will distribute them efficiently. However, if the market fails, then "measures need to be adapted that work with the market and do not serve to frustrate it and throw up unintended consequences that make matters worse." The Committee concluded that the best way to achieve optimum use of land space in urban areas is through a combination of a formal planning system and a "market mechanism". Planning on its own would not provide solutions and must take into account market conditions. Getting the balance right was crucial.

While the 1963 Planning Act is generally regarded as hugely important in introducing planning to Ireland, it did, according to the Kenny Report, have the unintended consequence in its initial phase of causing house prices to rise while there were delays in going through the new planning process.

Role of Local Authorities

As previously stated, the current basis of the Irish planning system is the Local Government (Planning and Development) Act 1963 and subsequent Acts. Within the framework of these Acts, coupled with the role played by An Bord Pleanála and the Minister for Housing, Local Government & Heritage being in charge of policy-making, each local authority prepares, reviews and updates its own development plan taking into account the local factors and property rights. This is an extremely complex operation and each review usually takes a number of years. For example, the Dublin City Development Plan (2016 – 2022), the country's largest, ran to seven volumes.

Within the framework of the Planning Acts each authority is relatively free to adopt its own land use criteria which, therefore, reflects or should, the political will of the community in relation to type, mix and density of development permitted.

A key aspect of planning is to try to anticipate the amount of land which is likely to be required for development so that the necessary infrastructural services (generally water, sewerage and roads) can be put in place. Too little zoned land can result in spiralling prices while too much zoned land can result in the poor use of scarce resources. The effectiveness of planning depends on a myriad of factors, including interpretation of the Constitutional rights, issues of political, technical and administrative performance, legal powers and resource availability.

To allow for the orderly development of a sustainable community, local authorities need to be able to access the most suitable land at a reasonable cost. The Kenny Report put forward one such solution: acquire land at existing use value plus 25 per cent. A number of replies from local authorities to the 1985 Joint Oireachtas Committee on Building Land pointed to the difficulties in acquiring land under the existing legislation. In some cases, the desire on the part of the landowner not to sell may simply be to remain in farming and there is no speculative motivation attached (this was clear, for example, in the high profile 2017 Supreme Court case when Co. Kildare farmer Thomas Reid challenged the IDA - and succeeded - in keeping his 72-acre farm. It was later the subject of a documentary film entitled *The Lonely Battle of Thomas Reid*). In effect, in such a case, the use of the land to the individual concerned was considered higher than the going price for development land.

One example to the 1985 Oireachtas Committee quoted a council stating that it had been "forced to zone for residential development, amounts of land far in excess of those anticipated as being required within the plan period". Another stated that "a greater number of private dwellings had been erected outside the urban boundary than would have occurred had the land been available." [253]

Levies

Section 26.2 of the Local Government (Planning & Development) Act, 1963 authorised the imposition of planning conditions requiring contributions towards local authority expenditure on works which had facilitated, or would facilitate, proposed developments. However, the Act does not expressly authorise a general levy towards expenditure and leaves the decision to each local authority and to determine what services should be paid for and how much. Levies continue to vary widely and single houses were widely not liable for any levy. Most local authorities also attach levies in respect of specific works.

The 1985 Oireachtas Committee on Building Land considered the notion of the introduction of "holding costs" on undeveloped land. Holding costs are based on the idea of encouraging the release of serviced land by imposing a tax, or charge, either when the land is zoned or provided with services. However, the Committee rejected the notion on the basis that an individually applied tax could be unconstitutional because it was discriminatory and secondly, because in order to be effective, the tax would have to be variable to meet the circumstances of each particular case and so would be impractical. In the end,

---

[253] Report of the Joint Oireachtas Committee on Building Land (1985). Government Publications Office. Par. 6.17

the Committee concluded that compulsory purchase was the most effective method of acquiring development land.

The Committee accepted the principle of levies but that they should not be used as a tax on development which would be the case if they exceeded servicing costs. The Committee concluded that development levies are an appropriate method of recouping costs of providing main services, their level should be known to the industry well in advance and should not amount to a tax on development. [254]

Following the publication of the report, the Fine Gael/Labour Government applied a 60 per cent rate of Capital Gains Tax when the general level at the time was 40 per cent. However, it was later removed when it was seen to cause a blockage in bringing development land onto the market.

Nine years later, the 2004 All-Party Oireachtas Committee concluded that applying a higher rate of CGT was unlikely to bring down the price of development land and reducing the incentives to bring development land onto the open market were likely to be adverse.

Other Relevant Acts

Since the Kenny Report was published in 1973, a number of relevant Acts were subsequently passed by the Oireachtas, of which the Local Government (Planning and Development) Act 1990, the Planning and Development Act, 2000 and the Planning and Development Act 2018 are the most important.

Local Government (Planning and Development) Act 1976

This Act set up An Board Pleanála (the Appeals Board) on a statutory footing.

Local Government (Planning and Development) Act, 1990

The Local Government (Planning and Development) Act 1990 built on the 1963 Act by extending the rules for determining the rules for the amount of compensation to be paid. It also set out the rules for which the refusal of planning permission would not attract compensation as well as the reasons for which a refusal of planning permission would attract compensation.

---

[254] Ibid Par.7.34

The 2004 All-Party Committee on Property reported some concern had been raised at the time that parts of this Act might be unconstitutional, notably the restriction of the entitlement to compensation by landowners when planning permission was refused. The Committee went on to draw the conclusion that this 1990 Act provision "does provide some evidence that the Oireachtas was too cautious in this area in the past".

Planning and Development Act, 2000

As mentioned previously, this important piece of legislation repealed and replaced the 1963 and 1990 Acts. This Act states, in consolidated form, the majority of the compensation rules and the circumstances under which compensation is payable, or not payable, following the refusal of planning permission.

Part V of the Act was a mechanism, introduced by the Government, through which local authorities can obtain up to 10% of land zoned for housing development at "existing use value" rather than "development value" for the delivery of social and affordable housing. As previously outlined, it was referred to the Supreme Court by President Mary McAleese and found not to be in breach of the Constitution.

Planning and Development (Amendment) Act, 2018

The 2018 Planning and Development Act came into force on 1 January 2018, the principal purpose of which was the establishment of the Office of a Planning Regulator. It also provided for a National Planning Framework and provided for certain planning and development requirements to be taken into account by Irish Water.

Compensation

Compulsory Purchase has been used in Ireland since the foundation of the State as a mechanism for the acquisition of land for public infrastructural projects. Although the legislation surrounding it is extremely complex, it has proved a very successful policy tool for successive Irish governments in acquiring land for use for the common good. There is, of course, no express constitutional right for compensation in Article 43 of the Constitution, but such a right has always been found to be an implied right in order to balance the interests involved.

Ireland's compulsory acquisition and compensation law is based on 19th Century and early 20th Century legislation, most, but not all of which was common to both England and Ireland. However, since 1922 there has been a number of important developments in the relevant laws in the Republic. The compulsory purchase of land and the compensation rules associated with it trace their origin back to the Lands Clauses Consolidation Act, 1845 and a patchwork of other Victorian legislation which conferred on each householder the right to connect up to the public water and sewerage systems (Waterworks Clauses Act 1847, Section 53; Public Health (Ireland) Act 1878 (Section 27).

The Kenny Report described the law in this area as "a thoroughly confusing patchwork".

> Anyone who has to answer a question on this branch of the law finds himself compelled to start his enquiry with the Lands Clauses Consolidation Act, 1985 and then to work his way through a jungle of Acts extending over a century. [255]

Its complexity was eloquently expressed also, for example, by former Chief Justice T.F O'Higgins in *Portland v Limerick* Corporation:

> 'The various Local Government Acts, the Housing Acts and the Planning Acts for a code of interrelated statues in the drafting of which clarity of language is remarkably absent. The seeker for the true meaning of particularly statutory provisions is often sent from one statute to another and is frequently misled and confused by the use of different terms having the same meaning to a particular adaptation used in one statute which may be absent in another. These statutes are drafted for an elite *cognoscenti* – those who in either central or local government are accustomed to the exercise of the powers prescribed and the language used. For others, the ascertainment of what is laid down involves an arduous journey into the obscure'. [256]

---

[255] The Kenny Report, Par. 147

[256] *Portland v Limerick Corporation [1980] IILRM 77, 80.*

Irish compulsory purchase legislation was, like most other legislation, based on British laws where the onset of the Industrial Revolution moved the emphasis away from the agricultural area. But it was the coming of the railways in the 19th Century which provided the impetus to empower by statute undertakings of public utilities to compulsorily acquire property where attempts to negotiate a voluntary change of ownership had failed. The process set up throughout was a special Act of Parliament authorising the acquisition of specified land for a specified purpose and setting out the procedures for acquiring ownership, obtaining possession and for determining compensation.

The proliferation of railways led to heavy demands on Parliament and so to the passing in 1845 of the Lands Clauses Consolidation Act which set down a standard procedure for progressing the acquisition of a specific property and the assessment of compensation.

The procedure evolved in time into the 'provisional order' for specific cases. Section 203 of the Public Health (Ireland) Act, 1878 empowered the sanitary authorities established by that Act to compulsorily acquire land by means of a provisional order made by the Local Government Board. The provisional order proposal was to be given publicity in the newspapers, notices had to be served and objections had to be considered at a public enquiry. The main feature of the new CPO procedure was the dropping of the final parliamentary step, the referring of the provisional order to Parliament for confirmation. The new scheme was shown in the Development and Road Improvement Funds Act, 1909.

It was not until the 20th Century that the British Parliament recognised that assessment of compensation was a major element in its own right. The Acquisition of Land (Assessment of Compensation) Act, 1919 set out six separate rules for the assessment of compensation. While these have been added to over the years, replaced and consolidated as the compensation rules set out in the Schedules to the Planning and Development Act 2000, the basic principles remain the same, namely that the value of compensation should reflect the open market price. Dr Rachael Walsh of Trinity College Law Department stated:

> The 1919 Act and these are still the basic principles that we apply now. Added on to them have been bits and pieces of legislation that create distinctive compensation rules for particular issue so the planning context was one where a discreet set of rules were

developed for compensation, but very much drawing on the 1919 principles.... So actually, we have quite a patchwork system for working out what the rules of compensation are for acquiring land in contrast to let's say a lot of European countries where you would have one statute which deals with the rules applicable for compensation determination across the board.

The 1919 Act also abolished the assessment of compensation by jurors and replaced it by one under which compensation was determined by an arbitrator drawn from a panel of property arbitrators. The 1919 Act was added to in Irish law, initially by the Housing Act, 1966 and subsequently by the Local Government (Planning and Development) Acts 1963. These have since been replaced by their consolidation into the Planning and Development Act, 2000.

Local councils were first introduced in Ireland under the terms of the Local Government (Ireland) Act, 1898. Section 10 of the Act gave the newly-created councils power to acquire land by agreement or compulsorily inside, or outside, their districts. The main principle underlying the statutory provisions is that the owner of the land which is compulsorily acquired should get precisely what it was worth in money terms immediately before the acquisition.

Local Authorities and Compulsory Purchase

The concept of "the exigencies of the common good" and social justice, as outlined in Article 43.2.2° of the Constitution is the first hurdle in determining whether an action constitutes a disproportionate interference with property rights, or an unjust attack on same. With regard to CPOs, the acquiring authority must acknowledge the purpose for which the land is required. That purpose cannot solely benefit private parties and there must be an element of public benefit.

Compulsory compensation by local authorities is directed by the provisions of the Housing Act, 1966 which now must be construed by the provisions of the Planning & Development Act, 2000.

> While the 1966 Act, and other Acts that use the CPO process, can therefore be said to be relatively modern in approach, an important distinction between the UK and Irish systems of

compulsory acquisition is that when the UK legislation was reformed in the 20th century, when the CPO model was adopted, the 19th century legislation was repealed and replaced. In Ireland, while the 1966 Act followed the UK CPO model, no comparable exercise to repeal and replace the 19th century legislation has occurred to date. Thus, in Ireland the 1845 Act remains in force and continues to have some effect, though of decreasing significance.[257]

As pointed out previously, the 1966 Act overcame many problems which existed under the previous Local Government (Ireland) Act 1898. The relevant section (76) of the 1966 Act reads:

> *'A housing authority acquiring land compulsorily for the purposes of this Act may be authorised to do so by means of a compulsory purchase order (CPO) made by the authority and submitted to and confirmed by the minister in accordance with the provisions contained in the Third Schedule to the Act.'*

The power was subsequently extended in the Planning and Development Act, 2000. The power to use the procedures under the 1966 Act were also conferred on a number of other bodies other than local authorities e.g The National Roads Authority and Córas Iompair Eireann (CIE). An exception of course were religious and denominational and educational institutions due to Article 44.2.6° which states:

> *The property of any religious denomination or any educational institution shall not be diverted save for necessary works of public utility and on payment of compensation.*

At date of writing, this Article has not been amended.

Since 1976, appeals may be made to An Bord Pleanála and any decision by the Board relating to confirmation of a CPO is amendable by judicial review as governed by Section 50, 50A and 50B of the Planning and Development Act, 2000.

---

[257] Law Reform Commission (2017) *Compulsory Acquisition of Land.* (LRC IP13 – 2017).

Ten Rules on Compensation

The 1963 Local Government (Planning and Development) Act, which came into effect on 1 October, 1964 placed substantial legal constraints on the owners of development land as well as adding 10 new rules on compensation. Part of the new thinking of the time was reflected in Section 56 which provided that a developer should not be compensated where compensation was refused in respect of developments which consisted in the making "of any material change in the use of any structures or other land". (S56.1.a). Section 56.1.b also provided that compensation would not be payable where a development was premature having regard to factors such as deficiencies in water, or sewerage supply, or road system.

The statutory compulsory purchase of land, or other interference with property rights is a *prima facie* breach of the right to private property. The modern position on the extent to which such an interference is constitutionally permissible was set out in *Central Dublin Development Association Ltd v Attorney General* by Judge John Kenny (later to chair the Committee on the Price of Building Land) – and quoted in the Kenny Report (Paragraph 92)- as follows:

> The right of private property is a personal right. In virtue of his rational being, man has a natural right to individual or private ownership of worldly wealth. This constitutional right consists of a bundle of rights most of which are fundamental in contract. The State cannot pass any law which abolishes all the bundle of rights which we call ownership or the general right to transfer, bequeath and inherit property. The exercise of these rights ought to be regulated by the principles of social justice and the State accordingly may by law restrict their exercise with a view to reconciling this with the demands of the common good. The Courts have jurisdiction to inquire whether the restriction is in accordance with the principles of social justice and whether the legislation is necessary to reconcile this exercise with the demands of the common good. If any of the rights which together constitute our conception of ownership are abolished, or restricted (as distinct from the abolition of all the rights), the absence of compensation for this restriction, or

238

abolition, will make the Act which does this invalid, if it is an unjust attack on the property rights. [258]

A current guide to the steps in Compulsory Purchase is as follows:

A statutory body decides to make a CPO. Affected parties will be served with a notice and newspaper notices will be published, compulsory purchase order stating that the Order is about to be put on public display and submitted to An Bord Pleanála for confirmation. Objections can be made, but valid objections are generally on planning or legal grounds only.

A Public Local Enquiry is held at which affected parties can formally put their views forward (If no objections are made, An Bord Pleanála can confirm, amend, or reject the CPO without a Public Enquiry). An Bord Pleanála either confirms, amends, or rejects CPO order and publishes details of the decisions in this regard. After expiry of objection period, the CPO is operative. Acquiring Authority serves Notice to Treat on the affected parties and discussions commence regarding the level of compensation available.

The affected party lodges a claim for compensation. This can be made by the claimants' valuer. On reaching agreement, compensation is paid, otherwise the matter may be referred by either party to the Property Arbitrator to assess compensation. Acquisition is finalised and compensation paid.

The issue of compensation for land acquired under a CPO in default of agreement must be in accordance with the provisions of the Acquisition of Land (Assessment of Compensation) Act 1919 subject to the modifications of the Land Clauses Acts made in the Housing Act 1966.

Section 2 of the Act sets out six rules in accordance with which the arbitrator must act in assessing compensation. Ten more were added by Section 69 of the Local Government (Planning and Development) Act 1963. A further rule was added by Section 48 of the Planning and Development (Strategic Infrastructure) Act, 2006.

The rationale underlying the statutory provisions is that the owner of the land which is compulsorily acquired should get precisely what it is worth to him/her in money terms immediately before the acquisition. Rule 2 of the prescribed rules is regarded as the principle one which states:

---

[258] *Central Dublin Development Association Ltd v Attorney General [1975] 109ILTR 69 per Kenny J.)*

The value of the land shall, subject as is hereinafter provided, be taken to be the amount which the land as sold in the open market by a willing seller might be expected to realise: provided always that the arbitrator shall be entitled to consider all returns and assessments of capital value for taxation made, or acquiesced in, by the claimant (Rule 2 of the Land (Assessment of Compensation) Act).

The assessment of compensation will generally fall under a number of headings of claim which can include the following:

- Value of land acquired
- Diminution in value of retained lands, if any
- Costs resulting from acquisition
- Disturbance
- Loss of profits or goodwill
- Loss or depreciation of stock in trade
- Professional fees necessary for acquisition.[259]

In the event that there is failure to reach agreement between the local authority and the landowner, then the measure of compensation is fixed by an arbitrator. It is normal to take evidence on prices paid for similar properties in the neighbourhood that have been acquired as well as expert opinion on recent comparable sales.

The additional rules inserted by the 1996 and 2000 Acts set out matters which are either to be regarded or disregarded in assessing compensation but do not interfere with the basic principles set out in Rule 2.

The 1985 Oireachtas Committee concluded that the application of an undefined market value principle as the basis for compensation as set out in Rule 2, is unsatisfactory and contrary to the common good. It recommended that it should be modified to ensure firstly, that valuation of land would reflect its development potential and secondly, that any market prices used for comparability purposes in arriving at a valuation are discounted where there is evidence of distortion in the general trend of land prices. The Committee sought

---

[259] www.scsi.ie/documents/get_lob?id=402&field=file

legal counsel's opinion as to whether the recommendation was constitutional and the opinion confirmed it was.[260]

The 1985 Oireachtas Committee Report found that the compulsory purchase process was too cumbersome and too slow. An order, it stated could take between five and ten years to complete and the process was very open to legal proceedings. However, the Committee acknowledged that not all delays could be attributed to the process itself and that any changes would have to take account of the requirements of the Constitution which guarantees the property rights of citizens.

In recent years, various pieces of legislation have been added to create distinctive rules for particular issues but they are always rooted in the 1919 legislation to this day. In 2009 the NAMA Act, for example, had its own compensation principles but linking back to the 1919 Act. According to Dr Rachael Walsh of Trinity College Law School the disadvantage is that this patchwork-like nature to the compensation landscape makes questions on compensation rules in Ireland very complicated and often results in very long answers and court rulings as opposed to a straightforward answer as might be given in some other jurisdictions.

---

[260] *Report of the Joint Oireachtas Committee on Building Land (1985).* Government Publications Office. Par.7. 23

Appendix 2

Zoning and "Betterment"

Attempts to recoup increased value

In any formal planning system, development rights are granted to some land owners and denied to others. If the amount of zoned land is scarce, then the value of the zoned land increases and the cash bonanza given to the owner distorts the market.

'Residential' is the largest land zoning in any area. In Ireland, to this day, unlike many other countries, there is a preference to apply a bland residential zoning on suburban locations. In most cases, particularly in outer new suburbs, a bland residential zoning relies on the market and the developer's architect to decide the format of the compliant scheme.

The first attempt in Britain to tax the increase in the value of land was made in the Finance Act of 1910. This was a duty of £1 (€1.27) for each £5 (€6.35) increment value – known as an "increment value duty" – and was payable on any sale of any interest in land under a very complicated system of provisions. For example, a valuation of all land in the country and four different values of each parcel of land had to be made for the purpose of assessment of the duty. From the start, it was clear that the entire scheme was far too complicated - and unworkable - and it was repealed in 1920.

Subsequently, a number of schemes for the recovery by local authorities of some part of the increase in the price of land caused by betterment were submitted to the Commission on the Distribution of Industrial Population (The Barlow Commission). This body recommended that an expert committee should be appointed to consider the whole issue of compensation.

In January 1941, during the Second World War, a committee titled the "Expert Committee on Compensation and Betterment" under the chairmanship of Mr Justice Uthwatt was set up. The recommendations of this report heavily influenced the Kenny Report. (Uthwatt was, in fact, mainly concerned with the war damage and the need to carry out large scale redevelopment of poor accommodation and badly planned areas.)

242

This increase in value as a result of zoning is often referred to as "betterment". It also sends a signal to developers and would-be entrepreneurs to acquire as much zoned development land as possible and hoard it until the time is right to gain maximum profit. As a result, developers often compete with each other to acquire scarce development land in good locations leading to a distortion of the market and spiralling house prices. While zoning huge areas of land for development might seem an obvious solution, local authorities are reluctant to choose this route as it can result in servicing vast quantities of land that may not be required for a generation or more.

According to Tom Dunne, former Head of the School of Surveying & Construction Management, TU, Dublin, the "compensation betterment" problem arises when a city is growing as it is not possible to service all the land around the city. A decision has to be made on which land is going to be zoned and serviced. That is the job of planners. Zoned land in itself is not valuable as unless the land is serviced, it cannot be developed. The zoning is only a licensing arrangement.

> When you get planning, you confine the residential, you effectively take residential rights off some land-owners and concentrate them in one location. That means that those people with rights have monopoly powers in the sense that the people who own that land know they own land that is worth more. And the price of that land goes up because it attracts all the development rights that might have been more evenly distributed.

The 1963 Local Government (Planning and Development) Act introduced the notion that some people should be compensated for betterment and that other people should be compensated for the loss of their development rights. It is widely recognised that once zoning is introduced, the value of zoned land is inflated to the detriment of land that is not zoned or maybe for uses that do not have as high a value.

According to Dunne, the question as to how you compensate people was never really resolved in the UK. That question was never answered properly in the original British Town & Country Planning Act, 1954 which formed the basis for the 1963 Planning Act in Ireland.

Because it was not resolved, of course when the economy took off finally in 1964/65 land prices went up because house prices went up and there was immense speculation in land. The concentration was on getting your land rezoned, the local authority had an obligation to service your zoned land and you made a lot of money. There was a lot of complaint about that and the response by government was the Kenny Report.

Dr Rachael Walsh of Trinity College's Law Department says there was a landscape there when the planning system was introduced in Ireland it was understood to be a restriction of property rights and the compensation rules were designed to do that, to compensate owners for a restriction being imposed on their property rights.

Speculating on prime zoned land and hoarding some, or all, of it was a trend that emerged in urban areas in Ireland post the 1963 Planning Act one that the Kenny Report sought to tackle. It also tried to define "betterment".

When a local authority carries out a scheme for sanitary services or builds a road or does other improvements, the land which benefits from these will get a higher price when sold. This increase in price is called "betterment", an ambiguous term because it is sometimes used to describe the increase in price brought about all economic and social forces including planning schemes and sometimes to describe the part of the increase which ought to be recoverable from the owner.[261]

The Utwhatt Committee

One of the suggestions made by the Utwhatt Committee, when it reported in September 1942, was to give local authorities the right to acquire land compulsorily which had been, or would be, improved by local authority works at a price determined by reference to its use value before the works were carried out. Therefore, the increase in price value caused by the local authority works would accrue to the local authority which would get the benefit of it by

---

[261] The Kenny Report, Par. 27

selling the lands at their full market price. This method, known as recoupment, had never been practised in Ireland.

The principal recommendations of the Utwhatt Committee were that the development rights in all land outside built-up areas should, on payment of fair compensation, become vested in the state and that there should be a prohibition against development of such land without the consent of a Central Planning Authority. The Committee hoped that the Central Planning authority would be able to purchase land outside built-up areas at the existing use value as they believed the high price of land which local authorities had to pay was the main reason why many development works were not carried out. The Committee also recommended that, in the case of developed land, there should be a valuation of the site made every five years and that an annual levy should be made on the amount by which the new site value exceeded the original one.

The recommendation that all development rights in undeveloped land should be vested in the state was extended to all land, developed and undeveloped, in the 1947 Town and Country Planning Act. This Act introduced a new planning code under which all development rights were, in effect, nationalised. The Act set up a Central Land Board which was to levy development charges. The appropriation of the increase in value or 'betterment' by the owner was never the intention of the authors of the 1947 Act.

However, the system of development charges while very attractive, did now work out well in practice and showed in time that inevitably the purchaser had to increase the price of the houses to recover the price of the development charge and the price of the land. The system was ended the by the Conservative government in the 1954 Town and Country Planning Act.

> The failure of the development charge is instructive and lay in the inevitable resistance to it from landowners who faced binding restrictions on how they could use their land and could no longer profit when their schemes were approved. [262]

---

[262]Bentley, D. (2017) The Land Question: Fixing the Dysfunction at the root of the housing crisis. Civitas. London. P.42

However, from 1947 to the return of a free market in land under a new 1959 Act, local authorities in Britain were able to acquire land for their own development purposes at existing use value plus any development value at 1947 values. In 1962 a short-term capital gains tax was introduced in Britain followed by a general capital gains tax in 1965 but none survived.

Radical Proposal

The Kenny Report provided for the most radical proposal – before or since - for securing betterment for the community by allowing planning authorities to acquire development land at existing use value plus 25 per cent. In turn, the planning authorities would provide the betterment for the communities by the provision of service facilities along with social and affordable housing. Thirty-one years later, a number of submissions to the 2004 All-Party Oireachtas Committee favoured the approach taken by the Kenny Report. For example, in their joint submission, the National Roads Authority and the Railway Procurement Agency stated:

> Our fundamental submission is that the committee should act on the Kenny Report and by so doing, the Oireachtas can enact legislation measures which can provide for *inter alia* compulsory purchase, infrastructural development and land use development which will have a new, clear and unambiguous constitutional underpinning.

The principles of the Kenny Report were also supported by the Conference of Religious of Ireland (CORI) who, in their submission, argued for the introduction of a law confining the re-zoning of land to "those lands in the ownership of local authorities".

Over the years different methods were considered and applied to provide for the transfer of windfall gain to the government. The 2004 All-Party Oireachtas Committee Report recommended that the recommendation of the Kenny Report was the most secure scheme both for capturing betterment for the community and for controlling the price of building land. It suggested that it should be re-examined with a view to implementation "following such modifications as are necessary or desirable in the light of experience since its publication".

Appendix 3

The Rules for Assessment of Compensation.

Rule 1

No allowance shall be made on account of the acquisition being compulsory.

Rule 2

The value of land shall, subject as hereinafter provided, be taken to be the amount which the land, if sold in the open market by a willing seller, might be expected to realise; provided always that the arbitrator shall be entitled to consider all returns and assessments of capital value for taxation made or acquiesced in by the claimant.

Rule 3

The special suitability or adaptability of the lands for any purpose shall not be taken into account if that purpose is a purpose to which it could be applied only in pursuance of statutory powers, or for which there is no market apart from the special needs of a particular purchaser or the requirements of any government department or any local or public authority; Provided that any *bona fide* offer for the purchase of the land made before the passing of this Act which may be brought to the notice of the arbitrator shall be taken into consideration.

Rule 4

Where the value of the land is increased by reason of the use thereof or of any premises thereon in a manner which could be restrained by any court, or is contrary to the law, or is detrimental to the health of the inmates of the premises, the amount of that increase shall not be taken into account.

Rule 5

Where the land is, and but for the compulsory acquisition, would continue to be devoted to a purpose of such a nature that there is no general demand, or market for land for that purpose, the compensation may, if the official arbitrator is satisfied that reinstatement in some other place is *bone fide* intended, be assessed on the basis of the reasonable cost of equivalent reinstatement.

Rule 6

The provisions of Rule 2 shall not affect the assessment of compensation for disturbance or any other matter not directly based on the value of the land.

Rule 7

In the case of compulsory acquisition of buildings, the reference in Rule 5 to the reasonable cost of equivalent reinstatement shall be taken as a reference to that cost not exceeding the estimated cost of buildings such as would be capable of serving an equivalent purpose over the same period of time as the buildings compulsorily acquired would have done, having regard to any structural depreciation in those buildings.

Rule 8

The value of the land shall be calculated with due regard to any restrictive covenant entered into by the acquirer when the land is compulsorily acquired.

Rule 9

Regard shall be had to any restriction on the development of the land in respect of which compensation has been paid under the Local Government (Planning & Development) Act 1963.

Rule 10

Regard shall be had to any restriction on the development of the land which could, without conferring a right to compensation, be imposed under any Act or under any order, regulation, rule or by-law made under any Act.

Rule 11

Regard shall not be had to any depreciation or increase in value attributable to:

The land, any land in the vicinity thereof, being reserved for any particular purpose in a development plan, or

Inclusion of the land in a special amenity area order.

Rule 12

No account shall be taken of any value attributable to any unauthorised structure or unauthorised use.

Rule 13

No account shall be taken of:

- The existence of proposals for development of the land or any other land by a local authority, or
- The possibility or probability of the land or other land becoming subject to a scheme of development undertaken by a local authority.

Rule 14

Regard shall be had to any contribution which a planning authority would have required as a condition precedent to the development of the land.

Rule 15

In Rules 9,10, 11, 12, 13 and 14 'development', 'development plan', 'special amenity area order', 'unauthorised structure', 'unauthorised use', 'local authority', and 'the appointed day' have the same meanings respectively as in the Local Government (Planning & Development) Act, 1963.

Rule 16

In the case of land incapable of reasonably beneficial use which is purchased by a Planning Authority under Section 29 of the Local Government (Planning & Development) Act 1963, the compensation shall be the value of the land exclusive of any allowance for disturbance or severance.

Rule 17

The value of any land lying 10 metres or more below the surface of that land shall be taken to be nil, unless if it shown to be of greater value by the claimant.

Appendix 4

Rules for the assessment of compensation for land as proposed in the Kenny Report

The Court shall when assessing compensation for lands acquired under this Act apply the following rules:

No allowance shall be made on account of the acquisition being compulsory.

The compensation shall be the amount which the lands might be expected to realise if sold in the open market on the date when the application to assess the compensation is made to the Court when sold by a willing seller on the basis that the lands could never be used for any purposes other than those for which they were being used at the date of the application to the Court to assess the compensation plus 25% of such amount.

Without prejudice to the generality of Rule II, no account shall be taken of:

- The existence of proposals for development of the land or any other land by any person, or by a State or local authority,
- The probability, or possibility, of the land, or other lands, becoming subject to a scheme of development undertaken by any person, or by a State or local authority.

If the compensation assessed under these rules should be less that the price *bona fide* paid for the land before _____(the date of publication of this report), the price so paid together with such amount of interest as the Court shall think just, shall be the amount of the compensation.

If the land is subject to any rent or other payment, the said rent, or payment so far as it affects the land may, on the application of the local authority, be redeemed and extinguished on such terms as to the Court seems just.

If the land is subject to any easement or public right of way of to any *profit a prendre* or customary right, such easement, public right of way, *profit a prendre* or customary right may, on the application of the local authority, be extinguished on such terms as to the Court seems just.

251

The special suitability or adaptability of the land for any purpose other than that for which it was being used at the date of the application to the Court to assess the compensation shall not be taken into account.

If the land or any structures thereon are being used in a manner which could be restrained by any court or which is contrary to law, no compensation shall be awarded in respect of such use.

If any person shall be residing either as owner or tenant on land acquired by the local authority at the date when the application to assess the compensation is made, the Court may award to such persons such compensation for the expenses caused by the removal to other premises as it shall consider just.

Regard shall not be had to any depreciation or increase in value attributable to:

- the land or any land in the vicinity thereof being reserved for any particular purpose in the development plan, or
- inclusion of the land in a special amenity order.
- No account shall be taken of any value attributable to any unauthorised structure or unauthorised use.

Appendix 5

Democratic Declaration of the First Dáil

We declare in the words of the Irish Republican Proclamation the right of the people of Ireland to the ownership of Ireland, and to the unfettered control of Irish destinies to be indefeasible, and in the language of our first President, Pádraig Mac Phiarais, we declare that the Nation's sovereignty extends not only to all men and women of the Nation, but to all its material possessions, the Nation's soil and all its resources, all the wealth and all the wealth-producing processes within the Nation, and with him we reaffirm that all right to private property must be subordinated to the public right and welfare.

We declare that we desire our country to be ruled in accordance with the principles of Liberty, Equality, and Justice for all, which alone can secure permanence of Government in the willing adhesion of the people.

We affirm the duty of every man and woman to give allegiance and service to the Commonwealth, and declare it is the duty of the Nation to assure that every citizen shall have opportunity to spend his or her strength and faculties in the service of the people. In return for willing service, we, in the name of the Republic, declare the right of every citizen to an adequate share of the produce of the Nation's labour.

It shall be the first duty of the Government of the Republic to make provision for the physical, mental and spiritual well-being of the children, to secure that no child shall suffer hunger or cold from lack of food, clothing, or shelter, but that all shall be provided with the means and facilities requisite for their proper education and training as Citizens of a Free and Gaelic Ireland.

The Irish Republic fully realises the necessity of abolishing the present odious, degrading and foreign Poor Law System, substituting therefor a sympathetic native scheme for the care of the Nation's aged and infirm, who shall not be regarded as a burden, but rather entitled to the Nation's gratitude and consideration. Likewise, it shall be the duty of the Republic to take such measures as will safeguard the health of the people and ensure the physical as well as the moral well-being of the Nation.

It shall be our duty to promote the development of the Nation's resources, to increase the productivity of its soil, to exploit its mineral deposits, peat bogs, and fisheries, its waterways and harbours, in the interests and for the benefit of the Irish people.

It shall be the duty of the Republic to adopt all measures necessary for the recreation and invigoration of our Industries, and to ensure their being developed on the most beneficial and progressive co-operative and industrial lines. With the adoption of an extensive Irish Consular Service, trade with foreign Nations shall be revived on terms of mutual advantage and goodwill, and while undertaking the organisation of the Nation's trade, import and export, it shall be the duty of the Republic to prevent the shipment from Ireland of food and other necessaries until the wants of the Irish people are fully satisfied and the future provided for. It shall also devolve upon the National Government to seek co-operation of the Governments of other countries in determining a standard of Social and Industrial Legislation with a view to a general and lasting improvement in the conditions under which the working classes live and labour.

Appendix 6

Letter from Judge John Kenny to Minister Robert Molloy.

69 Nutley Lane
Donnybrook
Dublin 4.

AN ARD CHÚIRT
(The High Court)
BAILE ÁTHA CLIATH 7
(Dublin 7)

20th April 1972

Minister for Local Govt.
Robert Molloy Esq.

Inquiry into Price of Building Land.

Dear Mr Molloy,

I saw part of the Television Programme a few nights ago during which you said that you hoped that the Report would be in your hands in June. Some time ago I had written to you that I hoped it wd. be available in June.

The mountain of material I've read gets bigger each week. It is very unlikely now that the Report will be available in June. When I've finished I have started the drafting and I am not taking any holidays this Summer but am remaining in Dublin. I hope now that the Report will be available at the end of September if my drafting powers continue.

It is not easy to do hard work with the daily chronicle of horrors in Northern Ireland.

Yours Sincerely,   John Kenny.

255

Appendix 7

Summary of the Report of the Committee on the Price of Building Land (The Kenny Report)

In January 1971, the Minister for Local Government, Robert Molloy TD, commissioned a report on the price of building land, the most comprehensive report undertaken on the issue since the foundation of the State. The Committee were given the following terms of reference:

(1) To consider possible measures for: (a) controlling the price of land required for housing and others forms of development (b) ensuring that all or a substantial part of the increase in the value of land attributable to the decisions and operations of public authorities (including, in particular, decisions and operations relation to the provision of sewerage and water schemes by local authorities) shall be secured for the benefit of the community,

(2) To report on the merits and demerits of any measures considered, with particular reference to their legal and administrative practicality, and

(3) To advise on what changes in the present law may be required to give effect to any measure recommended. (Par 1)

The *Committee on the Price of Building Land* was comprised of six members, two from the Department of Local Government (Michael J. Murphy and Ted O'Meara) one from the Department of the Taoiseach (Dr Martin O'Donoghue) one from the Office of the Revenue Commissioners (L. Reason), one for the Valuation Office (D.F. Ryan) and was chaired by High Court Judge, Mr Justice John Kenny.

The Committee sought written submissions from interested parties and also wrote to organisations which it believed had a special interest in the area. In total, 42 submissions were received, including 16 from local authorities, three from Government departments (Agriculture & Fisheries, Lands and Transport & Power) and the remainder from interested parties and organisations including the IDA, the City and County Manager's Association and the

Construction Industry Federation. One TD, Fine Gael Deputy Mark Clinton made a submission. (See Appendix X).

A total of 59 meetings were held at which two heard oral evidence. (Par 5) The report was published in March 1973. It included a Majority Report and a Minority report written ironically by the two civil servants from the Department of Local Government, the commissioning department. In its introduction, particular tribute is paid to the Committee's secretary, Ms Beth Ann O'Byrne of the Department of Local Government who acted in a part-time capacity. (Par 4).

Following the Introduction, the Majority Report is divided into nine chapters with an addendum from Mr D.F. Ryan from the Valuation Office. The chapters look at the background to the rising price of building land; the causes of the increase; a definition of "betterment"; the role of local authorities in purchasing land; suggested methods for dealing with the problem; arguments for and against the Designated Area Scheme; issues with the Constitution; an overview of similar legislation in Italy and Northern Ireland; details of the proposed scheme and other suggested changes in the existing laws

The Minority Report is divided into six chapters. an Introduction, the reason for the disagreement with the Majority Report are enumerated, a possible alternative scheme is outlined in some detail with arguments for and against the alternative scheme. The final chapter suggests other legal changes.

The Report concludes with a list of the organisations and individuals who made submissions to the Committee.

Rising price of building land and the causes

The commissioning of the report was largely due to the increase in the price of for serviced land suitable for building. The Committee noted that between 1963 and 1971 the price of serviced land increased by 64%. In County Dublin, for example, it increased from £1100 per acre to £7,000. (Par 6). Similar increases occurred in other counties, the report noted. Factors cited include the increase in population, increase in the proportion of people living in cities, increase in household forming age group, increase in income and inflation. Also cited are improvements in food production methods, highrise, improved transport, planning uncertainty, lack of serviced lands, advance acquisition of greenfield sites. (Pars 13 – 20)

Attention is drawn to the existing system of how land compulsorily applied by a local authority is determined by official arbitration under the 1919 and 1963Acts, concluding that the system that must be applied "tends to inflate land prices" (Par 22).

It is the Committee's view that "if the present free market system of determining price is allowed to continue, the price of building land will continue to move in an upward direction." (Par 24)

Attention is drawn to a decision in 1967 that the three Dublin local authorities should get together and purchase land. A £3m fund made available and 1,902 acres bought at an average price of £1604. The Committee noted the process was slow in getting building moving at a satisfactory pace and it could only work "if there is a rapid and efficient disposal of lands purchased". (P25).

"Betterment"

In dealing with the term "betterment" in Chapter III, the Report describes it as an "an ambiguous term" used to describe various increases and which led to confusion. It is sometimes used to "describe the increase in the price caused by the works, sometimes used to describe the increase in the price brought about by all economic and social forces including planning schemes and sometimes to describe the part of the increase which ought to be recoverable from the owner. (Par 27). Various efforts for the recovery of betterment are described but nothing had even been collected when relevant sections were repealed under 1963 Planning Act. (Par 30)

The concept of a development levies is considered and rejected on the basis that they ultimately increase house prices. Furthermore, the cost of administering would outweigh the benefits.(Par 32)

British experience

The British experience is considered in Chapter IV. Particular attention is given to the Report of the Uthwatt Committee which was established in 1941 under the chairmanship of Mr Justice Uthwatt. (Pars 37 – 40). The Report concludes that "the British experience establishes that development charges and betterment levies are invariably passed on to the purchasers who have to pay them in the form of increased prices." (Par 42).

Suggested Methods

Chapter VI outlines 12 different legislative ideas (A – L) which would have the twin aims of "reducing, or at least stabilising, the price of serviced and potential building land and the acquisition by the community on fair terms the betterment element which arises from the execution of works by local authorities."

The suggestions are:

A. A system by which the price of all building land would be controlled.
B. Nationalisation of all building land and payment of compensation.
C. Nationalisation of the development rights in all building land and payment of compensation for these. The land when required for development would then be purchased by a Central Agency or a local authority at its existing use value.
D. A special gain on tax on profits arising from the disposal of land suitable for building.
E. A betterment levy on the difference between the price realised on the disposal of land after planning permission had been granted and the market price of its based on its existing use.
F. The right of pre-exemption.
G. An amendment of the Planning Act 1963 so that planning permission would be granted on the condition that the developer would pay the local authority the total cost of the works which have or will have to be carried out in connection with the proposed development.
H. A high rate of stamp duty payable by the vendor on the transfer or lease of land suitable for building.
I. The imposition of a new tax levied annually at a progressive rate on the site value of lands suitable for building for which planning permission (including outline permission) has been granted. The site value would not be the present rateable valuation but a modern assessment of the letting value.

J. A system under which land would be zoned by the planning authority for different uses and the compensation paid to owners on compulsory acquisition would be related to the specified use.
K. The pre-emption and levy scheme.
L. The Designated Area Scheme.

The Majority Report rejects options A to J with reasons. Option K is the one put forward in the Minority Repot but rejected by the Majority Report on the grounds that it would not stop the disproportionate increases in land prices and would not capture any of the increased prices for the community. (Par 66). Option L is the one proposed by the Majority Report as most appropriate.

Designated Area Scheme

This scheme would confer new jurisdiction on the High Court to designate areas in which, in the opinion of the Court, would likely be used for development over the following 10 years. The High Court judge would be obliged to sit with two other assessors, one of whom would have valuation experience and the other would have town planning qualifications. Once designated the local authority would have the power to acquire the land at existing use value plus 25 per cent. The 25 per cent increase was considered "a reasonable compromise between the rights of the community and those of the landowners". (Par 66)

It listed the advantages as follows:

1. Community benefits from most of the betterment element.
2. Unlikely anybody would pay more than existing use value plus 25%.
3. It would enable local authorities to make certain land available for reduced prices e.g. schools.
4. Local authorities could determine type of use in the leased of the land to the developer – necessitated amendment to the Landlord and Tenant (Ground Rents) Act, 1967.
5. It would give powers to LAs to proceed at a pace with regard to capital programme.
6. It would increase revenue to LAs from profits made on commercial and business lettings.
7. It would end disproportionate increase in land prices.

The main objection raised against the Designated Area scheme was that it could be repugnant to the Constitution, and in particular Articles 40.3 and 43 which relate to private property rights. These are dealt with in Chapter VIII where it is proposed that the President, when asked to sign the Bill into law, refer it to the Supreme court under Article 26 to determine whether or not it was repugnant to the Constitution. To avoid conflict with Article 44 Section 2.6, the Majority Report proposed that the property of any religious denomination, or educational institution, be excluded. (Pars 109 & 110).

Italy and Northern Ireland

Chapter IX examines broadly similar legislation passed in Italy and Northern Ireland. In relation to Italy, the Majority Report cites and a law passed by the Italian Parliament on 22 October, 1971 where the principle that land which is suitable for building should be acquired by the local authority at a price which ignores the development potential and which is related to existing use value, is applied. (Par 111).

In relation to Northern Ireland, the Majority Report references the New Towns Act (Northern Ireland) 1965 whereby the Minister for Development had the powers to acquire land by agreement or compulsorily. Section 15 (7) reads: "no account shall be taken of any increase or diminution in the value of the land that is attributable to the existence of the new town." (Par 113).

Chapter XI suggest other changes to the law including a change in law for Land Registrar to allow public access to records, the introduction of a specific time limit for completion of building and the ability of the planning authority to get High Court injunctions for breach of planning.

Minority Report

The Minority Report drafted by the two representatives of the Department of Local Government proposed reject the main recommendation of the Majority Report and instead proposed that areas required for building would be designated by the local authorities. In a designated area, the local authority would have first option to purchase land put up for sale. A levy of 30% would be charged on all disposals of land in the area. A corresponding levy would be payable on development of land if there had been no levy on disposal within the preceding five years. The proceeds of levies would accrue to the local authorities to be used by them to finance capital works

It rejects the Majority Report recommendation on the basis that it was not just to abandon land being sold on the open market. (Par 2.1). It did not consider that there is "any justification for a radical departure from the basis compensation principle on which the present code is founded." (2.2). It said the Department had considered the issue of acquiring land on existing use value in the past and the idea was abandoned because of "insuperable Constitutional difficulties" and added "......it is virtually impossible to show how the common good requires that he (the property owner) should not be paid market value for it". The Minority Report predicts that a two-tier land price system would arise whereby land outside of designated areas would attract a premium. This would "almost certain" to be held repugnant to the Constitution." (Par 2.4)

Made in the USA
Columbia, SC
01 October 2023

23686734R00153